AF621950

ARCHAEOLOGY OF EASTERN INDIA

ARCHAEOLOGY OF EASTERN INDIA

(With special reference to Kakharua Valley, North Central Odisha)

RAJENDRA DEHURI

AGAM KALA PRAKASHAN
DELHI

First Published 2019

© Dr. Rajendra Dehuri

ISBN : 978-81-938457-0-7

All rights reserved. No part of this publication may be reproduced, stored in a retrieval system or transmitted, in any form or by any means, electronic, mechanical, photocopying, recording, otherwise, without the prior permission of Author and Publisher.

Published by:
Dr. Agam Prasad, M.A., Ph.D., Diploma in Museology
For **Agam Kala Prakashan**
34, Central Market, Ashok Vihar
Delhi - 110 052
Tel.: 91-11-27212194-95
Fax: 91-11-27212195
Email: agamkala101@gmail.com, agambook@yahoo.com
www.agamkala.com

Composed by:
Sushil Kumar
Delhi - 110 052
Mobile: 9891395309

Printed in India.

Dedicated

To

My Parents

Contents

Foreword

Right from the colonial period to the present time, Eastern India, comprising mainly present day West Bengal, Jharkhand, Bihar and Odisha, has drawn the attention of scholars like V. Ball, D. Sen, N. K. Bose, A. K. Ghosh, G. C. Mohapatra, K. C. Tripathy, Ranjana Ray and other scholars. The present work by Dr. Rajendra Dehuri is primarily based on his Ph. D. Thesis on the archaeological remains of the Kakharua Valley in the Angul and Keonjhar Districts of north central Odisha. Dr. Dehuri was introduced to the area as a result of a survey conducted by the Department of Anthropology, Utkal University under my supervision when he had opted for prehistoric archaeology as a special paper while pursuing his M.A. Subsequently, he did P. G. Diploma in Archaeology from Archaeological Survey of India and joined in the same organisation. He decided to work on the archaeological remains of the Kakharua Valley not confining to prehistory. Thus, the present work has some important features. Firstly, it aims at understanding the archaeological remains as a whole of a small river valley in North central Odisha giving a diachronic perspective for the archaeological heritage of a microregion. Secondly, it is based on intensive survey in a difficult terrain, - known also for leftwing extreme activities - yielding palaeolithic, mesolithic, neolithic and historical remains from more than thirty sites that he had reported. Thirdly, he has also discussed the salient features of different periods under study.

I sincerely hope that the book "Archaeology of Eastern India;with special reference to Kakharua Valley, North Central Odisha" will be welcomed by scholars of heritage studies including those of archaeology, anthropology and history.

2nd October, 2018
Bhubaneswar

Prof. Kishor.K Basa, Ph. D. (London)
Formerly Head, Department of Anthropology,
Utkal University, Formerly Director,
IGRMS, Bhopal
Indian Museum, Kolkata &
Anthropological Survey of India

Preface

The North Central Odisha is well known for its Archaeological evidence. There are number of prehistoric as well historic sites reported from Keonjhar and Angul districts. Sankerjang, Neo-Chalcolithic site is reported the bar celt compare to Vietnam's lithophone, and is important not only for the recovery of stone tools, copper artefacts and skeletal remains but for the C^{14} date which is the first radiocarbon date for an Odishan archaeological sites. Sitabinji another important site in Keonjhar district, represent painting of royal procession on natural rock shelter, the painting contains the name of Maharaja Disabhanja which is written in southern variety of Brahmi script datable to 5th century AD. Because of closeness to the region and belongs to one of them I am very much interested to prepare the comprehensive data. This is quite a modest attempt to reconstruct the archaeological prospect of North Central Odisha. The archaeological remains clearly imply that the area shows a sequence from Palaeolithic to Historical period, in which sites with the Microliths and Neolithic or ground stone tools are more numerous.

The present work would not have been possible without the help and inspiration of a number of benevolent minds and hands. It is my prime responsibility to express and acknowledge such help and inspiration.

Words are inadequate to express my deep sense of gratitude to Professor Kishor K. Basa, whose sincere effort, timely guidance and effective advice helped me in completing the present work. Needless to say, without his help it could not have seen the light of the day. I am deeply indebted to Mr. Daitari Sahoo, Senior Lecturer, Department of Anthropology, Utkal University, Bhubaneswar, for his valuable suggestions, and encouragement from time to time. My sincere thanks are also due to Dr. S.B. Ota, Joint Director General, (Retd.) Archaeological Survey of India for his encouragement. I am also thankful to Mr. Tapan Jyoti Baidya, the then Superintending Archaeologist, Ranchi Circle, ASI and Mr. Nizammudin Tahir, the then Director, Archaeological Survey of India for their encouragement in various ways.

I can never forget Dr. Basanta Kumar Mohanta, Asstt. Professor, Adi Keih College, Asmara University and Dr. Neeraj Kumar Sinha, Superintending Archaeologist, ASI, Sarnath Circle for their constant encouragement and moral support in every phase of my work. Thanks are also due to Dr. Sushanta Kumar Kar, Deputy Superintending Archaeologist, Amaravati Circle, ASI for his various suggestions and encouragement. Dr. Ramakanta Mahananda, and Dr. Manas Ranjan Dash, Research Scholars, Department of Anthropology, Utkal University, Bhubaneswar also deserve my thanks for their help while completing this work. My thanks are also due to Mr. Karunakar Mohanta, Ex. Sarpanch, Soida Panchayat, Mr. Jasketan Mohanta, Mr. Nakula Mahanta, Mr. Bhola Sahu of Dalo village, Dist. Angul, Mr. Mohan Munda and Mr. Niranjan Mohanta of Tala Birikala U.G.U.P. School, Dist. Keonjhar for their kind co-operation during my exploration in the thickly forested area.

I thank the librarian and the staff of Institute of Archaeology, Archaeological Survey of India, Ranchi University Library, Patna Circle Library of Archaeological Survey of India and Department of Anthropology Library and Central Library of Utkal University for the help I had received in my library work.

I fondly remember my days in the Department of Anthropology, Utkal University, Bhubaneswar because of the benign presence of my teachers Prof. K.C Tripathy, Prof. P.K. Nayak, Prof. S.K. Ghoshmoullik, Prof. J. Kanungo, Prof. P.K. Das, Dr. Basanti Rath, Dr. B.K. Behera, Prof. R. Mohanty, Prof. Jagannath Das, Prof. Sabita Acharya and Prof. U. Aparajita. I am grateful to all of them. Dr. Kanhu Charan Satpathy, Dr. P.K. Patra and Dr. S.K. Mohanty-all in the Department of Anthropology, Utkal University have also encouraged me and hence my thanks are due to them. I am extremely thankful to Mr. Sowmen Roy and Sanjay Yadav for their help and support in many ways. The maps, drawings and photography of antiquities have been prepared by Shri Mukesh Ekka and Rajnish Raj for which I am profoundly grateful. I am very much thankful to the staff of the Khajuraho Museum, especially Shri R.N. Singh and Shri Kamlesh Mishra for their co-operation in the hour of need. My special thanks are due to Dr. Arakhita Pradhan, Dy. Curator (Exhibition), National Museum for his help in going through the script and suggestions.

Needless to say, the moral supports of my parents (Sri Bira Dehuri and Smt. Sabitri Dehuri), Uncle Shri Digamber Dehuri and Aunte Smt. Sandhyarani Dehuri and friends such as Shri Prabin Tripathy, Smt. S. Samparna Mishra have made me overcome the moments of diffidence. I owe my gratitude to all of them. My wife Aparna has given me all moral and emotional support and has stood by me in every difficult situation while preparing the book and hence she deserves sincere thanks.

I am thankful to the staff of ASI, Delhi Mini Circle for their moral support and encouragement in the academic venture.

Dr. Agam Prasad & Shri Ashok Kumar Pandey of Agam Kala Prakashan, Delhi deserve all praise for their prompt and cordial efforts in publishing the book in very short time.

I am grateful to those authors of different books, journals, articles and reports which I have consulted in this present work. Finally, I thank Almighty God without whose grace; this work would not have been possible.

New Delhi **Rajendra Dehuri**

List of Figures

List of Plates

List of Tables

Introduction

The present book *Archaeology of Eastern India, with special reference to Kakharua valley, North Central Odisha,* is primarily based on an archaeological survey on the Kakharua valley which spreads over the districts of Angul and Keonjhar. A number of small streamlets like Sukha nala, Bada *nala*, Jalanda *nala*, Sati *nala*- which are basically the feeder channels to the Kakharua- are also important from the view point of the present study. There are both academic as well as personal reasons for carrying out a survey in the Kakharua valley. From an academic viewpoint, while much archaeological work–both prehistoric as well as historical - have been undertaken in major river valleys of Odisha, not much emphasis has been put on small rivers which are believed to have potentiality to yield the recovery of primary sites, and hence the present work. Besides, scholars depending on their interest and priority, confine their study to either prehistoric or historical aspects. However, in the present work an attempt has been made to document both prehistoric as well as relics of the historical period, is another important aspect. At a personal level, I was introduced to the Kakharua valley by participating in a surface exploration conducted by the Department of Anthropology, Utkal University around Kantala, Pallahara in Angul district in the year 1998 while an M. A. student and I had written a dissertation on it. Besides, the author native place is just 90 km away from this study region and hence the author had an intense desire to explore the thickly forest zone of Kakharua valley. Such micro area approach would hopefully help reconstruct the past of the local area by providing archaeological evidence as a primary source with regard to the prehistory and history of North Central Odisha.

Aims and Objectives

The following are the main objectives of the present study

i. To begin with, the present work aims at studying major feeder channel and its surrounding hilly landscape in micro aspect to locate prehistoric and historical archaeological sites.
ii. Attempt is made to prepare map of distribution of archaeological sites.
iii. No comprehensive work on the prehistoric archaeology of North Central Odisha has been made as yet, especially from the high undulating Kakharua Valley, and hence the present work.
iv. Except reference to bar celt, neolithic evidence from Sankerjang, Pallahara in Angul districts and Balisahi from Telkoi region of Keonjhar district, nothing is known about the artefacts. Therefore, an account of neolithic evidence in North Central Odisha is also the need of the hour.
v. Historical sites are not much known from this area. Therefore, the sculptural remains, potsherds and other structural remains are also to be documented.
vi. With regard to the surrounding area some attempts have been made around Bonaigarh, Pallahara, Telkoi and Keonjhar where as the hilly tract has not been focused from the prehistoric point of view. Hence, this may bridge the gaps between coastal plain land culture and with the high land environmental adaptation.

Methods of Study

To fulfil the aims and objectives of the study, the following methods have been adopted:

1. **Study of Topo-sheet and Maps:** Study of maps and topo-sheet is essential to get a broad idea about the location, geomorphology, latitude, longitude, altitude, communication system and settlement pattern of the site. Therefore, the maps of the studied region (district, block, village etc) available in different levels and the topo-sheet of 1: 25,000 and 1: 50,000 scales, published by the Surveyor General of India are studied.
2. **Surface Exploration and Material Recovery:** Intensive surface exploration is essential in archaeology for locating sites, including the primary ones. Therefore, an intensive surface exploration has been done for six field seasons from 2006-2011 in different parts of the field and its neighboring area. The exploration covers the areas of hills, foothills, piedmont and river valley areas. Emphasis has also been made to visit the earlier reported sites to see the present condition of the site and to collect new finding.
3. **Section Scraping:** Some sections were studied at different places and on the river banks to know the cultural deposition and stratigraphy of the site. These sites include Bankadar near the confluence of the Kakharua and Mankara, another one is near the site Baisnavadar Neolithic site.
4. **Grid:** A grid of each 5 x 5 square meter has been taken at Baisnavadar to show the distribution, plotting and systematic collection of artefacts. The grid was divided into 10 cm x 20 cm each units for proper measuring of the artefacts. The horizontal axis of grids are named with English alphabets, like A, B, C, D and E where as the vertical axis are number with English numerical like 1,2,3,4 and 5.
5. **Mapping and Plotting:** To show the broad geomorphology of the site mapping of each and every site has been done at the field. To show the artefacts along with the associated features and their distribution pattern plotting of some important sites and grids have been done.

6. **Interview for the Ethnographic Data: -** Ethnographic data relating to modern usages of 'Neolithic' artefacts has been collected.
7. **Analysis and Interpretation: -** The primary analysis of lithic and ceramics are made at the field which are later finalized in laboratory. Inter-site comparison of these collected artefacts is done and attempt has been made to compare these with other published and unpublished materials.
8. **Drawing and Photography: -** Drawing of lithics, ceramics and other collected antiquities are made at laboratory to give a clear idea about the morphological feature of the antiquities. Photography of the important morphological features of the sites and antiquities are taken separately for more relevant information.

The book comprises six chapters along with an introduction as well as summary and conclusion. Chapter-1 is basically a review of literature on Archaeology of North Central Odisha: An outline. To begin with, an outline on the history of archaeology in India as well as Odisha is discussed in an outline. In particular the limitations of the study on archaeology of Odisha are pointed out. Chapter-2 describes about the study area and the present environment. The description of the region of North Central Odisha includes the location, the administrative background, and present environment, such as physiographic features, forest, hill, drainage, system, geology, climate, rain fall and population. The river systems include the Baitarani and the Brahmani river system along with small streamlets. The Chapter-3 contains descriptions of sites discovered in the Kakharua valley by the author from surface exploration and an account of the stratigraphy of the area. The total number of artefacts recovered from various sites is presented in a tabular form. Chapter-4 deals with the Palaeolithic and Mesolithic cultures of Kakharua valley, North Central Odisha. The chapter is divided into two parts to deals with the problem of Palaeolithic culture and Mesolithic culture. For Mesolithic culture, the distribution of sites has been divided into four eco-zones, i.e. sites on the foot hill area, sites on river bank, site on river bank cum foot hill area and sites on the piedmont area. Site-wise tool typology has been presented in a tabular form. Both morphological and metric analysis of tools are made at the end of the chapter. Chapter-5 describes about the Neolithic cultural relics, i.e. the ground and polished stone artefacts of the study area. Like the Mesolithic culture, the distribution of Neolithic sites has been divided in to four eco-zones, i. e. sites on the foot hill area, sites on the river bank, sites on river bank cum foot hill area and sites on the piedmont area with the detail analysis. Site-wise tool typology has been presented in a tabular form. The metric analysis of Neolithic artefacts has also been included in the chapter. Chapter-6 contains description of archaeological sites of the historical period. The artefacts discovered from historical sites of the studied region are described. Analysis of findings i.e. ceramics, lithics, beads and other antiquities are made in this chapter. In the summary and conclusion, the salient features of different chapters are given. It ends with a note on the scope for future work in this region.

CHAPTER 1

Archaeology of North Central Odisha: An Outline

The present chapter aims at providing an overview of the Archaeology of North Central Odisha with small introduction to archaeology of India in order to provide broad view to the study aspects. Archaeology may be simply defined as the systematic study of antiquities for reconstructing the past. Renfrew and Bahn considered archaeology as a discipline both a physical activity in the field and an intellectual pursuit in the lab (1991). The study of archaeology has gone a long way from the days of the 18th century German art historian Johan Wincklemann, who had worked on Rome and is often called the 'Father of Archaeology' He was very much interested in the Greek classical art. In later period more study had been carried out on Greek, Roman and Biblical archeology.

However, in the 19th century, tradition developed in the natural and social sciences brought together the uniformitarianism in geology by Charles Lyell, evolutionism in biology by Charles Darwin and the concept of three age system i.e. stone age, bronze age and iron age by Thomsen. The Three Age system of classification was first published in a guide book to the Danish National museum in 1836 and later translated into English in 1840 (Daniel 1968,1971:47). This was followed by the theory of cultural evolutionism by Morgan (1877), Spencer (1867, 1870) and Tylor (1871).

In respect of prehistoric archaeology, Sir John Lubbock (later Lord Avebury) in his book **Pre-historic Times** has used the terms 'Palaeolithic' and 'Neolithic' for two separate ages. On the basis of technology, he has classified the total human cultural remains into four distinct phases, such as, Palaeolithic, Neolithic, Bronze Age and Iron Age. He described that the wooly mammoth, cave bear, rhinoceros and other extinct animal flourished during the Palaeolithic period.

Archaeology of India

The study of archaeological evidences as academic interest in Indian archaeology can be traced back to middle of the eighteenth century. It was the period of initiative taken up for a systematic and scholarly study of Indian antiquities. A French geographer J.B.D' Anville's approach was based on possible location of the famous sites of Pataliputra to understand this specific geographical interest but Pataliputra was incorrectly identified with Prayag. James Rennell along with J. Tieffenthaler and Du Perron produced three-volume study of Indian geography in the year 1786-88.

With the establishment of the Asiatic Society by Sir William Jones on 15th January 1784, emphasis was put on archaeological study, the traditional system of Indian Jurisprudence, the study of Sanskrit literature and the in-depth study of linguistics. Although archaeological discoveries were very less till the 1830, important publications include that of Francis Buchanan's three –volume report on his Mysore Survey in 1807 and his survey of Bengal presidency, submitted in 1816. A three volume summary of the latter was published in 1838. Apart from that Colin Mackenzie had also studied the antiquities of south India through his collection of inscriptions and manuscripts. In 1830's James Princep became the Secretary of the Asiatic Society and played a major role in the initiation of field research and contribution of decipherment of the two most important historical scripts of India such as Brahmi and Kharoshthi. This was a great achievement in the field of epigraphy and numismatic studies. An important result was the discovery of the name Piyadasi or Asoka and two Indo-Greek kings Agathocles and Pantaleon.

In these years much of attention was paid by European Generals. The Manikyala stupa in Punjab was excavated by Lieutenant Alexander Burnes and Charles Masson. Unlike that, Markham Kittoe dug up ten cart loads of Buddhist images at Kurkihar near Gaya in Bihar. Another interesting feature of this period was the excavation of megaliths in south India. Captain Meadows Taylor published his excavation results with sections. Alexander Cunnigham, a Young military engineer had travelled extensively and wrote detailed descriptions of the areas and indentified major archaeological sites. After the establishment of Archaeological Survey of India in the year 1861, with Alexander Cunningham as its head, the target of reconstructing the ancient historical geography of India rested with J.D. Beglar, A.C.L. Carlleyle and H.W. Garrick. James Burgess was interested in architectural surveys. These monographs on the monuments of west and south-east India are monuments to his pioneering endeavour in this regard. The important research in Epigraphy during this period includes the volumes of Corpus Inscriptionum Indicarum. In field archaeology, the excavation at Kankali Tila in Mathura was a major discovery and in exploration, the Tarai region of Nepal gave broad idea of the topographical features of the area.

Besides the European scholars, the native scholars like Babu Rajendra Lal Mitra, Ram Raz, Bahu Daji, R.G. Bhandarkar and P. Mukharji were also experts in diverse branches on archaeological pursuits. For example R.L Mitra edited Sanskrit manuscripts, RG Bhandarkar worked on the antiquity of sites like Sopora and Kolhapur, Ram Raz on the south Indian architectural principles and Bhau Daji published western Indian inscriptions.

Prehistory

Robert Bruce Foote, a geologist of Geological Survey of India discovered hand axes of Lower Palaeolithic period at Pallavaram near Madras in

1863 (Foote 1966, 1916). His collection of prehistoric implements from Andhra, Tamilnadu, Karnataka and Gujarat were published as catalogue in the year 1914 and 1916. It was during this period again that an archaeologist A.C.L. Carlleyle, an assistant of Alexander Cunningham, discovered Mesolithic remains from Kaimur hill section of Uttar Pradesh.

With regards to prehistory, authors like D. Terra and T.T. Paterson published their studies on the Ice age in India and associated human culture which was a significant one. Another study was based on tools collected in the Eastern Ghats of the Andhra region by L.A. Cammiade with M.C. Burkitt of Cambridge University (Cammiade et al 1930, Burkit 1958). These were more significant studies because of the geo-chronological scale on the European model that influenced prehistoric research for a long time. As for the lithic material it is well known that the western sub-Himalaya region had a distinct lithic cultural tradition throughout the Pleistocene. This tradition which is known by the name "Soanian" evolves at least through three stages beginning with the Middle Pleistocene and ending up with the Pleistocene itself or a little later.

Among the noteworthy discoveries that gave a stimulus for research in this direction at the turn of the second half of this century, mention should be made of (1) the assemblage with Upper Palaeolithic traits brought to light by Sankalia (1956: 35-53) from the river Parvara (Maharashtra), Sharma in the Belan valley Uttar Pradesh (1955-56), Soundara Rajan (1958) from Nagarjunakonda (Andhra Pradesh), Issac (1960) in the Kurnool district (Andhra Pradesh) confirming the findings of Cammaiade and Burkitt and the blade and burin industry from Salvadgi in Bijapur district (Karnatak) described by Seshadri (1962). Subsequent findings made around this time from sites around Renigunta in Chittoor district, Andhra Pradesh (Murty 1966) and in Salvadgi and Meralbhavi (Bijapur and Gulbarga districts, Karnataka) Paddayya (1968, 1970 and 1973) widened the scope for a fresh evaluation of the data in a pan – Indian context. Blade tool industries have a wide geographical distribution and are known from several open air sites in the states of

Karnataka, Maharastra, and Uttar Pradesh and both open air and cave sites in Andhra Pradesh (Murty 1985).

It was also supposed that the microlithic Industries of the Mesolithic might have developed from the Levalloisian tradition of the Middle Stone Age. The suggestion of Subbarao thought was accepted as a working hypothesis yet a large number of scholars pleaded against it (Misra, 1962: 113-124). In the meantime, similar industries were reported from besides Allahabad and Mirzapur (Varma. 1970:30,1985) Chittoor district (Murty 1968: 83-101), Shorrapur Doab in Gulbarga, district Mysore (Paddayya 1968): Singhbhum near Chakulia, Palamau district (now in Jharkhand), Bihar etc (Ghosh 1965). In the Lekhania Excavation also thick and broad blades were noticed in the bottom most layers (Sharma 1965). Cockburn (1894) had also noticed similar blade element in the bottom most layers in his diggings.

Pottery has been reported from a number of excavated sites such as Langhnaj, Bagor Phase II, Nagarjunakonda, Morahana Pahar, Baghai Khor, Lekhahia, Chopani Mando, Ghagharia Rock shelter I in the Son valley. The pottery of both the types such as handmade and wheel turned is reported. At most of the sites the pot-sherds are very small and it is difficult normally to make out shapes.

Burials have been excavated at a number of Mesolithic settlements – Dorthy Deep and Jambudvipa Rock shelters in the Mahadev hills in Madhya Pradesh, Langhnaj in Gujarat, Bagor in Rajasthan, Baghai Khor and Lekhahia rock-shelters in district Mirzapur and Sarai Nahar Rai and Mahadaha in Pratapgarh, Uttar Pradesh. Extended burials have been reported from Dorothy Deep and Jambudipa rock shelters (Hunter 1935: 28-57, 1936: 127-144), Baghai Khor (Varma 1965:73-74), Lakhahia (Sharma 1965: 77-78) Bagor Phase I (Misra 1973), Sarai Nahar Rai (Sharma 1973: 129-144) and Mahadaha (Sharma et al 1980: 80-98).

The whole of Indian sub-continent is rich in Neolithic artefacts. The occurrence of Neolithic culture in the Indian sub-continent is not very late in comparison with the rest of the world. On the basis of the radiocarbon dates, Mehrgarh in Pakistan, the earliest Neolithic site in South Asia, is dated to the sixth millennium BC with both aceramic and ceramic traditions (Allchin 1996: 1(5). Numerous polished celts (ordinary and shouldered), potsherds of kiln-backed, painted pottery have been discovered from the different Neolithic sites of Kashmir, Madhya Pradesh, Chhotanagpur plateau, Orissa, Andhra Pradesh, Assam, Mysore, Gujrat, Madras and West Bengal. The evidences of the antiquities of various cultivated plants and domesticated animal remains from the Neolithic levels, barley *(Hordeum vulgare)* and rice *(Oriza Sativa)* were discovered from the Neolithic levels of Chirand in Bihar (Mittre 1972:18; Verma 1970-71:19-23; Agarwal 1981:93, 1992). Only the evidence of collection of wild fruits and seeds such as *Lithespernum arvensi, Ipomea, Euphorbia, Medicago denticulata, M. alcata, Lotus corniculata* have been reported from the early phase of Neolithic Burzaham (Agarwal 1984). It was believed that the animals comprising cattle, sheep, goat, horse seem to have been domesticated (IAR 1981-82:10-11; 1983-84:12-13; Agarwal 1984: 115; Chakrabarti 1988:87; Singh 2001: 136).

Majority of Chalcolithic cultures flourished in the black cotton soil zone. This according to Leshnik (1968: 295) "clearly represents an ecological adaptation dictated by available technology, knowledge and means. It has been presumed that there early farmers could not have cultivated the black cotton soil in the absence of iron plough (Kosambi 1963:315-16, 1989) and may have confined their agriculture to the alluvial strips along the river banks (Agrawal 1982 :218). In recent years a number of Chalcolithic sites have been reported and excavated to know more about its significance, in order to its artefacts, pottery form, bone objects, smelting process of copper and its objects etc. In recent years a good number of Chalcolithic sites has been reported in eastern India.

While the concept of an Indian "Iron Age" is from N.R. Banerjee's publication on the subject in 1965 (Banerjee 1965a, 1965b), the academic interest in Indian iron goes back to the eighteenth century and possesses a much broader dimension than a narrowly archaeological one. The most significant feature of this phase was the publication of N.R. Banerjee's The Iron Age in India in 1965. Although this book was much criticized on account of diffusionary framework and of interpretation of some archaeological data, however it must be acknowledged in retrospect that this was the first attempt to define the scope of Iron Age studies in India and deserves as such full recognition as a pioneering work in the context of modern Indian archaeology.

In 1979, Sahi published his analysis of the occurrences of Iron objects in Phases Ib and Ie of the Chalcolithic Ahar on the basis of data presented by the Ahar excavation reports. It may be observed that the idea of different each iron using centers with an indigenously evolving base of iron technology has been accepted with some modification in two recent interpretations of Indian prehistory and protohistory (Agrawal 1982, Allchin and Allchin 1982) B. Allchin and F.R. Allchin (1982:345, 1984,1989a,1989b) now put the first period of iron in the subcontinent between 1300 and 1000 B.C. but they prefer to correlate the spread of iron in subcontinent with " the secondary spread of the Indo Aryans". A similar metallurgical opinion has recently been expressed in the Indian context by K.T.M. Hegde (1981) who believes that the Indian iron working developed indigenously. Shaffer (1978 unpublished) has strongly questioned "the assumed vital techno economic role played by iron tools in the settlement of the Gangetic Plain". Dilip Chakrabarti has questioned the diffusionary frame work of Indian Iron Age and believes that it is a product of indigenous evolution in India (Chakrabarti: 1976, 1992)

Historical Sites

Historical archaeology indicates relations in the use of language and materials like ceramics, and other features and explains many aspects of this trend, by its continuous search. Archaeological examination, however, gives a clue to understand this legend in its religio-historical context.

The central India comprising the state of Madhya Pradesh has given evidence of numerous early historical sites, right from Mauryan times onwards. Several urbanized religious and trade centers like Maheswar (Dikshit 1952, IAR 1965-66), Ujjain (IAR 1956-57), Eran,

Tripuri, Vidisha, Besnagar (IAR 1977-78) and Malhar (IAR 1974-77) which served as the link between the north and the south and seems to have received the impact of urbanization from urbanized centre of Uttarapatha and a channel of transmitting Buddhism further south.

In southern extension Andhra Pradesh has proved to be one of the richest areas so far early historical sites are concerned. So far as the sites with Buddhist are concerned, the place of pride of course goes to Nagarjunakonda followed by Yelleswaram. Huge stupa mounds have also been reported from Kalingapatnam (IAR 1976-77: 10), Dhulikatta in district Karimnagar (IAR 1975-76 :2-3), Kondapur in district Medak (IAR 1973-74: 6), Dupadu in district Guntur, Chandavarman in district Prakasam (IAR 1976-77:3) Viratraj Gudda, or Erradibba in district Khammam and Satanikotta in district Kurnol (IAR 1977-78: 3-11). Further south, in Karnataka, Vadgaon-Madhavapur in district Belgaum has proved to be most promising site where extensive structural remains of the Satavahana period have been unearthed. Another similar centre, has been evidenced at Chandravalli, district Chitradurga (IAR 1977-78: 27-29) where well built structures, coins and a range of sophisticated antiquities like beads, terracotta and metal objects have been found. In Tamilnadu, Literary sources give a picture of a very prosperous township in the early centuries of the Christian era subsequently Kaveripatnam (IAR 1973-74:25, IAR 1977-78: 50) exposed viharas and shrines along with structures of moulded bricks and decorative stucco figurines. The excavation at Kuchipuram in district Chingelput has given more significant evidence.

The excavations at Ter and Bhokardan (Deo & Gupte 1974), Tagarpura and Bhogavardhana of ancient times stand testimony to the same social and economic conditions. Pauni (Deo & Joshi 1972) in the Vidarbha region of Maharastra has brought to light an extensive Hinayana Buddhist establishment going back to the period of the NBP and subsequent times. Paunar, in Dist. Wardha, well known for the series of Vakataka sculptures of Ganga, Ramayana panels, panels of Siva and the Seshasayin Vishnu, gave evidence of brick-built structures indicating that it was an important centre in the 5th -6th Century A.D.

(Deo & Dhavalikar 1967). In western India Somnath, Dwarka, Devni mori and Prabhas Patan have brought to light noteworthy evidence. Prabhas Patan gave evidence of the massive fortification of stones assignable to 4th cent. B.C. to 1st cent. B.C. whereas Dwarka on the sea-coast evidenced its occupation in the initial centuries of the christian era. Devni mori (Mehta et al. 1966) has, on the other hand, evidenced a large scale Buddhist establishment with quite a range of terracotta and stucco statuary.

Kausambi (Sharma 1960 and 1969), the capital of Vasta and present day Kosam, has given some remarkable evidences. Equally important has been the site of Rajgir, ancient Rajagriha, the capital of Magadha (IAR 1953-54). Another important site from Bihar is Vaisali (Deva and Mishra 1950) the birth place of Mahavir, the 24th Tirthankara of the Jainas. Antichak which has been excavated since 1973 has given reasonable idea of the nature of the Vikramshila establishment (IAR 1973-78). The excavations at Champa (IAR 1974-77) for several seasons, though attesting habitation from pre- NBP period, seem to indicate a prosperous phase only in the Mauryan-Sunga times culminating in the Gupta period when the town becomes a jewellery-manufacturing centre. Similar seem to have been the case with Balirajgarh (IAR 1972-75) which became a centre of terracotta and bead production. Remains of a slightly later period were exposed at Nalanda (IAR 1975-76: 8-9) where a brick-built temple, rectangular on plan, with moulded decoration, niches for images, votive stupas and corbelled drains were uncovered giving an idea of the religious establishment of 7th – 8th century and later. The excavator identifies Piprawa (IAR 1973-74: 27-28) with ancient Kapilavastu which played an important role in Buddhism. Mathura is another famous sacred city exposed number of antiquities dated back to the pre-NBP period.

In Odisha, Sisupalgarh has been identified with Tosali of the Asokan records and Kalinganagara referred to in the inscription of Kharavela. Through the settlement here goes back to Mauryan period, subsequently it developed into a well fortified town, one square kilometer on plan with each side of the fortification having majestic gateways (Lal

1949: 62-105, Mohanty and Smith, 2006: 27-32). Another site having fortifications was Jaugada in district Ganjam (IAR 1956-57), Bangarh (IAR 1973-74: 32-33, 1974-75: 51), Bharatpur, Chandraketugarh (IAR 1956-57: 29-30) and Tamluk are some of the notable historical sites in West Bengal. Of these, Tamluk identified with ancient Tamralipti has given evidence of human occupation right from the Mauryan period till the medieval Pala times (IAR 1954-55: 19-20, 1975-76: 51-52). In Assam, Ambari, a suburb of Guwahati gave evidence of habitation which might go back to the initial centuries of the Christian era (Ansari and Dhavilkar 1977:79-87).

Archaeology of North Central Odisha

The North Central Odisha is confined to the region of southern part of Keonjhar, south eastern part of Sundergarh, western part of Mayurbhanj, Angul, Dhenkanal, northern part of Jajpur, eastern part of Sambalpur and Deogarh district (Fig.-1). Archaeological research in the region during the colonial phase received attention with the work of British scholars on the monuments and other cultural materials of the region. Following Valentine Ball, Palaeolithic sites have been reported by Acharya (1923-29), Bose and Sen (1948) which were confined to Mayurbhanj District. Mohapatra (1962) started systematic exploration of the river valley in north and central Odisha in order to locate prehistoric sites, particularly in the districts of Mayurbhanj, Keonjhar, Sundergarh and Dhenkanal. He explored the river valleys of Brahmani. Baitarani, Mahanadi and Burhabalang, covering an area of approximately 25,000 sq. km and located a number of prehistoric sites of Lower and Middle Palaeolithic, Mesolithic and Neolithic cultures. These studies were also important due to the stratigraphical feature, with reference to Pleistocene climate. They have focused the morphological and technological parameter of stone artefacts.

Palaeolithic Culture

It was the discovery in the year 1939 that gave a new dimension to Palaeolithic archaeology of the north Odisha in general and Mayurbhanj in particular. The study focused and laid foundation of scientific prehistory of India at Kuliana through an excavation. It was a mile stone for India as well as Odisha for the first excavated palaeolithic site and truely focuses on systematic approach to Palaeolithic study.

P.K. Singh's (1980-1985) systematic investigation of the central Odisha focused on the Stone age cultures of the region. His study was confined to Denkanal, Angul, Talcher, Kamakshya nagar and Pallahara sub-division, which resulted in the discovery of 53 Lower Palaeolithic, 06 Mesolithic and 19 Neolithic sites. There are 1599 Lower Palaeolithic tools recovered from central Odisha which includes 88 (5.50%) chopper, 1302 (81.42%) hand axe and 33 (2.06%) scraper. Typologically Central Odisha is dominant with hand axe and cleavers. Except choppers, the other tool types are smaller in their occurrence and they do not have much typological significance. However, they suggest the multi-implemental behaviour of the early human folk in the area.

Fig.1: Google map showing the Study area, North Central Odisha.

Khilar (1997-99) has reported 833 lithic artefacts of different cultural periods from the 14 sites of Deo basin around Karanjia. The findings include four lower palaeoliths, 86 middle palaeoliths, 144 upper palaeoliths, 465 microliths and 134 neoliths. The Deo basin, which is a tributary to Baitarani, was dominated by palaeolithic artefact as a whole. During the year 1992-93 Mohanta has surveyed in Manada (Mohanta 1997-99) area. The finding comprised Lower Palaeolithic, Middle Palaeolithic, Microlithic and Neolithic artefacts. The Palaeolithic artefacts were basically made out of quartzite.

It the field session of 1996-97 in Kantala area of Pallahara, students of the Department of Anthropology, Utkal University have reported 612 artefacts of which four are indentified as Palaeoliths, 338 as Microliths, and 270 as Neoliths (Mishra 1997).

In the western margin of Similipal massif study by Chakrabarty (Chakrabarty 2000) in Khiching plateau, the sites are divided into open air sites, channel-bed sites and cliff section sites. The Lower Palaeolithic artefacts in the first instance are divided into two groups; shaped tools (65: 37.35%), and simple artefacts or debitage (109: 62.65%). The shaped tools are represented by hand axes (17 : 26.15%), cleavers (14: 21.53%), knives (4: 6.15%), choppers (8: 12.30%), pick (1: 1.53%) scrapers (18: 27.69%), chisel (1: 1.53%) point (1:1.53%) and a non-descriptive flake tool (1: 1.53%). The simple artefacts consist of flakes (13: 11.93%), cores (5: 4.59%), and other wastes (91: 83.36%). The Lower Palaeolithic assemblages on ground of their techno-morphological features have been designated as Acheulian.

The Middle Palaeolithic comes from three sites. The tools are made usually on fine-grained raw material like chert, chalcedony, jasper etc. and include various types of scraper borers and scraper–combination tools.

In the field session of 1999 in Sankerjang 411 artefacts were collected. These include Palaeolithic (lower and middle), Microlithic, Neolithic and Iron implements. There are only three types of Lower Palaeolithic artefacts i.e chopper tools, hand axe and anvil, whereas the Middle Palaeolithic artefacts are 10 in number which include 4 hand axes, 2 scrapers and 4 flakes constitute the tool types.

Mesolithic Culture

A number of Microlithic tool assemblages have been identified in different parts of India. The study of the Belan stratigraphical section resolved the problem of its position in Indian context. In brief discussion, the entire section from bottom upwards has been divided into ten deposits consisting of the three gravels and the intervening deposits. Cemented gravel II or the deposit marked (7) and overlying reddish silt deposit (6) have yielded Middle Palaeolithic assemblage. Over the reddish silt (6) rest yellowish silt numbered as (5) has yielded an industry which can be called transitional between the Middle Palaeolithic and the Upper Palaeolithic. Cemented Gravel III or deposit number (4) is the true Upper Palaeolithic horizon followed by overlying layer (3) which has yielded Upper Palaeolithic blades along with Microlithic blades and flakes. Layer (2) and (1) have yielded Microliths associated with geometric shapes. The Belan stratigraphy further co-relate with Chopani Mando excavated site (Sharma 1980), Lakhania (Sharma 1965).

In case of Odisha, the Microliths are reported from different places. The Microlithic study by Mohapatra (1962) was done in a systematic exploration of the river valleys in north and central Odisha in order to locate pre-historic sites, particularly in the district of Mayurbhanj, Keonjhar, Sundargarh and Dhenkanal. After a decade gap, Singh identified Mesolithic phase near Sarang, Meramandali, Talchar, Gotamora, Balaram Prasad and Kundale (Singh 1985). All these sites are open air sites and the artefacts were collected from the loose rocky surface which rests above the Kankarised layer. All the sites except Gotamora are located close to the Brahmani river and its tributaries Nadira and Lingana. At the site of Gotamara a large number of flakes, blades, cores, reject material and fragments of crude potteries have been recovered in large quantities, and are spread over a wide area, whereas the finds from other sites are distributed over a small area. It suggests that the former one was workshop-cum-habitation site whereas the later sites were used for temporary purpose. The Kuchai excavation (IAR 1961-66) in north Orissa has some evidence of microliths but it does not give any clear-cut picture either of its age or the environmental condition at the time of the microlithic industry (Thapar 1976).

The upper Mahanadi valley in the Sundargarh district, specifically on Koel near Misankund, Shigudighat near Birsa town and Pitamahal and other sites have yielded a large number of microliths on compact reddish brown weathered sandy silt deposits. These tool types comprised of blunted backed blades and bladelets, lunates, micro-gravette points, borers, burins, a variety of side and end scrapers and a solitary trapeze. Typical geometric forms are completely absent. The raw material used for manufacturing these tools is mainly metamorphosed shale's and milky quartz (Behera 1983-84).

Explorations in Ghasipura and Harichandanpur Tahsils of the Keonjhar district by P. Mohanty (1983-84) resulted in the discovery of 12 primary Mesolithic sites. The majority of the sites are in association with the granite outcrops and a few are on the foot hills close to the tributary rivers. The sites are Karadapal, Tahsil, Noapara, Kachildarah, Karadabani, Sanahudi in Ghasipura Tahsil and Palarpur (Rebna), Golibeda, Chilikadah and Bhagamunda in Harichandanpur Tahsil. Four of these sites are quite large with the artefacts found spread in an area measuring 100m x 100m. Beside the above sites, at a few rock outcrops stray microliths and heavy artefacts were reported. Although these spots cannot be called as sites but their significance for interpreting the working of the Mesolithic cultural system cannot be ruled out. The microliths consisted of retouched blades, truncated blades, blunted backed blades, points, borers, crescents, triangles, trapezes, side scrapers, scrapers, hollow scrapers, knives, flake cores, blade cores, worked nodules and chips. Chert was the principal raw material found in most of the sites along with quartz, chalcedony and agate also utilized. All these site have heavy duty tools made of dolerite and quartzite in association with microlith artefacts. Their types included uni and bi-facial choppers, points, discoid cores having steep edges, scrapers, flakes, lunates, knives and celts.

Further in the exploration work at Champua, Ghasipura, Ghatangaon, Harichandanpur, Palaspal and Patana Tahsils of Keonjhar district Mohanty (1986-87) reported 58 Mesolithic sites. Most of the sites discovered are located in the granitic outcrops, whereas others were found in the foothill regions close to streams. The sites are ranging from the small ones, have an extent of 100m^2 whereas the largest size measures about 20,000m^2. The sites are now under dense forests. Most of the sites were primary and undisturbed by nature. The lithic industry of Keonjhar has been divided into two category (i) microlithic (ii) heavy-duty tools. Out of the total sites, 14 sites yielded only microlith, 5 sites yielded heavy duty components and the remaining 39 sites are of both components. There is no stratigraphical evidence to separate the two components. Thus, it is clear that the heavy duty tools found in this area, according to Mohanty form an integral part of the Mesolithic culture. The microlithic assemblages have the most outstanding feature of a well developed blade technology industry. The main tool types reported are backed blades, obliquely truncated blades, retouched blades, burins, knives, triangles, trapeze, crescents, lunates, side scraper, steep scrapers, thumb-nail scrapers, flake core, blade-core, micro blade core, utilized blades, flakes and chips. The techniques used were soft hammer of bone or wood, punch, or by pressure technique and then various type of retouching were done on them. Chert was the main raw material used. Besides these, quartz, chalcedony and dolerite were also used. Along with these tools, heavy duty artefacts made of dolerite, quartzite and lime stone are found. These differ from the microliths both in terms of raw materials and their typo-technological features. The heavy duty artefacts comprise of chopper-chopping tools, horse-hoof scrapers, picks, knives, large scrapers, limaces and flakes. Celt fashioned by means of flaking grinding and polishing is another interesting category of artefacts. However, the lithic data from Keonjhar are divided into four major classes as per its area of occupation, concentration and distribution of artefacts, artefacts of heavy duty and implement along with light scatters of microliths and pre-dominancy of heavy duty artefacts. In the North Central Odisha, this is possibly for the first time that a full attempt has been made to account for it in functional-ecological terms. As no fossil or organic remains were available at the site, it is not possible to give absolute dates to the culture but on the basis of the blade technology and edge-ground tools, these sites are dated tentatively between 5000 to 2000 BC (Mohanty;1989, 1992, 1993).

In the district of Boudh, Mesolithic sites occur in three contexts (1) river bank deposits (2) foothill region and (3) raised land / upland deposit of the rivers and small nallahs. In this phase the sites yielded artefacts assemblages of two different kinds namely microlithic artefacts (both geometric and non-geometric shapes) made of siliceous materials like chert, chalcedony etc. All the Mesolithic sites found in the region are associated with the alluvium deposits of about 1m to 3m determined forms different exposed section (Tripathy 1996).

An intensive exploration in Telkoi region of Keonjhar district was made by the Department of Anthropology, Utkal University in 1998 (Dehuri 1998, 2004). The reported artefacts include 287 microlithic artefacts from Madhusudanpur, Charigarh College area, Tungur Pahar, Balisahi, Nuagarh and Telkoi. The microlithic artefacts are dominated by fluted core, flake, blade, awl, borer, burin, point, scraper and notch. It is variety of crypto crystalline silica used as main raw material.

Apart from these, the above mentioned Department surveyed around Pallahara region (Basa 2000:16-61, Basa et al 2000:264-284) on the Mankara river basin which is a tributary of Brahmani from where a good number of microliths are reported. The important sites are Samiapalli, Subarnapalli, opposite SEDP, Pallahara College area, Bajpur, Muktapur and Kainsaripalli. The microliths are geometric and non-geometric type. In a trial trench at Bajpur, a microlithic horizon of Mesolithic culture was identified, in which bladelet, blade, crescent, burin and flake are recovered below 45cm of present surface. It is interesting to note that the microlithic implement concentration noticed just under the Neolithic horizon.

Besides the above mentioned explored microlithic site, during the field session 1996-97, the Department of Anthropology, Utkal University has conducted a field work around Kantala near Pallahara which revealed 270 microlithic artefacts, characterized by blade, flake, crescent etc. (Mishra 1997).

During the field session of 1999 in around Sankerjang area 411 artefacts were collected. These include Palaeolithic (lower and middle), Microlithic, Neolithic and Iron implements. There are 193 microlithic implements reported from the different sites. The dominant tool types are simple blade (66), flake (32), fluted cores (21), chips (18), backed blade (18), points (8) and borers (7) etc. The site Biraka shows the highest number of microliths and Barkhal shows only one microlith.

The Kardi locality of Boudh district has resulted in the discovery of six sites pertaining to prehistoric evidence, characterized by lithic tools, ceramics, terracotta relics, metal objects, and objects on faunal remains.

There are 273 mesolithic remains characterized by simple and shaped artefacts which have been collected from the six sites. Almost all the Mesolithic sites in the area have yielded microliths characterized by worked nodules, flake, burin, borers, notches and lunate. This suggests that both non-geometric and geometric forms of microliths were produced during the Mesolithic period for various functional purposes. These microliths are generally made of cryptocrystalline and crystalline rocks of opaque, translucent in natural, and characterized by chert of different shades, quartzite, jasper, agate, chalcedony and carnelian as well as mineral like quartz. It has been observed that various flakes and blade flakes were primarily made out of selected cores of different rocks by means of pressure flaking and fluting techniques (Sahoo 2013).

Neolithic Culture

In 1958-59, Mitra and Ghosh also reported some Neolithic artefacts in Keonjhar district (Mitra & Ghosh 1958-59). In the recent years scholars have paid much attention on the region after 1971 with a herdsman, Shri Somnath Biswal from the revenue village of Sankerjang, who spotted some curious large and smooth stone artefacts which protruded out of the side of a small hillock near his home, which now is displayed in State Museum (Census 1971). In the following years, P.K. Roy, Superintendent of the State Archaeology, Orissa undertook an excavation and revealed the materials of Neo-chalcolithic culture (Ray 1977). The important

Neolithic artefacts are variety of knapped and ground stone adze, which proved the finest technically and artistically yet to be excavated in South Asia (Yule & Rath 2000; 288).

In 1985, Behera has made extensive survey in Bonaigarh region of Sundargarh district (Behera 2000), reported 18 major workshop sites and minor workshop site. Geographically the area is an isolated hilly track, surrounded by rugged forest clad hill, intersected by a few narrow valleys, which are the only outlet to the neighboring regions. Most of the sites here are open air sites and located in two geographical contexts, viz; sites on the alluvial surface of the river banks and those in the foot hill or piedmont area.

Out of the 18 sites, the minor workshop sites are confined to southern part of the Bonai region and are generally found on the cliff surface of the river and foot hills as well as piedmont areas, usually not very far from the river Brahmani. From these sites, mainly finished and semi-finished celt of different types along with pebble tools, axes, adze, chopper-chopping, bored-stones, spearhead, grain pounders, elongated knife on pebble etc and debris were found of these axes of various types and chisels formed the main tools types in these workshops.

In major workshop sites, only one has yielded evidence for mass production of semi-finished celts, located near village Sulabhdihi. Behera argued that on the basis of the dimension of the site, it is presumed that this site must have served as a very large Neolithic celt manufacturing center. In a trial trench near Bargaon village three layers have been identified. The layer one had a deposit of 30 cm and yielded wheel made pottery and some iron objects. The second layer yielded wheel made potteries with red ware, grey ware and few potsherds of black and red ware whereas the third layer reported shapeless, coarse and gritty red ware sherds, several celt, dressed flakes and a broken semi-finished chisel were reported.

The result of the excavation suggest that the Neolithic culture complex of the Bonaigarh sub-division belonged to pre-iron phase and was associated with a coarse gritty-tempered red ware, a feature also noticed at Kuchai in the Mayurbhanj district of Orissa (Thapar 1985;

45). Thus the Bonaigarh neolithic is datable to second half of the 2nd millennium B.C.

Singh (2000) during the course of his survey carried out in between 1980-85 in the district of Angul and Dhenkanal covering a total area of 10,826 sq km had identified 19 Neolithic sites. The sites are mostly found along river Brahmani and its tributaries. The Neolithic people of this place generally preferred the locally available rocks, which are not locally available and it is presumed that they might have been quarried from the adjoining localities. All together 211 tools have been picked up from these sites, which includes axes, adzes chisels, bar celts, scrapers, ring stones, shouldered-celts, chopper and hand made pottery with grain impressions. There imply about the traits of incipient agricultural and social life of the early man in this region.

Pallahara, a small town is the sub divisional head quarters of the Angul district. In the exploration carried out in the Mankara river valley which is a major tributary to the river Brahmani (Mohanta 1995, Basa et.al. 2000). The survey resulted in the discovery of pre-historic sites yielding artefacts belonging to the Palaeolithic, Mesolithic and Neolithic cultures. Of these the Neolithic were found at Somiapalli, Subarnapalli, Pallahara College area, Bajpur, Muktapur, Illisuan, opposite S.E.D.P. office and Udaypur.

In all, 205 Neolithic artefacts were recovered from the surface exploration and the excavation. The main tool types of the Neolithic culture are axe, chisel and dimple-scarred rubber, flakes and chips. The axes were usually made with rectangular butt, but a few are also found with irregular butt. Their working edges are beveled and made sharp ended. Chisel, both finished and unfinished along with blank of quadrilateral shape are found. The dimple-scarred rubber stone have shallow marks on one side and also on both the sides. The raw material used for making the tools here is predominantly dolerite.

The trial trench at Bajpur revealed habitation deposit upto 85 cm. and divided into three distinct layers. The 1st layer is 13 cm thick and is yellow reddish in colour. The layer 2nd is 30 cm thick; layer 3rd is 42 cm thick and is reddish in colour. The first two layers belong to the

Neolithic culture and the third one has yielded microliths. The Neolithic artefacts include Neolithic flakes and chips without any finished tool, whereas the Mesolithic tool assemblage consists of blade-lets, blade and crescents made on chert. Another important trait i.e. potsherds also recovered from the surface as well as excavation are prepared on slow wheel on coil method with two main types identified as coarse red ware and black and red ware. The potteries found here can be compared with those found at Kuchai (the first ever excavated Neolithic site in Orissa), scholars have tentatively tried to date them on the basis of chronology of the Early Metal Age sites in the same region to around 2nd millennium B.C.

Another important site Sankerjang was visited by members from the Excavation Branch IV, Bhubaneswar and reported a few Neolithic tools which comprised ring stones and small celts.

In Boudh district, the Neolithic phase has not been firmly established. However the excavations at Manamunda also yielded some implements of Neolithic culture, but the main problem lies in the fact that without a clear cut cultural phase one cannot ascertained a particular nomenclature to a cultural phase. Only one site named Salekata, 30 km south from the Boudh town properly yielded some polished stone implements and a variety of crude red ware (Tripathy 1996).

In the year 1997-98, an intensive exploration in the Telkoi region has resulted 532 artefacts, out of which 221 are of Neolithic period. Typologically, the ring stone, axe, chisel are important one. In a trail trench T1, near Telkoi resulted potsherds of red ware and another trench T2, exposed west to the previous resulted 4 flakes, 1 axe in upper layer, whereas the lower layer reported microlithic tools (Dehuri 1998, 2004).

Ranjana Ray of Calcutta University reported a Neo-chalcolithic site near Kanjipani locally known as Kuanr which is located on the right bank of Masani nallah and surrounded by another nallah i.e. Ghumura nallah. The northern side of the mound is highly dissected. There are a number of channels on this side, in which a large quantity of tools and potsherds are coming out. The findings were axe, adze, saddle quern, ring stone, hammer stone, various type of scraper, blade, points, awls, borers, knives as well as large quantity of flakes and chips. All the celts were made by chipping, pecking and grinding technique. But the Kuanr celts are chipped and ground and very much akin to what had been found from Barudih and Dugui (Ghosh et al 1982, 1984a, 1984b).

Apart from these, the Department of Anthropology, Utkal University explored the central as well as north-central Odisha and reported a number of Neolithic sites specifically in Malikhojha area (Sankerjang locality) in Angul district. The Pallahara region has also yielded a number of Neolithic sites in which adze, axe, ring stone are dominant varieties (Mohanta 1995, Mishra 1997). An exploration in Sankerjang region of Angul district was made by the Department of Anthropology, Utkal University in 1999 (Mohanty 1999). The sites have resulted Neo-chalcolithic artefacts and yielded 196 specimens out of which lithic artefacts are 194 and 2 copper objects. The lithic remains include axe, adze, chisel, ring stone, muller, hammer cum polisher, bar axes and bar adzes. The waste products of Neo-chalcolithic tools are flakes and chips. Among the neo-chalcolithic materials groove marked flake (54), simple flake (40), chisel (26), axe (16), ring stone (14) are dominant varieties. The bar axe (7) and bar celt (2) are collected from the Sankerjang localites.

Altogether only three Neolithic artefacts have been yielded from the Kardi region. All these three are chisel and remnant of chisel, made out of dolerite rock. The tool types found from the study area have typo technological similarities with the Bonai and Pallahara material (Sahoo 2013).

Chalcolithic Culture

The site Kuanr reported Chalcolithic remains which consist of large quantity of potsherds, terracotta pieces, burnt clay pellets, charcoals and metal ornaments. Potsherds are too fragmentary. They are red and buff in colour but some are with slips, coarse to medium fabric. Metal objects found from the site are ornaments. These include nine bangles and two rings. Apparently the ornaments are made up of bronze. The bangles are of design with parallel lines engraved at equal intervals along the width of the bangle. The site is very rich one. It suggests the presence of chalcolithic culture in Orissa in a wider scale. The archaeo-metallurgy points out to the possibilities of great antiquity for brass as an alloy in this region. The findings from Kuanr may broadly be placed after Neolithic and before the Iron age (Ghosh et al 1984).

In the survey during the field session (1999) of Department of Anthropology, Utkal University around the Sankerjang has reported Neo-chacolithic remains have been reported in the form of copper objects. The copper objects are identified as bangles (Mohanty 1999).

Historical Period

Unlike the other aspect of archaeology, the historical perspective has played an important role to shape history with the help of textual sources and archaeological remains located in the geographical context. In last century, scholars have attempted to map out the historical significance at regional level and to highlight its cultural evidences.

A cave shelter inscription in Sitabinji is an eye opener to the north-central and north Orissa, in which referring to Maharaja Sri Disabhanja and Brahmi script belonging to 5th century A.D. (Senapati 1986:42). A natural rock shelter locally known as 'Ravanachhaya' contains an ancient rock painting depicting a royal procession where a king riding on an elephant holding water lily in his left hand and a goad in right hand along with well decorated attendant, horse man, dress of the soldiers, ornaments and floral motifs are important. Apart from these the other reported archaeological finds of the site include female figurines, bronze ornaments, beads, ear studs, terracotta, copper cast Puri-Kushana coins, lamp stand, elephant figures and brunt bricks. Another important evidence of the site is the Chaturmukha Sivalinga that shows the ancient Shiva shrine at the site. (Ramachandran 1951:5-25; Panigrahi 1981:369, Mohanti 1988; Senapati 1986: 42 and 433-434; Mohapatra 1986: 173-174).

In recent years an early historical site has been reported at Telkoi on the left bank of river Somakoi, a tributary of the river Brahmani. The mound covered an area of 150 x 100 meters and height is about 6 meter from the present river bed level. It is undisturbed and scattered with a large quantity of potsherds, a few iron artefacts, a dimple scar rubber, spout, dish on stand and flake of deprival fine grained granite (Dehuri 1998). A large amount of iron slag is noticed to the west of the site across the stream with a distance of about 500 meter. Along with brick bats a good number of polished quartzite pieces have also noticed.

The excavated early historic sites of Manmunda, Asurgarh, 50 km west of Boudh town yielded cultural material dating back to 3rd century BC to 1st century AD. The findings, especially pottery helped in reconstructing the trade activity of the region. The finding of black polished ware and lids with knob in a large quantity is significant for the comparison and dating of the sites. Apart from these the site has also yielded pig iron slag (Tripathy 2000).

Out of nine sites reported from Kardi region of Boudh district only four sites have yielded early historical evidence which includes various types of ceramics remains, terracotta remains and metal object. The forms of the ceramic remains include those of vase/handi, bowl, dish, basin, vase, lids. The other terracotta remains include smoke stand, toy wheel, Hopscotch/discs, leg of animal figurine and unidentified cylindrical objects. The metal objects in the collection include an interesting female figurine made of copper (Sahoo 2013).

Sankerjang has been well known as neo-chalcolithic site from 1970. However, the present survey by the Department of Anthropology, Utkal University in around the Sankerjang and from trial trenches yielded evidence of Iron artefacts. Besides the iron evidence the site has yielded the evidence of secondary mortuary practice belonging to the Iron age. In all such cases iron artefacts have been unearthed (Nayak 1999).

The above review contains a summary of lithic tradition and historical archaeology of Orissa reconstructed on the basis of survey, excavation and analytical observation of cultural archaeological edifice. However, in spite of the attempts and progress made in archaeology of Odisha, both in prehistoric and historical archaeology, there are some major limitations (Basa 1994, 1997, 2000).

Limitations of Archaeological Research in Odisha

1. The surface explorations has been made in various regions of Odisha with excavation at few places. These excavations are basically of vertical nature to throw light on relative chronology with diachronic perspective. In the absence of horizontal excavation, it is difficult to reconstruct a comprehensive history of the society at a synchronic level.
2. Chronology is the major problem in Odishan archaeology, in which radio carbon dates available from the site of Sankerjang (2590+60 B.P. (KN 3753), Cal-795 BC (Basa 1997: 40-41). Sinha (2000:344) has reported a radio carbon date from Golbai Sasan for the beginning of Period IIa which is 4100+100BP (PRL No. 1637). Behera has reported some dates from western Odisha site.
3. The adoption of inter-disciplinary approach is very limited to the Odishan archaeology. However, the techniques like remote sensing and X-ray diffraction analysis would be a great help to archaeological research. In Odishan archaeology, problems still remain on various issues. These include the site formation process, domestication of plants and animals, identification of port sites from early historic period onwards, etc. Inter-disciplinary approach is the answer to all these problems (Basa 1997:47) with the recent advances in Odishan archaeology, which had travelled from the period of romanticism of the nineteenth century.
4. The early historical archaeology study was confined to coastal as well as a few urban sites only whereas rural sites of the early historical period can serve to understand the approaches like catchment analysis, state formation process and ancient trade.

With this background it is appropriate to discuss the study area and its present environment which is the content of the next chapter.

CHAPTER 2

The Study Area and Present Environment

In the present Chapter the study area and its environment has been delineated. Besides, the aims and objectives as well as the various methods followed are also stated. Then the sites which were discovered during survey have been described. The stratigraphy of the area has been reconstructed on the basis of two sections. In the end, various artefacts recovered have been presented in a tabular form.

Geographically the North Central Odisha, comprises the districts of Angul, Deogarh, southern-western part of Keonjhar, north part of Dhenkanal, north part of Jajpur, western part of Mayurbhanj and eastern part of Sambalpur. These districts are vastly covered with dense mixed jungle with rich mineral resources such as vast deposits of iron, manganese, coal and chrome ore. Anthropologically, the land is inhabited by a number of tribal groups like the Juang, Bhumij, Hos, Kisan etc. The North Central Odisha contains old rocks covering an area of 100 sq. km. at Asanpat in Keonjhar district. The Keonjhar district was sequel to the integration of the feudatory state with Odisha on the 1st January 1948 where as the Angul district is very much newly created in the year 1995 from the Dhenkanal district. Before its merger with

Odisha the whole North Central Odisha districts were princely state. The early history of the area is not adequately known. It was most probably a part of the Bhanja dynasty ruling over Keonjhar district and Bhanja of Angulaka-Pattana of modern Angul district with its head quarter old Angul or Purana garh.

The present study area covers two districts, namely, Keonjhar and Angul. The Keonjhar district lies between 21° 1' N and 22° 10' N Latitude and 85° 11' E and 85° 22' E longitudes the Angul district lies between 20° 29' N and 21° 42'N Latitudes and 86° 29' E and 86° 21' E Longitudes. It is bounded by the districts of Sundargarh, Sambalpur in west; Dhenkanal, Jajpur in south; Mayurbhanj, Baleswar in east and the Singhbhum district of Jharkhand state in north. The area covered around 12593.05 sq. km. (of Keonjhar and Angul district) (Fig.3).

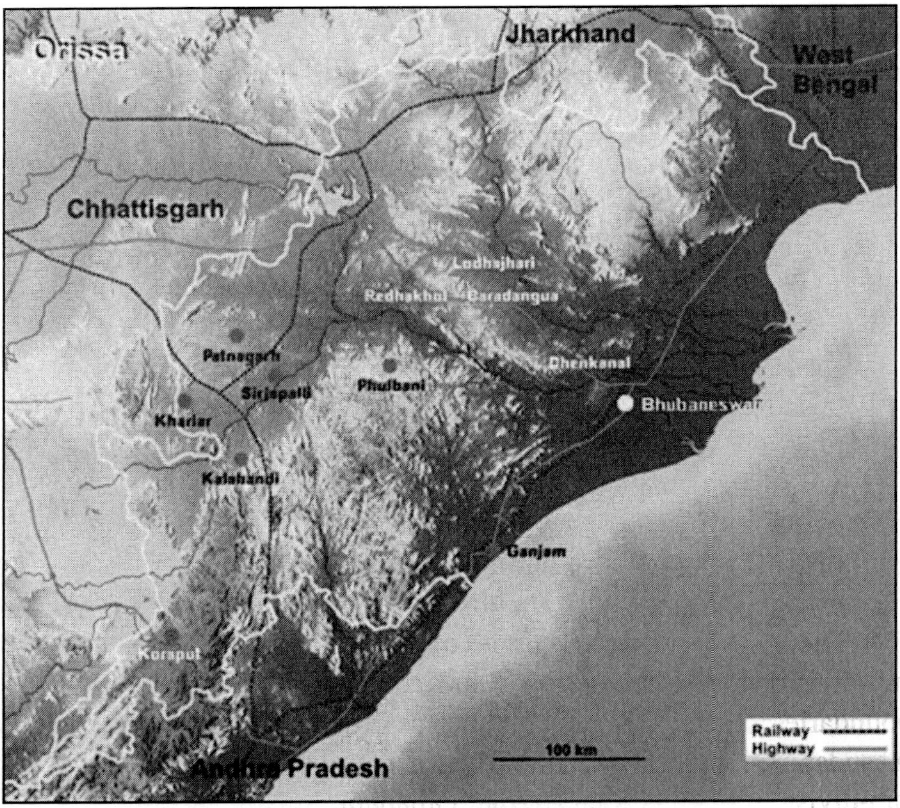

Fig.2: Google map showing Odisha.

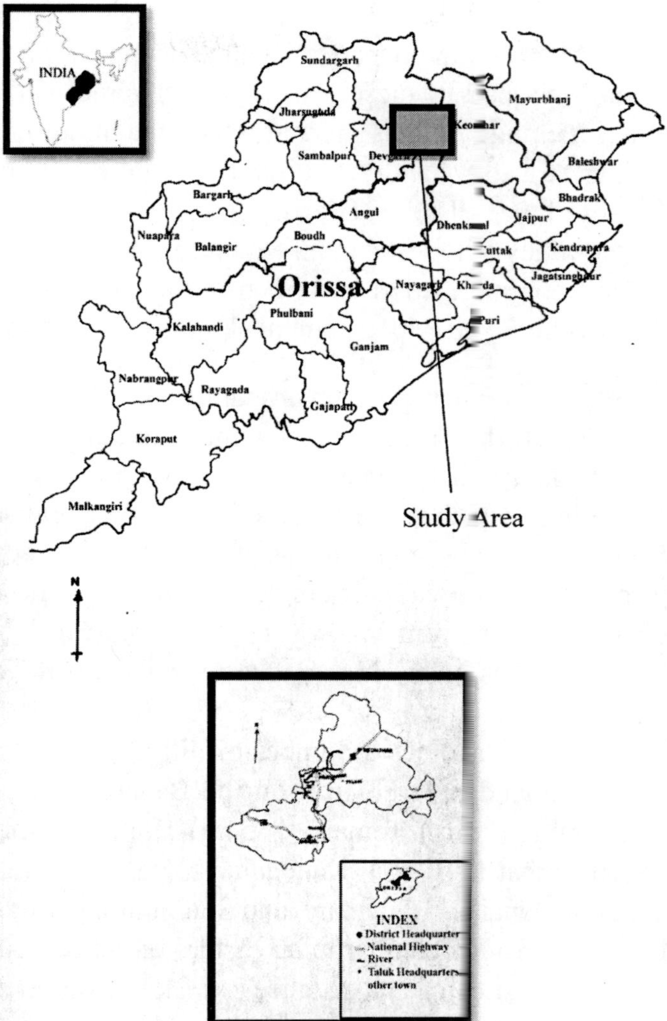

Fig.3: Map of Odisha showing the district Angul and Keonjhar.

The administrative boundaries of the district are further divided into sub-division and tahsil. In respect of Keonjhar district, the sub-divisions boundaries are divided into three such as, Keonjhar sadar, Champua and Anandapur. Similarly, the Angul district is also sub divided into four sub-divisions such as Angul Sadar, Pallahara, Athamallik and Talcher.

Topography of the Study Area

The area consists of southern part of Keonjhar and northern part of Angul district. Most part of these districts are covered with the dense jungle and a vast range of hills. The area is undulating and contains a number of fertile valleys and the soil varies from a rich loam to the gravelly detritus of the hill slope. Broadly speaking the district of Angul is formed of the valley of the Brahmani which has hilly tracts to its south and north. The Keonjhar district is formed of the valley and low lands and mountainous highland with a general slope from north to south.

Hill & Mountain System

In the Angul district, the northern mountainous regions cover the east and north of Pallahara sub-division. Here a magnificent hill called Malaygiri (1.187mt), which is one of the loftiest peaks in Odisha, towers above the hill ranges. The high hills to the north of the region form the Central portion of the mass of tangled hill ranges which stretched towards Keonjhar. Apart from Malaygiri the Banmundali is 790 mt. in height. The district has a few high peaks in Pallahara region having elevation of over 762 meter.

The Keonjhar district has a number of hill ranges. The principal peaks are Gandhamandan (1.117 mt) on the Banai Border, Gonasika (978 mt), Thakurani (915 mt), Tomaka (785 mt), Bolat (554 mt), Khajaru (918 mt), Mahaparbat (716 mt), Kandadhar Parbat (915 mt) situated near the border of Bonai and Pallahara, and Sitabinji (670 mt) situated at a district of 19 km. from Keonjhar in an eastern direction. Chakratirtha and Baula Parbat are situated at a distance of 16 km. from Anandapur in north-easterly direction.

River System

The study area comes under the river basin of Brahmani and Baitarani, which have major source from Chotanagpur plateau and the Keonjhar plateau. These rivers are perennial in nature and have their own local importance. On the basis of their location and the direction of flow, these river can be broadly divided into two division, namely; (a) the river of Brahmani basin includes Brahmani, Mankra, Kakharua, Somakoi, Ramiala, Singda and Nigra. (b) the Baitarani basin includes the rivers like Aradei or Ororai, Kanjhari, Kukurkata, Kusai, Musal and Salandi. Brief descriptions of some important rivers are given below to understand the drainage system of the area (Fig.4).

Rivers of the Brahmani Basin

(1) **Brahmani-** It is the largest river which originated from the Chotanagpur plateau by primarily two rivers called south Koel and Sankh and both have joined together near Panposh in Sundargarh district and from downward called as Brahmani. The Brahmani has also the usual religious sanctity attached to it which has received recognition in some Puranas. The name Brahmani appears to be a modern one but its old name is Sankhajyoti. The Brahmani enters Angul district 3 km. west of Banor in Pallahara sub-division. In southward the river marks the border of Pallahara and Talchar sub-division. The Somakoi, Tikra Singlajor, Nigra and Ramaila are major tributaries of Brahmani which join with the river at different places. The river has uncertain course which changes occasionally but generally it flows in south ward direction and then finally drain into Bay of Bengal. The length of the river within Angul·district is about 75 km. Apart from these above tributaries the river Brahmani has a number of other tributaries in lower part.

(2) **Mankara**- It takes its origin in sadar sub-division of Keonjhar district then flows westward. The Kukhra or Kakharua is the major tributary of this river which joins about 7 km. east of Pallahara.

(3) **Tikra**- The River Tikra rises in Rairakhol sub-division of Sambalpur district and after passing through a portion of Rairakhol and Deogarh sub-divisions enters into the Angul district and joins river Brahmani near Kaniha.

(4) **Nigra-** It rises from the hills which forms the boundary between Angul and Athmalik subdivisions, joins the Brahmani at Kharga Prasad near Meramandali railway station in Dhenkanal sub-

division. The Nigra has two principal tributaries known as Bauli and Mutkuria with a length of 48 km. and 45 km. respectively.

(5) **Somakoi**- The river Somakoi takes its origin near Gendachaua hill of Kalapat reserved forest area of Keonjhar district. It follows a zigzag course almost in a westerly direction and falls into the river Brahmani in Angul district. Telkoi, one of important place is situated on its bank, its length is about 50 km. in Angul district.

Rivers of the Baitarani Basin

(1) **Baitarani-** Baitarani is regionally regarded as holy as Ganga, so it is also called as Gupto Ganga in Odisha. It is the largest river in Keonjhar which originates from Gupta Ganga Pahar in Keonjhar plateau of Janghira-Dhinkikot region of sadar sub-division of Keonjhar district. After flowing from the hills it flows towards the north as a hill stream up to the border area of the west Singhbhum district of Jharkhand state near Champua and Jaganathpur and from where it immediately turns towards south. Finally, it drains into the Bay of Bengal at Dhamara in the district Balasore. The total length of the river is 344 km. Its major tributaries are Kanjhari, Kukurkata, Kusai and Musal etc.

(2) **Aradei (Ororai)**- The river Aradei takes its origin from the hill regions near Bararoan pahar in the south-east of Keonjhar and finally joins with the river Baitarani near Champua. The major tributaries of the river are Machakandana, Kadai and Sothi or Kasia.

(3) **Kanjhari**- The Kanjhari rises near Gonasika hill and joins Baitarani south of Udaipur. In its 56 km. way it crosses important villages named Ramchandrapur, Raghunathpur and Poipani.

(4) **Kukurkata**- Kukurkata is another important river rising in the forest near Jhalbera and flowing in easterly direction and falling into the river Baitarani. Two important historical sites i.e fresco painting and inscription at Dongaposi and Sitabinji are located on the bank of this river.

(5) **Kusai-** The Kusai rises from the Rebna reserved forests south of Meghanada parbat and flows in south-easterly direction and merges

in the river Kukurungi. Then it takes almost an easterly direction and follows a zigzag course until it finally debouches into the river Baitarani. It's important tributaries are Remal, Sindhu and Ganda. The mediaeval temple site of Kosaleswar Siva temple is located in the Deogaon village on the river bank.

(6) Musal- It rises from Meghanada parbat and follows the east and south east direction and joins in the river Baitarani near Simria.

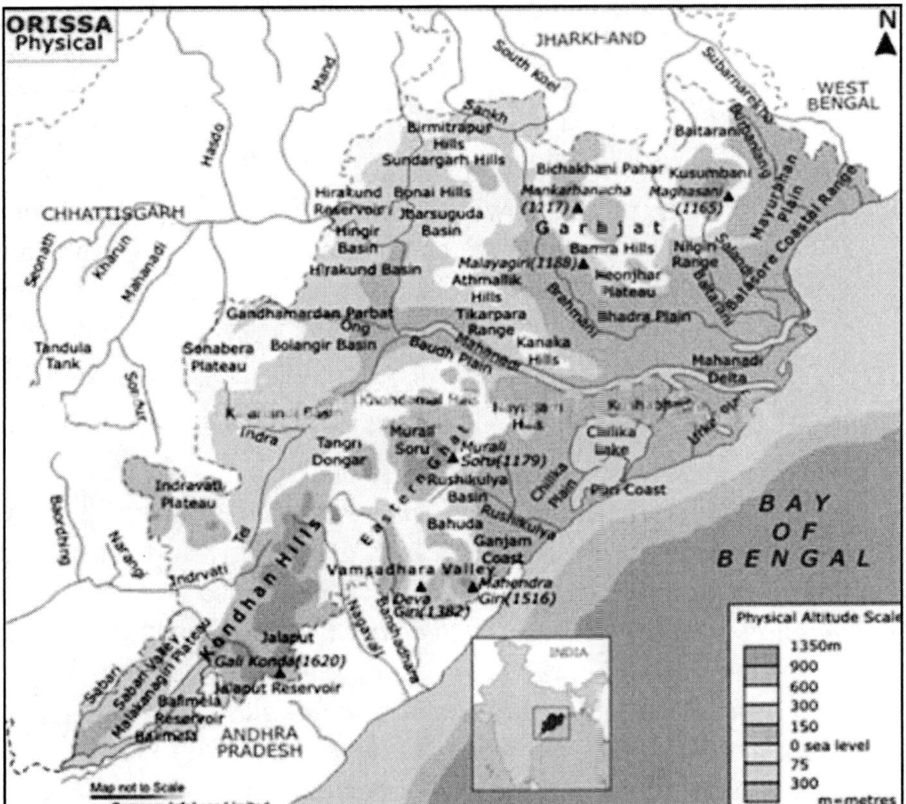

Fig.4: Physical profile of Odisha.

(7) Kakharua- The river Kakharua rises from Giri parbat of Gandhamardan massif. It follows west and south-west direction and follows a zigzag course until it finally merges into river Mankara near Pallahara. The length of this river is about 25 km long and flows through densely wooded tract. The important village falling in the course of the river is Birikala, Champajhar, Jamudiha, Kadadiha, Rugudidiha, Nagira, Jolanda, Atanaka, Jamardiha, Gopapur. After running through the Keonjhar, Angul district the river joins with small river Mankara other joins the Brahmani.

Forest

The North Central Odisha has covered a vast land of forest cover and hill tract. The two districts Angul and Keonjhar comprise mostly of steer hills and narrow winding valleys, in which Sal (*Shorea Robusta*) trees are dominant in present. On the basis of relief, rainfall and vegetation the forest are classified into (a) tropical moist deciduous forest (b) tropical semi- evergreen forest (c) mixed deciduous hill forest (d) high level Sal forest (e) dry deciduous Sal forest (f) plain Sal forest and glass land savannahs.

In the Angul and Keonjhar district, the forest areas are scattered throughout the district but they occur generally in Pallahara and Athmalik sub-divisions in Angul district, and Champua and Keonjhar sadar sub-division in Keonjhar district.

The tropical moist deciduous forest or the monsoon forests are located in the lower elevations. Sal (*Shorea Robusta*) is the predominant species found in this area. It gives a high grade charcoal for different types of smelting activities. The other associate important trees are Asan (*Terminalia tomentosa*), Kusum (*Schleicher trijuga*), Champa (*mycelia champa*), Amba (*mangifera indica*) Simuli (*Bombox malabarica*), Jam (*Eugenia Jambolena*) and Chara (*Buchanaia latitolia*) etc.

The tropical semi-evergreen forests occur in the lower hills and valley areas. The important tree species include Jam (*Eugenia jambolena*), Karanja (*pangamia glabra*); Arjun (*terminalia arjuna*), Simuli (*Bobmox Malabarica*), Kadamba (*Anthrocephalus kadamba*) and Nageswar (*ptereosper-mum suavedens*) etc.

High level Sal occurs at the flat topped hills and piteous of 1830 ft to 2745 ft. Dry deciduous Sal forests are noticed at the shallow infertile exposed hill slopes. Very poorer quality of Sal in association with Kendu (*disophous melanoxylon*), dum kurudu grows in this area. Sal forests occur both in flat plains and slightly undulated areas, where as the grass land seen at the hill-tops, hill slopes and valley area.

Fauna

The extensive and dense forests of these districts harbor a great number of wild animals in which the carnivorous animals include, leopard, bear, hyena, wolf, wild dogs and fox. Herbivorous animal, sambars, spotted deer (harina), barking deer (kutura), porcupines, (jhinka), wild boar (barha) are found throughout the district. Elephants are found in the dense forest area.

There are various kinds of birds found is this area. The pea fowl, jungle fowl and common spur fowl are fairly common. The whistling teal and the little cotton teal are common resident. The aqua-fauna comprises rivers rohi (*Labeo rohita*), bhakura (*Catla Catla*), mirkali (*Cirrhina Mrigala*), magura (*claries batrachians*) and seul (*Ophicephalus striates*).The principal snakes and reptiles are cobra, (*Bara tripudians*), vipers (*Viprera russeelli*), krait (*Bangarus Ceruleus*). Sometimes the little thantia are found in large rivers.

Climate

The climate of Keonjhar and Angul district is more like that of the Deccan plateau than of the east coast region and characterized by an oppressive hot summer, high humidity and well distributed rainfall during the monsoon season. The hot season is from March to May. The period from June to September is the south-west monsoon season. October and November constitute the post-monsoon and the cold season is from December to February.

Rainfall

About 76 percent of the annual rainfall in the Angul as well as Keonjhar district is experienced during the south-west monsoon season, July being the rainiest month. The hot season commences at the beginning of March when the temperature begins to rise rapidly. May is the hottest month when the mean daily maximum temperature is about 38° C, and the mean daily minimum temperature is about 25° C. The maximum temperature may sometimes reach 46° C with oppressive heat. During the monsoon the temperature comes down to pleasant condition. December is usually coldest month in the year and the mean daily minimum temperature is about 12° C. The relative humidity is generally high and it is about 75 percent winds are generally light to moderate with some increase in force in the summer and monsoon season.

Agriculture

Keonjhar and Angul are primarily agricultural districts. The practice of cultivation is still primitive and lands are mostly rain fed. The whole region can be broadly divided as plain region of Brahmani and Baitarani belt in which the soil type is alluvial with loamy structure. The hilly region of Bhuyanpirh, the region comprises the part of Pallahara region and the Bansapal area. This region lies between the hills ranges of Gandamardan of Bansapal area to Malayagiri of Pallahara region. The soil type is red laterite with high iron content and acidic in nature. The soil is subject to heavy erosion; and lacks fertility; moreover, shifting cultivation is done by the local tribal cultivators. The crop production in the district is mostly dependant on rainfall and the chief crop of the district is rice, both wet and upland, winter crops of almost all the cereals grown in Odisha are cultivated here. Minor millets are sown by the poor people on deteriorated land to supplement their food before rice is harvested. Maize is extensively grown both in Bansapal and Pallahara uplands. Agriculture in the study area of the district is not mechanized. The age old wooden plough and several other implements suit the local condition of soil and crop are in use. The country plough is the most commonly used implement.

Generally the cultivators follow the rotation of some crops and rational cropping pattern required due to absence of sufficient irrigation facilities the agriculture of the districts depend upon natural rainfall.

Geology

The Angul district falls in the hill area towards the boundary of Keonjhar. These hills and ridges are separated by broad valleys and low hilly areas. The higher hills of this region are composed of quartettes (Iron ore series and Kolhan series) while the lesser hills are made of quartz-mica schist's and other rocks. The broad valleys are mostly of gneisses. The district Keonjhar comprised of the quaternary to recent formation. The Iron formation of Gandhamardan hill (west of Kendujhar) with associated quartette, ferruginous shale, basalt and tuff forms the south-eastern boundary of this group in the district. Laterite, alluvium and soil cover all the formation of the district (Fig.5).

Mineral Resource of the Districts

In respect of Angul district, the best rock formation are Khandalites, Charnockites and their variants. They are succeeded by a series of younger formation of iron ore series. Both the formations were, however, grouped in the pre-Cambrian age. These are in turn succeeded by the rocks of Gondwana system belonging to upper Paleozoic to Mesozoic. The laterite and alluvium were deposited during Quaternary period.

Iron Ore

On the basis of physical setting of Odisha, the distribution of Iron Ore is divided into five distinct zones namely: Tomka-Daitari, Bonai-Keonjhar, Gorumahisani – Badampahad and Hirapur (Chakrabarti 1992:32). Besides, there is enough lateritic capping outside the Mahanadi – Baitarani Delta (Ball 1881; 361-362). The iron ore production is very high in Keonjhar and presently a fair reserve status iron ore also marked in Angul district. In Keonjhar, the Singhbhum-Kendujhar- Bonai iron ore belt run through the district. The usual type of ore is massive, hard and compact, steel grey to dark and brownish black in colour. The varieties include (1) hard ore (steel grey to brownish, massive and laminated) (2) moderately hard ore (laminated) (3) soft ore (flatly, friable and powdery) and (4) laterite ores. Another major iron deposits are Gandhamandan and Khandadar zones in which a part extended to Pallahara sub-division of Angul district. The parent rocks of these iron ore deposits are Banded Iron Formation (BIF) and, more precisely the Banded Hematite Jaspur (BHJ) or Banded Hematite Quartz (BHQ) and ferruginous shale's. Hematite constitutes the predominant band

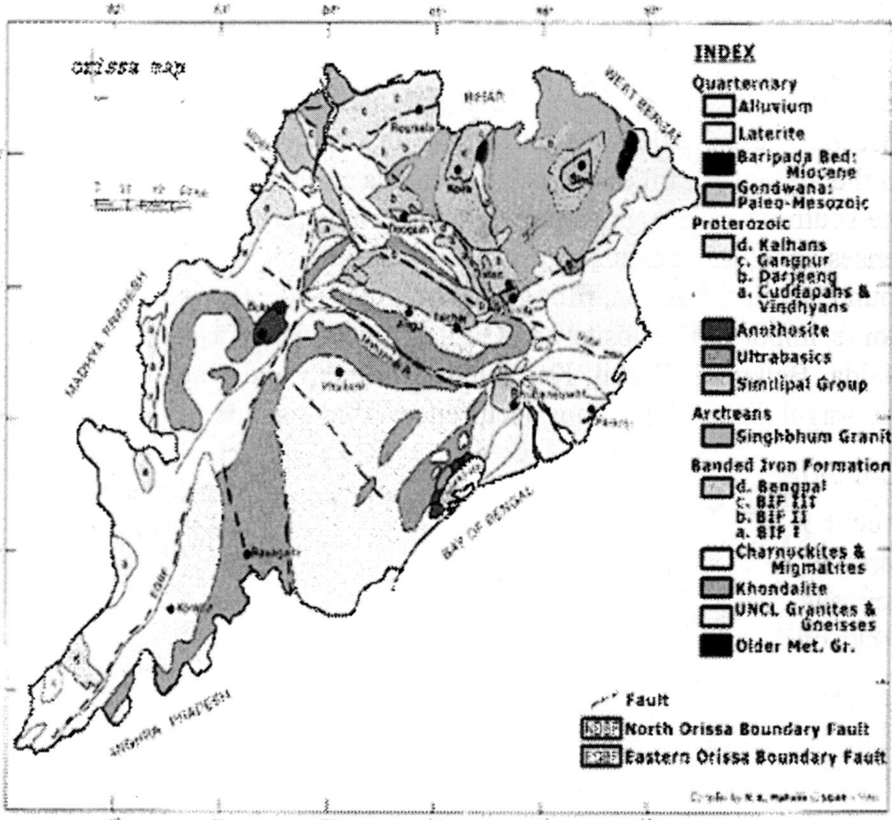

Fig.5: Geological map of Odisha.

in layered BIF, over magnetite's, martite, geothite and magnetite. The ore types include massive (often hard and compact, widely jointed and containing 64-68% Fe), laminated (biscuit-like when in fine lamiae, medium hard to soft, porous, friable, exhibit folding and crumpling, containing 62-65% Fe), Shaley (Shaley textured and brittle, containing 61-63% Fe), lateritic (product of alteration of the former types, porous, containing 5658% Fe), Powdery (Fine grayish blue, occurring in bands and pockets, containing 65-68% Fe), and the recommended ore or conga (Braciated flat beds with sub-angular hematite boulders and embedded in lateritic matrix, overall grade 58-60% Fe) (Mohanty1998).

Manganese Ore

Keonjhar is very rich in manganese. More than 90% of manganese ores of Odisha are extracted from Keonjhar and Bonai area of Sundergarh district. These ore deposits found over an area of 500 sq kms. Confined to the area of Barbil in the north, Dhubna in the south and Bhutura in the south-west through some workable ore deposits are found in small lenses irregular pockets, thin bands etc, a few high grade deposits are found in veins, fraction, fillings and irregular bodies in brachiated chert. Some important deposits are Gurda, Raida, Bhadrasai, Sidhamatha, Nalda, Belkundi, Barbil, Karo, Joda, Kalimati and Dhubna, where as the Angul district has minor occurrences of manganese ore.

Chromite

About 90% of Chromite in India is present in Odisha of which total reserve of about 0.33 million tones are in Keonjhar. The chromite deposits of this district are found in association with the ultra basic rocks of Boula, Nausali and Phulinjhorhuli areas.

Distribution of Other Minerals

Other important minor minerals are china clay, gold, talc and soap stone, pyrite, bauxite etc, also noticed in the Angul and Keonjhar district (Fig.6).

Population

According to the 2011 census there is 3,075,480 people in the two districts. Among these people 1,802,777 are residing in the district of Keonjhar and rest 1,272,703 are in Angul district. The literacy rate is respectively 78% and 69.00% in Angul and Keonjhar district. Schedule tribes including primitive tribes constitute the major group in this area. The scheduled tribes of this area are mostly Santhal, Ho, Munda, Bathudi, Gond, Saunti, Bhumij, Bhuiyan, Kolha, Sarara, Oraon and Vodha. The tribes like Juangs are inhabitants in the high land of Keonjhar plateau. They are basically depending upon shifting cultivation. Apart from their traditional occupation they also depend highly on other forest product

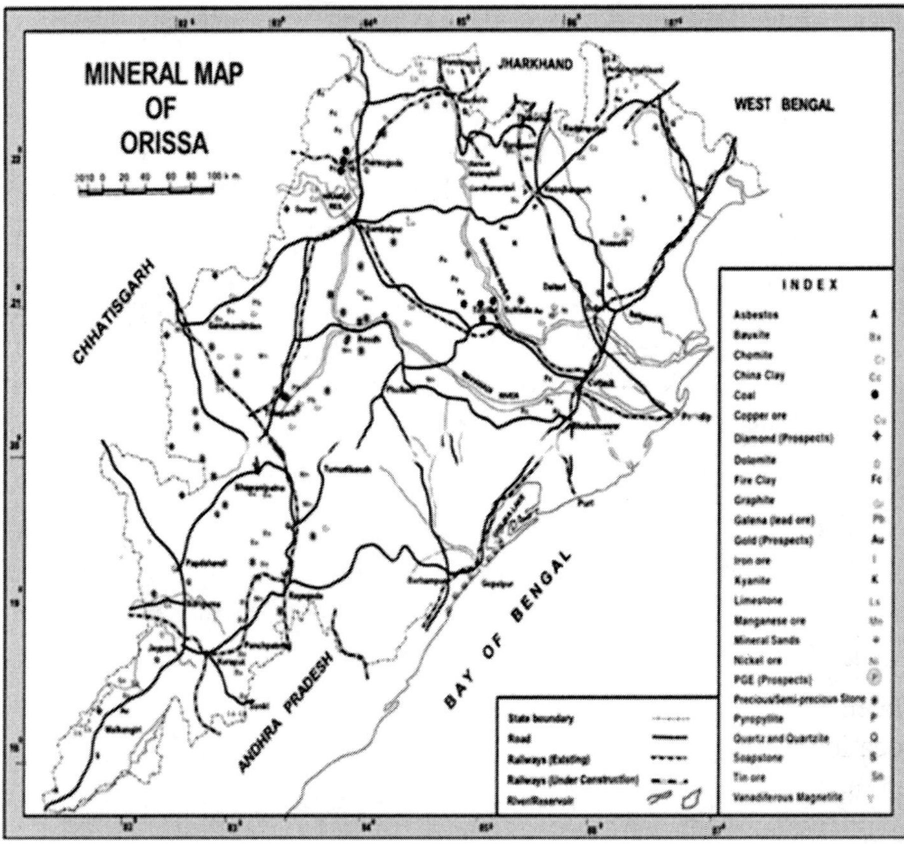

Fig.6: Mineral Map of Odisha.

and collect honey, resin, wax, gum, myrobalan, arrow-root, lac, kendu leaves, sal seed, neem seed, kusum seed and karanj seed from different parts of jungle. Though some of the tribes like Santhal, Ho, Munda, Oraon etc. are settled agriculturists, they also collect different forest products during their free time.

CHAPTER 3

Archaeological Sites in the Kakharua Valley

During the field survey for the present work, an emphasis has been given to locate the maximum number of sites from different geophysical locations for which an intensive field exploration has been conducted on the river valley, piedmont areas and on the foot hills. However, after an intensive survey 30 archaeological sites have been discovered on the Kakharua valley. Details descriptions of the sites are given below in alphabetical order.

Atanaka Reserve Forest Area (ARF) N. 21° 30.545' E. 85° 16.183', Alt. 691 ft.

The site is on a high elevated land located just west of Atanaka reserve forest. The river Kakharua is flowing left to the site. The site extends 200 mt. x 100 mt. area in north-south and east west direction within a bushy jungle. A large amount of Neolithic and small chips were scattered over the area. Along with the Neolithic chips a good number implements such as, axe fragment of ring stone are also collected. Apart from these Neolithic tools a few microliths have also been collected (Fig.7, pl. 7).

Bhaluguda:- (BLG) N- 21° 28.980' E- 85° 15.882', Alt. 617 ft.

A highly erosional channel is located on the left Dalo-Jolanda, just 300 mt. north-west of iron crusher. The site is locally known as Bhaluguda, which comes under Soida village boundary and about 1.5 km. west of to the left bank of Kakharua. The site extends to 200 x 100 mtr. in east-west and north-south direction. The exposed channel has yielded a few microliths of non-geometric variety (Fig.11 & 16).

Barikaguda – (BRG) N. 21° 30.541' E. 85° 17. 009', Alt.757 ft.

The site is located north to the Soida hudi or Soida hill, which is locally known as Barikaguda. It falls in the Jolanda village boundary. The site extends about 200 x 200 mtr. in north-south and east-west direction. The northern side of the site is covered by paddy land of Jolanda village, eastern by the paddy land of Jalanda Munda sahi, west by the Dalo-Jolanda road and Jalanda Hatapada and south by Soida hill. Chopper and some other tools of Lower Palaeolithic period have been reported from this site (Fig.9 & 15, Pl.3).

Baisnavadar (BND) N- 21° 31. 322' E- 85° 17. 872', Alt. 791 ft.

The site is located on the left bank of the river Kakharua at Baisnavadar. It is a slightly elevated land now developed as agriculture field. The site extends about 500 x 200 mtr. north-south and east-west as Baisnavadar to Magardar in north-south direction and Kadadiha Munda Sahi in west to Kakharua left bank in east (Plate-4). The site was chosen for a systematic collection of tools from an area of 4.50 x 3 mtr. by following a grid pattern, as there is a good evidence of prehistoric activities noticed. A good number of Neolithic flakes and chips with a chipped axe are noticed from this site. The grid is again divided into 10 cm. in north-south and 20 cm. in east west to plot the exact location and nature of implements (Fig.9, Pl.14 & 15). The other Neolithic implements of this area are collected randomly from surface. A good number of chipped axe is present in this site.

Bisriguda (BSG) N- 21° 31.188' E- 85° 17 307', Alt. 720 ft.

The site is located at the Bisriguda ghat of the right bank of the river Kakharua. Due to rain gully and river action the site is partly exposed and heavily eroded. After a few years the site may be lost forever due to these above activities. A large amount of Neolithic flake and chips has been recovered from this small eroded area. The site extends 100 x 50 mtr. north-south and east-west direction. The site is bounded by Charan sahi in north, Kakharua river is east and south and road to Jamardiha to Rugudiha in western direction (Fig.9 & 30, Pl.16 & 17).

Bijagotha Hatapada (BHP) N-21° 30.199' E- 85° 14. 963', Alt-675 ft.

The site is located on a highly elevated erosional channel on Bijagotha Hatapada of right bank of Rentna nala or Sukhanala, a tributary to river Kakharua fall in the village of Jamardiha to Patamunda passes through the site. Due to heavy erosion of the soil from this site it is observed that a large amount of Neolithic flake and chips with chipped Neolithic axe scattered on surface. The cross section of most of the chipped axe is squares in nature (Fig.7&35, Pl.32&33).

Bankadar (BKD) N-21° 27.308' E-85° 14.340', Alt. 514ft.

The site is situated 1 km. west to Sorbeda Juanga sahi in Bankadar forest on Sorbeda to Bankadar minor project non metallic road. Two Neolithic implements were collected from the road side. Due to deep bushy jungle it is difficult to survey the area (Fig.8).

Dalo Puruna Diha (DPD) N-21° 28.878' E-85°15.943', Alt. 618 ft.

On the left bank of Kakharua and north-west of Dalo-Munda Sahi the site Dalo Puruna diha is situated. This is an open flat surface scattered with a good amount of potsherds with stone polisher and grinder fragments. It spreads 200 x 100 mtr. area. Recently the cultivation of maze and different grams are noticed. Eastern part of the site has been changed into paddy field, where as the north part is bounded by bushy jungle (Fig.11, 43&44, Pl.4, 45 & 46).

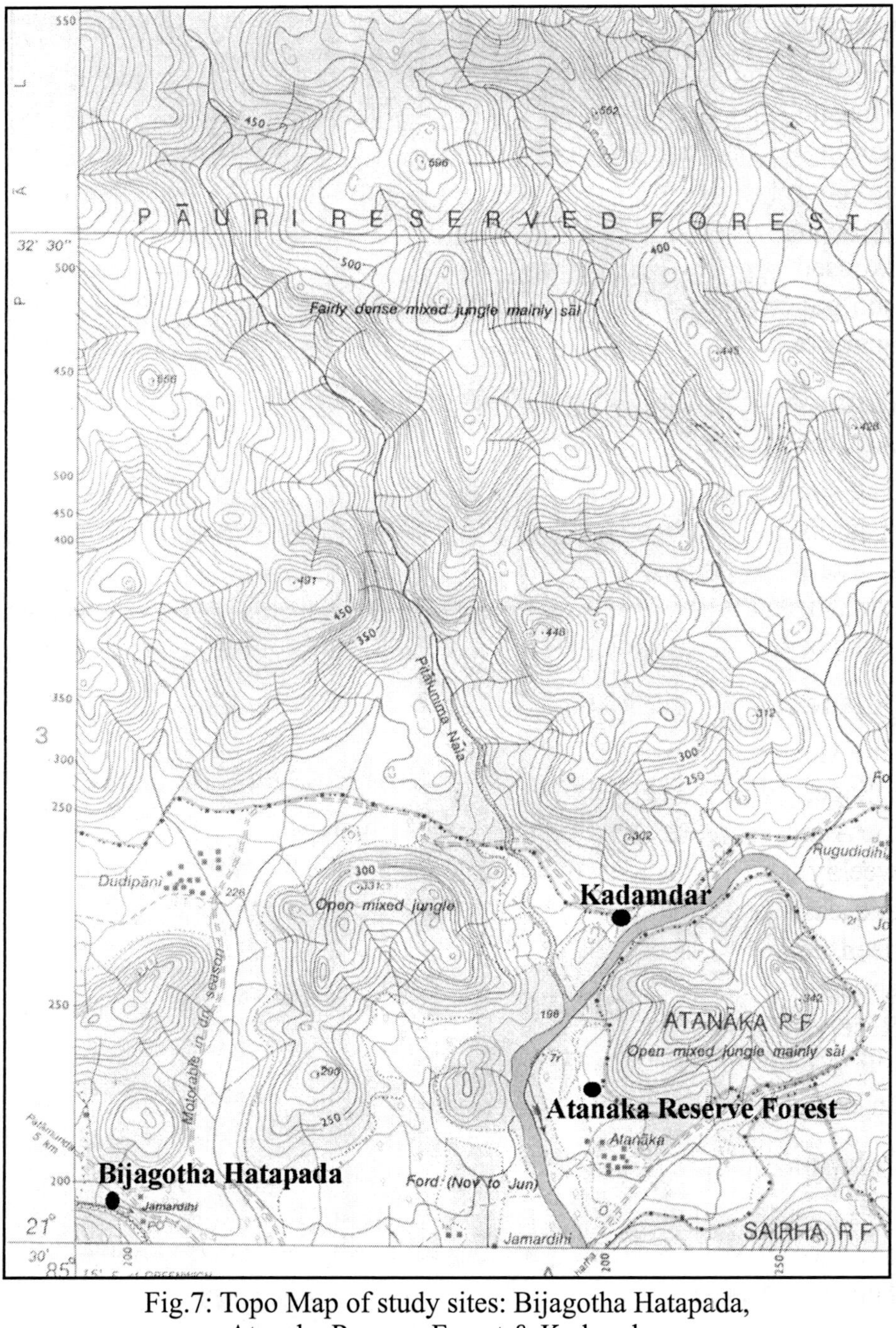

Fig.7: Topo Map of study sites: Bijagotha Hatapada, Atanaka Reserve Forest & Kadamdar.

Gopapur Gadhuaghat (GPG) N-21° 30. 169' E-85° 16. 074' , Alt. 677 ft.

The site is 100 mt. east to the Gopapur village near the Gadhua ghat or bathing ghat. The site has been surrounded by paddy field in western direction and the site extended upto 100 x 50 mtr. north-south and east-west. The erosional channels which originated in the nearby field have exposed a good quantity of microliths which include geometric and non-geometric microlithic tool. The raw materials of the implement are quartz and chert (Fig.11).

Gopapur Munda Sahi (GMS) N-21° 28. 878' E-85° 16.141' , Alt. 692 ft.

The site lies to the east of Munda sahi on the right bank of Kakharua. It is observed that a large quantity of Neolithic flakes and chips are scattered in about 50 x 50 mtr. area. The site has yielded two unfinished core. It is open flat land, probable used in agricultural purpose a few years back (Fig.11).

Jolanda Hatapada- (JHP) N. 21° 30.564' E. 85° 17', Alt. 725 ft.

The site Jalanda Hatapada is located ½ km. south-east to the Jolanda village, on the left of Dalo-Jalanda road on north-eastern foot hill of the Atanaka Reserve Forest. It is known as Jaolanda Hatapada due to a weekly market. The site covers an area of 100 x 50 mtr. in north-south and east-west direction. A small amount of Neolithic tools have also been noticed in the erosional surface. The northern part of the site is covered by a flat agricultural land and the southern part by Atanaka Reserve Forest, east by Soida Hudi/Hill and the west by Atanaka Jolanda hill. A good number of Neolithic implements have been recovered from an eroded channel (Fig.9, Pl.23).

Jolanda Munda Sahi- (JMS) N-21° 30. 360' E- 85° 17.305', Alt. 770 ft.

The site is locally known as Gaiguthani Hudi of Jolanda Munda sahi. The site extends an area about 300 x 50 mtr. on the foot hill area the site has very low amount of Neolithic implement reported. The southern part of the site is bounded by a small seasonal nalla, the eastern part of Gaiguthani hill the western part by seasonal nalla and by the Jolanda Munda sahi. The Neolithic implement has been found from the erosional surface of the foot hill area of the site (Fig.9 & 33, Pl.24).

Khalinala (KLN) Vill- Jamudiha N-21° 31. 291' E- 85° 17.817', Alt. 768 ft.

The site is located close to a culvert connected to village Kadadiha and Jamudiha road, south-west of village Jamudiha. The prehistoric artefats were collected from an erosional surface of 500 x 300 mtr. near dry channel flowing from east in right bank of river Kakharua, south-west to village Jamudiha (Fig.9, Pl.18).

Kadamdar (KDD) N-21° 30.970' E-85° 16.571', Alt.852 ft.

The site is named after the nearby gorge, which is locally known as Kadamdar. The site extends in an area of 100 x 50 mtr. North-South and East-West direction. To reach the site one has to follow the Judipani-Rugudidiha road upto the gorge because the road is closed at the gorge and again it is away from the river. Lithic implements of Mesolithic and Neolithic culture are exposed in an eroded surface. South and South-West parts covered are with the river whereas the other part is covered with Sal jungle. The site is located on the left bank of the river which has a gentle slope towards the river (Fig.7 &17, Pl.5).

Karadapal-I (KDP-I) N- 21° 28. 324' E- 85° 15.486', Alt. 590 ft.

The site is situated 100 mt. north of Karadapal village. It is a plain surface with erosional channel at a distance. The site extends 50 x 50 mtr. Ring stone fragments were collected from this erosional surface. The site is surrounded by Tomkia Reserve Forest in west, Kakharua in east, agricultural filled in north and village in south (Fig.11, Pl.8).

Karadapal- II- (KDP-II) N- 21° 28. 681' E- 85° 15. 472', Alt. 576 ft.

In the extreme north-west of Karadapal village, or on the north Munda sahi the site is located on the foot hill of Tomkia Reserve Forest. The site is covered with mixed Sal jungle. Presently the site has been developed into banana plantation. The site extends 50 x 50 mtr. A good number of microliths have been collected from eroded land (Fig.11, Pl.12).

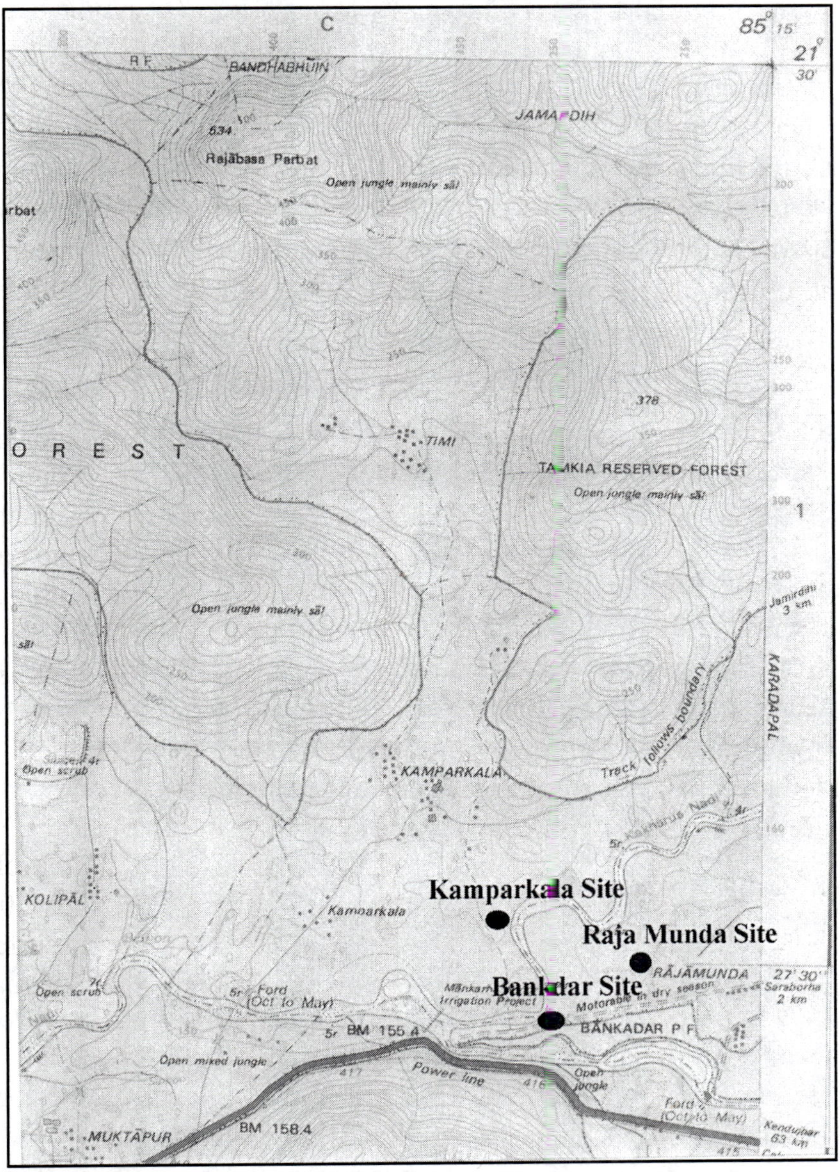

Fig. 8: Topo Map of study sites: Kamparkala, Bankadar & Raja Munda.

the site which include blades, points, borers etc.

Kamparkala (KPK) N- 21° 27. 664' E- 85° 14. 113', Alt. 540 ft.

The site of Kamparkala is situated on the right bank of river Kakharua surrounded by Sal forest on the south-east of Kamparkala village. The village is about 1 km. away from the site. Near the banana plantation field, the area extends 100 x 100 mtr. area. In a small rain gully a good number of Neolithic tools have been collected, which include axe, ring stone or hammer stone with dimple mark. Moreover, a polisher is noticed in which groove mark or depression is clearly indicative of prehistoric period. A large number of rubber stones are noticed at the site. Out of these two are picked up for studies (Fig.8 & 31, Pl. 19).

Katiragarh (KGH) N- 21° 35. 821' E- 85° 19. 379', Alt. 1754 ft.

The Katiragarh site situated on the confluence of Dhanatupa *nala* and Katira *nala*, which are again join satinala, a tributary to Kakharua. The medium elevated mound extends 400 x 200 mtr. east-west and north-south direction. Presently the mound has been used as agricultural field of Barogora villagers. To reach the site one has to follow Boragora-Katiragarh muroom road. A large amount of potsherds and stone implements are found including polisher grinding stones etc. The site is interesting since two small temple replica and two stone image one of which partly damaged are noticed. A mandap made out of laterite is noticed to the north part of the site or locally known as Duarsuni. The mound has more than one meter deposit of a single culture site (Fig.10, 38-41, Pl.40-43).

Kakharua Protection Forest (KPF) N- 21° 29.185' E- 85° 16.057', Alt. 638 ft.

The site is named after the nearby forest. It is located near the Dala-Jolanda road on the right of the Dangadhar village. On the north the site is bounded by Dangadar to Dangadhar Munda sahi, east by Kakharua protection forest, west by Dalo-Jolanda road and south by the forest itself. The site has small hillock with dolerite out crops and a large amount of big Neolithic flakes which indicated that the dolerite outcrop was used in prehistoric period as epicenter of dolerite raw material for preparing the heavy duty tool. These flakes are fan shaped with large in size. Possibly these are the primary flakes for Neolithic implements especially of celt or axe. The site has also yielded unfinished tool (Fig.11, Pl.25-27).

Kadamdiha (KDD) N- 21° 31.674' E- 85° 18. 070', Alt. 822 ft.

The site is located north-east side of Shri Durga Suri's house of Kadamdiha village. It covers an area of 200 x 100 mtr. area. Large amount flake-blade tools of Mesolithic period have been collected from the area. The site is open to an eroded murram bed. There is a road from Kadamdiha to Taldih which passes through this site. Presently the whole site is converted into agricultural land which slopes from west to north-west direction. The site is bounded by Kadamdiha village in west, Chatpani hill in east, small local *hudi* or hill in north and Jamudiha village in south (Fig.9 & 23, Pl.11).

Mohanpur (Manpur) Shiva Mandir (MSM) N- 21° 29. 919' E-85° 16. 282', Alt. 674 ft.

The site is located south and south-east of Mohanpur (Manpur) Shiva mandir on murram surface. It is a small elevated high land covered with bushy jungle. The site is very much close to the Kakharua river which is about 200 mtr. away. The site has yielded a large amount of microliths of Mesolithic period. A Neolithic celt has also been collected form this site. Both geometric and non geometric shapes are noticed in microliths (Fig.11 & 24, Pl.13).

Nemliloti (NLT) N- 21° 34. 208' E- 85° 18. 589', Alt. 1694 ft.

The site Nemliloti is situated on the confluence of Kakharua and Bada Nadi. The implements distributed in an area of 25 x 25 mtr, which include blades, points etc. It is very difficult to reach the site, however the villagers have foot path to reach the site for worshiping their God known as Mahadev Munda which is originally a Shiva linga, possibly existing from historical period. The whole area is covered with Sal forest (Fig.10, Pl.43).

Rugudidiha (RGD) N- 21° 31.622' E- 85° 17.762', Alt. 770 ft.

This site is located on the right bank of the Kakharua in the south of Tala Rugudi sahi. It extended about 300 x 200 mtr. north-south and east-west direction which is presently disturbed by means of agricultural activities. It is slightly elevated in nature. A large amount of microliths and a few Neolithic flakes and chips have been noticed on the exposed murrams. The area is inhabited by Bhuinya tribal people (Fig.9 & 21, Pl.9).

Rajamunda (RMD) N- 21° 27.929' E- 85° 15.425', Alt. 648 ft.

The site is located in the north-eastern side of village Rajamunda. The site is bounded by a Sal forest. The site extends 100 mtr. north-south and 50 mtr. east-west direction. The site has yielded a good culture. The microliths include blades, borers, points etc. River Kakharua is 200 mtr. west to the site (Fig. 8, 18, Pl. 6 & 20).

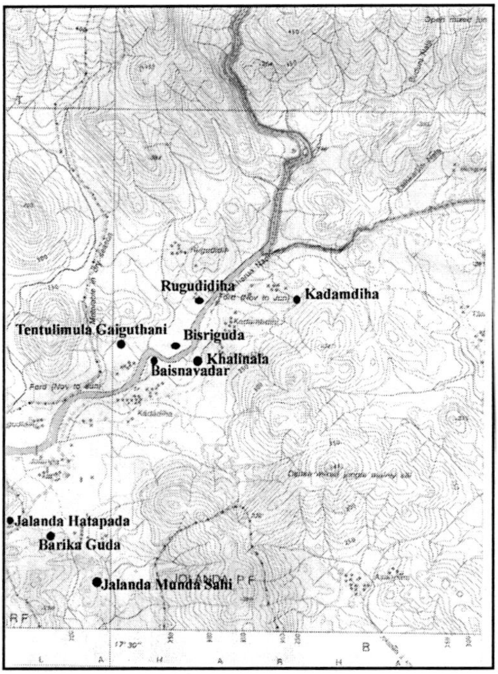

Fig.9: Topo Map of study sites: Rugudidiha, Jalanda Hatapada, Jalanda Mundasahi, Baisnavadar, Kadamdiha, Tentulimula Gaiguthani (Jamudiha), & Khalinala.

Rado diha (RDH) N- 21° 35.295' E- 85° 20.208', Alt. 1876 ft.

The site is named after a small streamlet Radon *nala*, which is a feeder channel to Kakharua through Satinala. It is on the right bank of it and about 400 mtr. south-east of foot hill of Saranda forest. The site has yielded one Neolithic axe from the elevated agricultural field. It is interesting to note that on a stone outcrop a few engravings have been marked in horizontal and vertical line (Fig.10, Pl.28 & 29).

Rado MIP (RMP) N- 21° 35.373' E- 85° 20.048', Alt.1841 ft.

South to the Rado minor irrigation project, the eroded soil has exposed a good number of potsherds along with a small amount of terracotta beads and glass bangle. The site has also yielded iron implements (fragments). The site is partly damaged due to the irrigation project and it extends upto 150 mtr. east-west and 100 mt. north-south direction. The deposition of the site is 1 mt. thick section in which potsherds have been observed frequently (Fig.10 & 42, Pl. 38 & 44).

Sarbeda Dautasala (SBD) N-21° 27.418' E- 85° 16.021', Alt. 561 ft.

The site is located on a high erosional channel south to Sarbeda Dautasala. The site has implement ferrous and a large amount of Neolithic flakes and chips with Neolithic tools reported along with microlithic tools. The tools include scraper, blade, borer and points etc. The site extends 50 x 50 mtr. area (Fig.11 & 22, Pl.10).

Sarbeda Kudur (SBK) N- 21° 27.464' E- 85° 16.184', Alt. 533 ft.

It is an erosional surface located south-west of Godaradiha village. it is about 300 mt. away, on the left bank of Godaradiha nala perennial stream fall in Mankara river which is a tributary to Kakharua river. The site is extended 100 x 50 mtr. in north-south and east-west direction. A large amount of Neolithic flakes and chips along with two bar Celts have also been found from the erosional channel (Fig.11 & 34, Pl. 30 & 31).

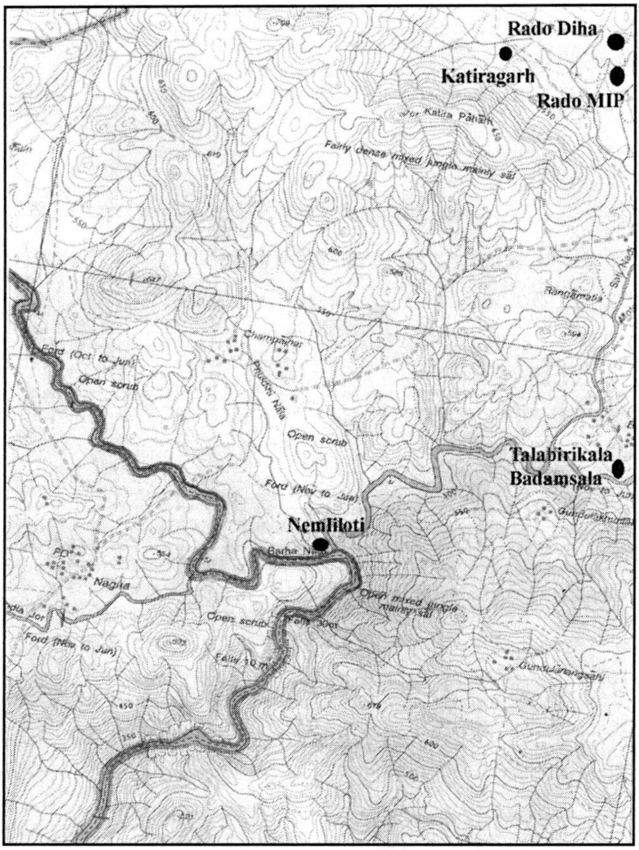

Fig.10: Topo Map of Study sites: Katiragarh, Talabirikala Badamsala, Rado diha, Rado MIP and Nemliloti.

Tala Birikala Badamsala (TBB) N- 21° 34.632' E- 85° 19.574', Alt.1677 ft.

The site is located south-west of Badamsala of Tala Birikala village on the right bank of river Kakharua. This is relatively a small site scattered with potsherds of fragile condition. South part of the site is damaged due to riverine action. Part of it extends 25 x 50 mtr. in north-south and east-west direction. Potsherds have been recovered upto 20 cm. depths, which are clearly noticed in river section, but the distribution is very limited in number. Presently the site is covered with bushes and partly turned into cultivable land (Fig.10).

Tentulimula Gaiguthani (Rugudidiha) (TMG) N- 21° 31.096' E- 85° 17.085', Alt.720 ft.

This is an open air site having flat land with little erosion in eastern side. It extends 200 x 100 mtr. east west and north-south direction. The site is located about 250 mtr. south of the Bisriguda. The site is bounded by Bisriguda in north, local jungle in south, the Jamadiha- Rugudiha road in west and river Kakharua in east direction. Presently a Kaju jungle or Kasurina plantation has developed in this site by forest department. The site falls under Rugudidiha village area. A good number of Neolithic Axes have been collected from this site (Fig.9 & 32, Pl. 22).

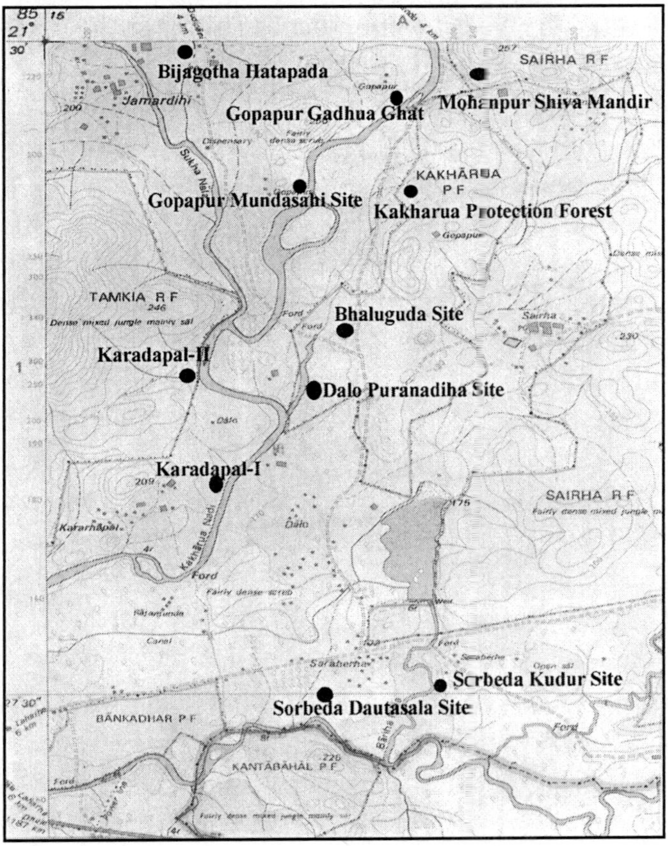

Fig.11: Topo Map showing the study sites: Dalo Puranadiha, Karadapal I, Karadapal II, Sorbeda Kudur, Sorbeda Dautasala, Mohanpur Shiv Mandir, Gopapur Gadhuaghat, Gopapur Munda Sahi, Bhaluguda, Rajamunda & Bijagotha Hatapada.

Stratigraphy

During the field survey in the Kakharua valley, about 35 km areas have been observed in different section profile. In fact much effort has been made to recover the in situ artefacts and to reconstruct a possible chrono-cultural sequence and composites stratigraphy of the area by section scanning. Only two sections were taken into consideration such as; near the site Bankadar and second one near the Baisnavadar site. The Bankadar is end of the river (confluence point of Mankara and Kakharua) where as Baisnavadar is middle of the Kakharua valley. In all respects from bottom to top these two sections show their sequences of deposition so the Bankadar section deposit show silt (Recent Humus), red silt, yellowish clay soil, loose gravels with laterite, yellowish clay with pebble and laterite bed rock, where as the Baisnavadar site section is quite different with deposit of red silt, loose gravel with laterite, dolerite cobble and resemble with Bonaigarh regions of Sulabhdihi exposed section of the mound 1.

The Bankadar section deposition are showing four depositional unit and resting on the lateritic bed rock. From bottom to top the depositional layers are identified as lower loose gravel mixed with laterite and a thin band of boulder in lower part, yellowlish clay, red silt and the top cover with recent silt deposit. The lower loose gravel layer is measuring 1.02 mtr. in thickness. This layer is resting on lateritic bed rock and the loose gravel comprises gravel of various shaped pebble amalgamation with sand and grits of quartz and quartzite. The second bottom one is yellow clay is also non implementiferous and showing 1.10 mtr. thick deposit. The red silt shows the occurrence of artefacts in different exposed areas, it is 1.12 mtr. deposit. The top most layer is comprises with thin deposit of recent silt, which is acted as cover and preserve the antiquarian remains of the region.

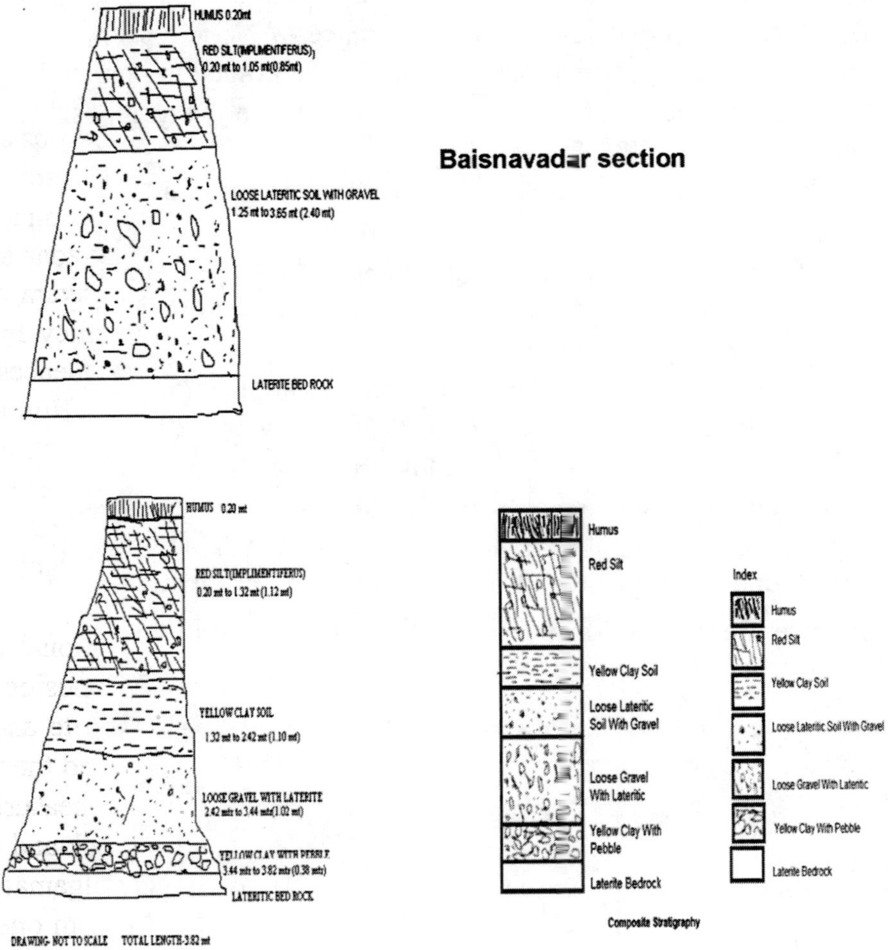

Bankadar section

Fig.12: Stratigraphy around Kakharua valley.

The second section has been taken at mid of the Kakharua river near at Baisnavadar in Kadadiha village. The lower most strata is resting on the lateritic bed rock. From bottom to top the depositional layer are identified as loose gravel with lateritic and dolerite cobble, red silt and a thin layer of recent silt. The lower most strata is identified as loose gravel with lateritic and doloritic cobble. It is 2.40 mtr. thick deposit resting on lateritic bed rock. The immediate top stratum is red silt which is associated with the occurrence of Neolithic implements. The exposed rain gullies nearby the section yield such implements. It is 1.05 mtr. deposit. The top layer is very thin and showing deposit of the recent silt (Fig.12, Pl.1&2).

It is interesting to note that the Bonaigarh region is very close to present study area and both fall in the same ecological set up. Geographically, both are located in an isolated hill tract, shut in all sides by rugged forest clad hills, intersected by a few narrow valleys, which connect it with the adjoining areas.

The two sections are different in nature but occurrence of the red silt is the common one. The red silt deposit is about 20 cm below the present surface. So the red silt exposed area is implementiferous. But the microliths which have been collected from the upper surface or lateritic surface can not be related stratigraphically to any other cultural relics found from the area. And in view of their production, microliths might have been manufactured and used by the Mesolithic people prior to emergence of the Neolithic.

Table No-2.1: Distribution of section profile at Bankadar and Baisnavadar site.

Sl. No.	Depositions	Bankdar		Baisnavadar	
		Height in mt.	**Colour**	**Height in mt.**	**Colour**
1.	Silt (Humus)	0.20 mt	Silt (Humus)	0.20 mt.	Silt (Humus)
2.	Red silt	1.12 mt.	Red silt	1.05 mt.	Red silt
3.	Upper loose gravel silt	1.10 mt.	Yellowish clay	--	--
4.	Lower loose gravel silt	1.02 mt.	Loose gravel with laterite	2.40 mt.	Loose gravel with lateritic and dolerite cobble
		0.38 mt.	Yellow clay with pebble	--	--
5.	Laterite bed rock		Lateritic bed rock exposed		Laterite bed rock exposed
	Total	3.82 mt.		3.65 mt.	

Site Representation

The survey has resulted in the discovery of thirty sites. These are recorded through GPS system and plotted on the topo-sheet with its proper longitude, latitude and altitude. It is noticed that the sites are located in different eco-zones of the region. The artefacts are represented in a table format for the benefit of the readers.

Table No- 2.2: Sites their longitude, latitude and Eco-zonal distribution

Sl. No.	Micro area (site)	Latitude	Longitude	Altitude	Eco zonal distribution	Total no findings LITHIC
1	Atanaka Reserve Forest (ARF)	21°30.545'	85°16.183'	692 ft.	Piedmont	19
2	Bhaluguda (BLG)	21°28.980'	85°15.882'	61[illegible] ft.	River bank	16
3	Barikaguda (BRG)	21°30.541'	85°17.009'	75[illegible] ft.	Piedmont	3
4	Baisnavadar (BND)	21°31.322'	85°17.872'	79[illegible] ft.	River bank	56
5	Bisriguda (BSG)	21°31.188'	85°17.307'	72[illegible] ft.	River bank	61
6	Bijagatha Hatapada (BHP)	21°30.199'	85°14.963'	67[illegible] ft.	River bank cum foot hill	61
7	Bankadar (BKD)	21°27.380'	85°14.340'	51[illegible] ft.	Piedmont	2
8	Dalo Puruna diha (DPD)	21°28.878'	85°15.943'	613 ft.	River bank	27
9	Gopapur Gadhuaghat (GPG)	21°30.169'	85°16.074'	67[illegible] ft.	River bank	22
10	Gopapur Munda Sahi (GMS)	21°28.878'	85°16.141'	6[illegible]2 ft.	River bank	13
11	Jalanda Hatapada (JHP)	21°30.564'	85°17.000'	7[illegible]5 ft.	Foot hill	22
12	Jalanda Munda Sahi (JMS)	21°30.360'	85°17.305'	7[illegible]0 ft.	Foot hill	3
13	Khalinala (KLN)	21°31.291'	85°17.817'	7[illegible]8 ft.	River bank	3
14	Kadamdar (KDD)	21°30.970'	85°16.571'	8[illegible]2 ft.	River bank	39

contd...

15	Karadapal I (KDP I)	21°28.324'	85°15.486'	590 ft.	Piedmont	19
16	Karadapal II (KDP-II)	21°28.681'	85°15.472'	576 ft.	River bank cum foot hill	24
17	Kamparkala (KPK)	21°27.644'	85°14.113'	540 ft.	River bank	4
18	Katiragarh (KGH)	21°35.821'	85°19.379'	1754 ft.	River bank	-
19	Kakharua Protection Forest (KPF)	21°29.185'	85°16.057'	638 ft.	Foot hill	36
20	Mohanpur Shiva Mandir (MSM)	21°29.919'	85°16.282'	674 ft.	River bank cum foot hill	46
21	Nemliloti (NLT)	21°34.208'	85°18.589'	1694 ft.	River bank cum foot hill	10
22	Rugudidiha (RGD)	21°31.622'	85°17.762'	770 ft.	Piedmont.	33
23	Rajamunda (RMD)	21°27.929'	85°15.425'	648 ft.	River bank	36
24	Rado diha (RDH)	21°35.295'	85°20.208'	1876 ft.	Foot hill	1
25	Rado MIP (RMP)	21°35.373'	85°20.048'	1841 ft.	River bank cum foot hill	-
26	Sarbeda Dautasala (SBD)	21°27.418'	85°16.021'	561 ft.	Piedmont	29
27	Sorbeda Kudur (SBK)	21°27.464'	85°16.184'	533 ft.	Piedmont	2
28	Kadamdiha (KDH)	21°31.676'	85°16.072'	840 ft.	Piedmont	74
29	Tala Birikala Badamsala (TBB)	21°34.632'	85°19.574'	1677 ft.	River bank	4
30	Tentulimula Gaiguthani (TMG.)	21°31.096'	85°17.085'	720 ft.	River bank	5
					Total	**664**

The above table indicates that the total number of sites explored in the study area is 30 and the total collected lithic implements are 664. The table also indicates the longitude, latitude, altitude with eco-zonal distribution. Out of of 30 sites, three sites are of historical significance and represent medieval period antiquities and one site represents Palaeolithic culture, the rest others are predominantly occupied by Mesolithic and Neolithic artefacts (Fig.14). Considering the above, we can approach the eco-zonal distribution with the finding tools. So, that one could understand the culture of Kakharua valley and other features of this region in a systematic way.

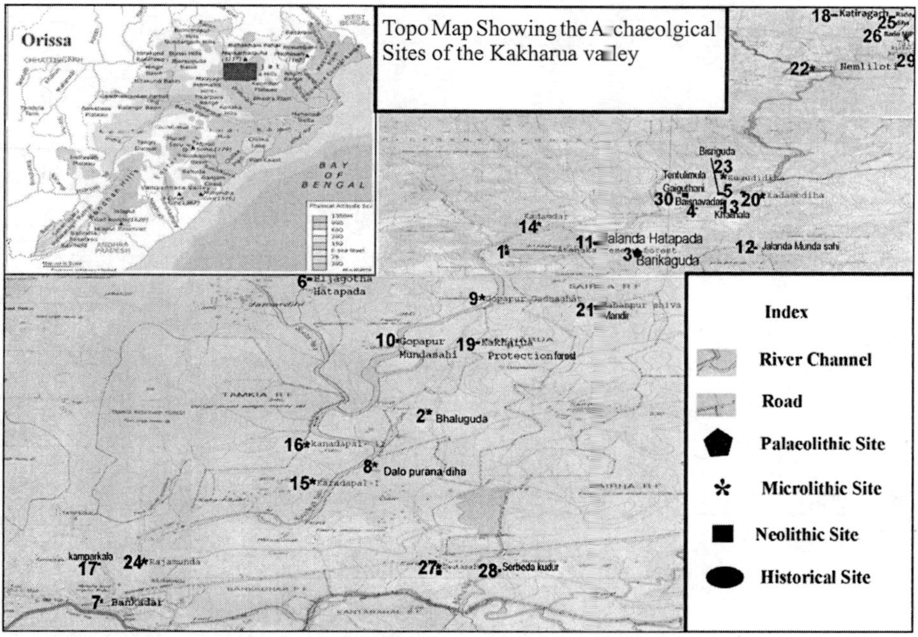

Fig.13: Topo map showing the archaeological sites of Kakharua valley.

Table No-2.3: Site-wise and culture-wise distribution of lithic artefacts

Sl. No.	Name of the sites	Lower Palaeolithic	Microliths	Neolithic	Total	Percentage
1	Atanaka Reserve Forest	-	16	3	19	2.86%
2	Bhaluguda	-	16	-	16	2.40%
3	Barikaguda	3	-	-	3	0.45%
4	Baisnavadar	-	-	56	56	8.43%
5	Bisriguda	-	-	61	61	9.18%
6	Bijagotha Hatapada	-	-	61	61	9.18%
7	Bankadar	-	-	2	2	0.30%
8	Dalo puranadiha	-	22	-	22	3.31%
9	Gapapur Gadhuaghat	-	22	-	22	3.31%
10	Gopapur Mundasahi	-	-	13	13	1.95%

contd...

11	Jalanda Hatapada	-	17	5	22	3.31%
12	Jalanda Mundasahi	-	-	2	2	0.30%
13	Khalinala	-	-	3	3	0.45%
14	Kadamdar	-	38	1	39	5.87%
15	Karadapal I	-	18	1	19	2.86%
16	Karadapal II	-	24	-	24	3.61%
17	Kamparkala	-	-	4	4	0.60%
18	Katiragarh	-	-	-	-	-
19	Kakharua Protection Forest	-	-	36	36	5.42%
20	Kadamdiha	-	74	-	74	11.14%
21	Mohanpur Shiva Mandir	-	46	-	46	6.92%
22	Nemliloti	-	10	-	10	1.50%
23	Rugudidiha	-	27	6	33	4.96%
24	Rajamunda	-	33	3	36	5.42%
25	Radodiha	-	-	1	-	0.15%
26	Rado MIP	-	-	-	-	-
27	Sorbeda Dautasala	-	25	4	29	4.36%
28	Sorbeda Kudur	-	-	2	2	0.30%
29	Tala Birikala Badamsala	-	4	-	4	0.60%
30	Tentulimula Gaiguthani	-	-	5	5	0.75%
	Total	**3(0.45)**	**392(59.03)**	**269(40.51)**	**664**	**99.99%**

The above table contains the lithic remains and the distribution of sites. The intensive exploration of the river valley has brought to light 27 lithic sites, which show the Stone Age tradition. The lithics show the recovery of 3 palaeoliths, 392 microliths and 269 neolithic artefacts from 27 sites spread over the Kakharua valley. Besides, three sites belonging to the historical period are also discovered. They include sculptures, Iron implements, beads, glass bangles etc. The Barikaguda is the only palaeolithic site. The evidence of Mesolithic culture comes from 15 sites in the study area. These are located in river bank, foot hill area, piedmont area and river bank cum foot hill area. All these microlithic materials are homogeneous in nature and blade is the dominant variety. The Neolithic remains are found from 19 of sites yielding 269 artifacts, in which axe is of dominant variety unlike the other central, north-central

Odishan Neolithic. The evidence of shoulder axe marks the links with north-eastern Indian Neolithic culture as well as the main land South East Asia (Sahoo-2000). The occurrence of large amount of flakes and chips imply such site as a workshop site. However, it is to be noted that there are no prehistoric ceramic remains.

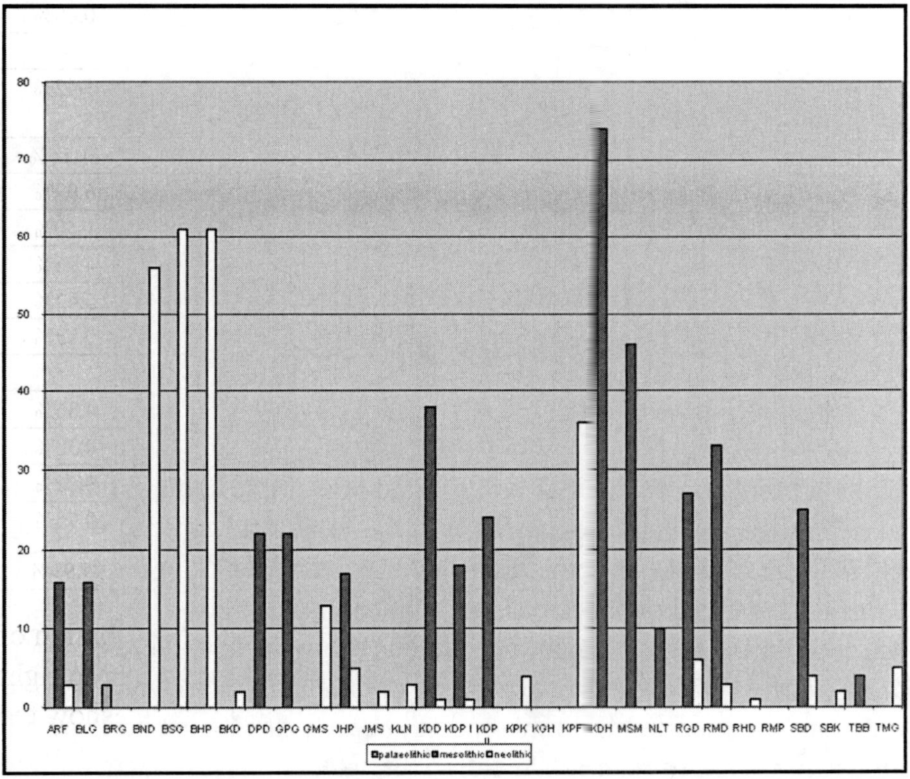

Fig.14: Site-wise distribution of artefacts of Kakharua valley.

With this general background, it is important to discuss culture-wise recoveries, which is the theme of the next chapter.

CHAPTER 4

Palaeolithic and Mesolithic Cultures of Kakharua Valley

In the present chapter the Palaeolithic and Mesolithic cultural relics will be delineated. While surveying the area, the author had come across some Palaeolithic and Mesolithic artefacts along with Neolithic implements. Considering the abundance of lithic implements at these sites, it can be inferred that the sites containing the above might have been used for a long period of time. The availability of palaeolithic is very few and only one site reported from this region, because the palaeolithic people are mainly concentrated on major river valley whereas later cultural people adopted the small feeder channels of river. As per typological and morphological analysis the microlithic artefacts are studied broadly under (a) the flake components and (b) the blade components.

The Palaeolithic Artefacts

From the review of literature, it is noticed that a limited study has been conducted by scholars in the northern as well as in central Odisha too. So the present study in the Kakharua valley would focus on the recent discoveries and the extension of the Palaeolithic boundary in north central region.

The following table contains the palaeolithic implements from Barikaguda site in Kakharua valley.

Table No-3.1:- Distribution of palaeolithic artefacts in Barikaguda (BRG)

Sl. No.	Typology	Mean measurement (in cm)			Mean ratio			Material	No	Percentage
		L	B	T	T/L	B/L	T/B			
1	Bifacial chopper	11.3	11.0	4.4	0.38	0.97	0.4	Quartzite-1	1	33.33%
2	Cleaver	12.0	8.8	4.6	0.38	0.73	0.52	Quartzite- 1	1	33.33%
3	Pick	16.6	8.6	5.3	031	0.51	0.61	Cherty quartz-?1	1	33.33%
Total									**3**	**99.99%**

Thus from the piedmont site lithic implements have been collected such as bifacial chopper, cleaver and one pick. It is important to note that all these are made out of quartzite and cherty quartzite raw material. All these tools are basically of palaeolithic culture. The bifacial chopper is 11.3 cm, 11.0 cm. and 4.4 cm. in term of length, breadth and thickness where as cleaver is 12.0 cm., 8.8 cm. and 4.6 cm. Lastly the pick is 16.6 cm., 8.6 cm. and 5.3 cm. in respect of length, breadth and thickness (Fig.15, Pl.3).

The Microliths Artefacts

During the present survey, emphasis has been given to locate maximum sites from the Kakharua river valley and its small feeder channels. An intensive field exploration has been conducted on the foot hills, piedmont areas and river bank to locate prehistoric sites. On the basis of the geomorphological locations the microlithic sites are divided into four categories, such as, the sites on river bank, the sites on foothill, the sites on piedmont area and the sites on foot hill cum river bank. From this survey conducted, 15 sites have been discovered with microlithic assemblages from this region, from which the left bank yielded eight sites and the right bank also yielded seven sites of Kakharua and its tributary.

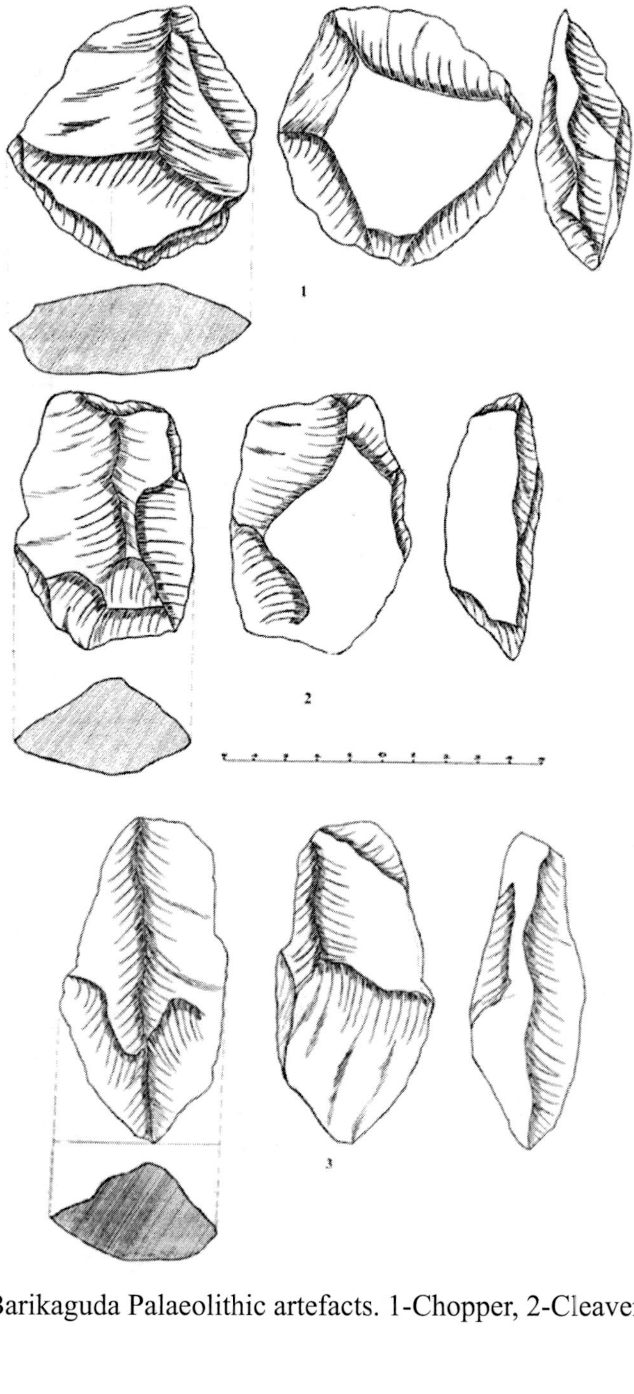

Fig.15: Barikaguda Palaeolithic artefacts. 1-Chopper, 2-Cleaver, 3-Pick

The river bank sites implies that such sites are close to the river or partly exposed by the reverine action and include Bhaluguda, Dalo Puruna diha, Gopapura Ghadhuaghat, Kadamdar, Rajamunda and Tala Birikala Badamsala. The foothill site includes Jalanda Hatapada. The Piedmont sites include the undulated erosional sites of this ecozone, namely Atanaka Reserve Forest, Karadapal-I, Rugudidiha, Sorbeda Dautasala, Kadamdiha. The river bank cum foot hill site includes Karadapal-II, Mohanpur Shiva Mandir and Nemliloti.

Sites on River Banks

Microliths have been found from six sites on river bank. They are Bhaluguda, Dalo Puruna diha, Gopapura Ghadhuaghat, Kadamdar, Rajamunda and Tala Birikala Badamsala. The microlithic recoveries are presented in tabular form.

Table No-3.2 Distribution of microliths in Bhaluguda (BLG).

Sl. No.	Typology	Mean measurement (in cm)			Mean ratio			Materials	No	Percentage
		L	B	T	T/L	B/L	T/B			
1	Parallel sided blade	3.6	1.5	0.9	0.25	0.41	0.6	Chert-1	1	6.25%
2	Blade	2.0	2.0	0.7	0.35	1	0.35	Chert-1	1	6.25%
3	Thumb nail scraper	1.9	1.6	0.9	0.47	0.84	0.56	Milky quartz-2	2	12.50%
4	Side scraper	3.4	2.7	0.9	0.26	0.79	0.33	Milky quartz-2	2	12.50%
5	Borer	2.0	1.7	0.8	0.4	0.85	0.47	Chert-1, Milky quartz-1 Crystal-1	3	18.75%
6	Point	2.4	1.7	0.7	0.29	0.70	0.41	Milky quartz-1, Chert-1, Chert-1?	3	18.75%
7	Tanged point	3.0	1.6	0.8	0.26	0.53	0.5	Milkyquertz-1	1	6.25%
8	Crescent	1.7	0.7	0.4	0.23	0.41	0.57	Milkyquartz-2	2	12.50%
9	Blade core	3.2	3.1	2.2	0.68	0.96	0.70	Chert-1	1	6.25%
Total									**16**	**100%**

Table No-3.3 Distribution of microliths in Dalo Puruna diha (DPD).

Sl. No.	Typology	Mean measurement (in cm)			Mean ratio			Material	No	Percentage
		L	B	T	T/L	B/L	T/B			
1	Parallel sided blade	3.4	2.4	0.8	0.23	0.70	0.33	Quartz-1, Milky quartz-2	3	13.63%
2	Pen knife blade	2.4	1.3	0.5	0.20	0.54	0.38	Milky quartz-1 Chert-1	2	9.09%
3	Blade	2.9	1.5	0.7	0.24	0.51	0.46	Ash grey chert-1, Milky quartz-3, Chert-2	6	27.27%
4	Borer	2.2	1.4	0.4	0.18	0.63	0.28	Milky quartz-1	1	4.54%
5	Crescent	2.6	1.0	0.6	0.23	0.38	0.6	Milky quartz-2	2	9.09%
6	Crescent cum borer	2.2	0.8	0.4	0.18	0.36	0.5	Chert-1	1	4.54%
7	Round scraper	3.1	3.0	1.3	0.41	0.96	0.43	Chert-1	1	4.54%
8	Blade core	6.6	5.9	3.4	0.51	0.89	0.57	Chert-1	1	4.54%
9	Thumb nail scraper	2.1	2.0	0.6	0.28	0.95	0.3	Chert-1	1	4.54%
10	Tanged point	2.3	2.0	0.2	0.08	0.86	0.1	Chert-1	1	4.54%
11	Scraper	1.7	1.8	0.9	0.52	1.05	0.5	Quartz-1	1	4.54%
12	Flake?	1.6	0.9	0.2	0.12	0.56	0.22	Chert-1	1	4.54%
13	Utilized flake	2.3	1.5	0.5	0.21	0.65	0.33	Chert-1	1	4.54%
Total									**22**	**99.94%**

Table No-3.4 Distribution of microliths in Gopapur Gadhuaghat (GPG).

Sl. No.	Typology	Mean measurement (in cm)			Mean ratio			Materials	No	Percentage
		L	B	T	T/L	B/L	T/B			
1	Blade	2.4	1.5	0.9	0.37	0.62	0.6	Milky quartz-6, Grey chert-1	7	31.81%
2	Utilized flake	2.2	1.9	0.6	0.27	0.86	0.31	Milky quartz-3 Banded chert-1	4	18.18%
3	Point	2.5	1.5	0.6	0.24	0.6	0.4	Milky quartz-2 Chert-1	3	13.63%
4	Burin	2.8	2.1	0.6	0.21	0.75	0.28	Grey chert-1	1	4.54%
5	Pen knife blade	3.1	1.0	0.6	0.19	0.32	0.6	Grey chert-1	1	4.54%
6	Borer	2.6	2.7	0.9	0.34	1.03	0.33	Chert-1	1	4.54%
7	Point with deep notch	3.6	1.6	0.8	0.22	0.44	0.5	Milky quartz-1	1	4.54%
8	Blade cum end scraper	2.8	1.4	1.0	0.35	0.5	0.71	Milky quartz-1	1	4.54%
9	Borer cum end scraper	3.1	1.7	1.0	0.32	0.54	0.58	Banded chert-1	1	4.54%
10	Micro borer	1.6	0.6	0.5	0.31	0.37	0.83	Chert-1	1	4.54%
11	End scraper	2.8	1.5	0.9	0.32	0.53	0.6	Chert-1	1	4.54%
Total									**22**	**99.94%**

Table No-3.5 Distribution of microliths in Kadamdar (KDD).

Sl. No.	Typology	Mean measurement (in cm)			Mean ratio			Material	No	Percentage
		L	B	T	T/L	B/L	T/B			
1	Parallel sided blade	2.6	1.3	0.5	0.19	0.5	0.38	Milky quartz-3, Quartz-1	4	10.53%
2	Pen knife blade	3.2	1.6	0.6	0.18	0.5	0.6	Milky Quartz-2, Chert-1, Banded chert-1	4	10.53%
3	Lunate/ Crescent	3.5	1.5	0.9	0.25	0.42	0.6	Chert-1, Quartz-1	2	5.26%
4	Borer	3.0	1.4	0.7	0.23	0.46	0.5	Chert-2, Iron ore-1, Milky quartz-1, Grey chert-1, Quartz-1	6	15.79%
5	Point	2.8	1.6	0.7	0.25	0.57	0.43	Milky quartz-2, Quartz-1	3	7.89%
6	Tanged point	3.6	1.6	0.9	0.25	0.44	0.56	Chert-1	1	2.63%
7	Round scraper	3.4	3.1	1.6	0.47	0.91	0.51	Chert-2, Banded chert-1	3	7.89%
8	Blade core cum borer	3.9	1.7	1.2	0.30	0.43	0.70	Banded chert-1, Yellowish chert-1	2	5.26%
9	Blade core	3.2	2.2	1.4	0.43	0.68	0.63	Quart-1, Chert-1	2	5.26%
10	End cum side scraper	2.9	2.0	0.6	0.20	0.68	0.3	Quart-1	1	2.63%
11	Side scraper	1.9	1.5	0.5	0.26	0.78	0.33	Milky quartz-3	3	7.89%

contd...

12	Blade	3.4	1.8	0.5	0.14	0.52	0.33	Chert-1	1	2.63%
13	Blade fragment	1.7	1.5	0.5	0.29	0.88	0.33	Milky quartz-1	1	2.63%
14	Scraper	2.6	2.1	0.7	0.26	0.80	0.33	Chert-1, Milky quartz-1	2	5.26%
15	Thumb nail scraper	1.8	1.7	0.5	0.27	0.94	0.29	Milky quartz-1, Iron ore -1	2	5.26%
16	Burin (micro)	1.3	1.0	0.9	0.69	0.76	0.9	Chert-1	1	2.63%
Total									**38**	**100%**

Table No-3.6 Distribution of microliths in Rajamunda (RMD).

Sl. No.	**Typology**	**Mean measurement (in cm)**			**Mean ratio**			**Material**	**No**	**Percentage**
		L	**B**	**T**	**T/L**	**B/L**	**T/B**			
1	Blade	3.3	1.7	0.6	0.18	0.51	0.35	Chert-7 Grey chert-1 Vain chert-1 Ash grey-2	11	33.33%
2	Parallel sided blade	3.1	1.6	0.7	0.22	0.51	0.43	Milky quartz-2	2	6.06%
3	Point	3.4	1.6	0.8	0.23	0.47	0.5	Chert-1 Quartz-1	2	6.06%
4	Side scraper	3.4	2.2	0.9	0.26	0.64	0.70	Chert-3 Ash grey chert-1 Grey quartz-1	5	15.15%
5	Keel blade	3.1	2.3	0.8	0.25	0.74	0.34	Ash grey chert-1	1	3.03%
6	End scraper	3.7	1.8	1.0	0.27	0.48	0.55	Chert-1	1	3.03%
7	Borer	2.5	1.4	0.7	0.28	0.56	0.5	Chert-3 Quartz-1	4	12.12%

contd...

8	Blade core	4.0	2.3	1.8	0.45	0.57	0.78	Grey chert-2 Chert-1	3	9.09%
9	Thumb nail scraper	2.5	2.2	0.9	0.36	0.88	0.40	Chert-2	2	6.06%
10	Utilized flake	2.9	1.7	0.7	0.24	0.58	0.41	Banded chert-1 Quartz-1	2	6.06%
Total									**33**	**99.99%**

Table No-3.7 Distribution of microliths in Tala Birikala Badamsala (TBB).

Sl. No.	Typology	Mean measurement (in cm)			Mean ratio			Material	No	Percentage
		L	B	T	T/L	B/L	T/B			
1	Blade	3.5	2.1	0.8	0.22	0.6	0.38	Grey chert-1	1	25.00 %
2	Parallel sided blade	2.7	1.4	0.5	0.18	0.51	0.35	Chert-1	1	25.00%
3	Flake	1.5	2.2	0.5	0.33	1.46	0.33	Quartz-1	1	25.00%
4	Utilized flake	1.7	1.5	0.4	0.23	0.88	0.26	Chert-1	1	25.00%
Total									**4**	**100%**

There are six sites having mesolithic cultural relics from an open air river bank site. From Bhaluguda a large variety of blade artefacts including parallel sided blade, blade, thumb nail scraper, side scraper, borer, point, tanged point, crescent and blade core are recovered. The predominant raw material for this blade tool is milky quartz. Borer and point is dominant tool type which share 18.75% (Table-3.2, Fig.16). The cultural materials are recovered from the loose rocky surface of Dalo Puruna diha recorded lithic implements comprise parallel sided blade (3), pen knife blade (2), blade (6), borer (1), crescent (2) crescent cum Borer (1), round scraper (1), blade core (1), thumb nail scraper (1), tanged point (1), scraper (1), flake (1), and utilized flake (1). The raw materials used in the manufacture of these artefacts are mainly chert, milky quartz and quartz (Table-3.3, Plate-4).

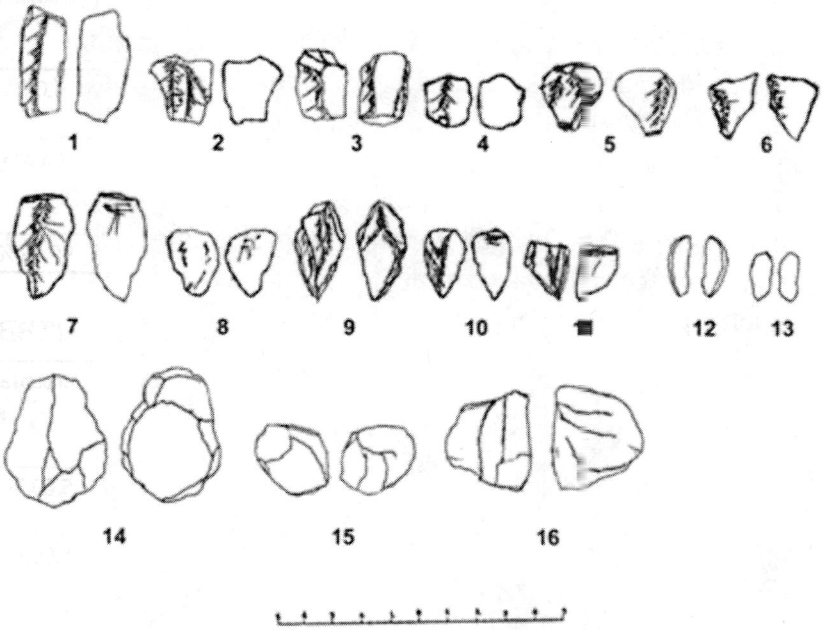

Fig.16: Bhaluguda microliths artefacts.
1-Parallal sided blade; 2-Blade fragment; 3,4-Thumb nail scraper; 5,8,11-Borer 6,7,10-Point 9-Tanged point; 29,30-Cresent/lunate; 14,15-Side scraper; 16-Blade core.

The microliths of Gapapur Gadhuaghat site are characterized by blade, point, burin, pen knife blade, borer, point with deep notch, blade cum scraper, borer cum scraper, micro borer etc. The blade is of dominant variety and covers 31.81%. The mean measurements extend from 2.4 cm.length, 1.5 cm breadth and 0.9 cm thickness. Chert is the dominant raw material variety (Table-3.4). The details distribution of Kadamdar lithic artefacts are including parallel sided blade (4), pen knife blade (4), crescent (2), borer (6), point (3), tanged point (1), round scraper (3), blade core cum borer (2), blade core (2), end cum side scraper (1), side scraper (3), blade (1), blade fragment (1), scraper (2), thumb nail scraper (2), micro burin (1), and adze (1) are important one. The principal raw material used for microlithic implement is chert, banded chert, quartz and milky quartz etc (Table-3.5, Fig.17). The details of Rajamunda microlithic artefacts are studied which include blade, parallel sided blade, point, side scraper, keel blade end scraper, borer, blade core, utilized flake and thumbnail scraper. The blade is dominant variety and constitutes 33.33% (Table-3.6, Pl.6 Fig.18). It is clear that different types of microliths including blade, parallel sided blade and flake have been recovered from Tala Birikala Badamsala sites (Table-3.7). The raw materials used in the manufacture of these artefacts are mainly black chert and some pieces are made of quartz, and grey chert etc.

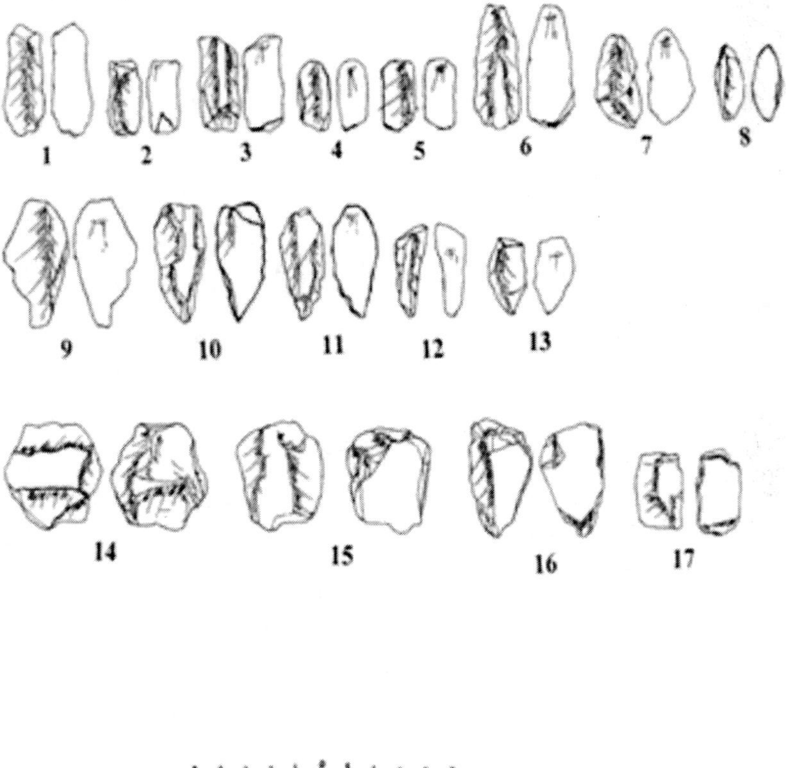

Fig.17: Kadamdar microlithic artefacts.
1,2,4,5-Parallal sided blade; 3,6,7-Penknife blade 8-Lunate; 9,10,12-Borer; 11-Tanged point; 13-Point; 14,15-Round scraper; 16, Blade core cum borer; 17-Blade core.

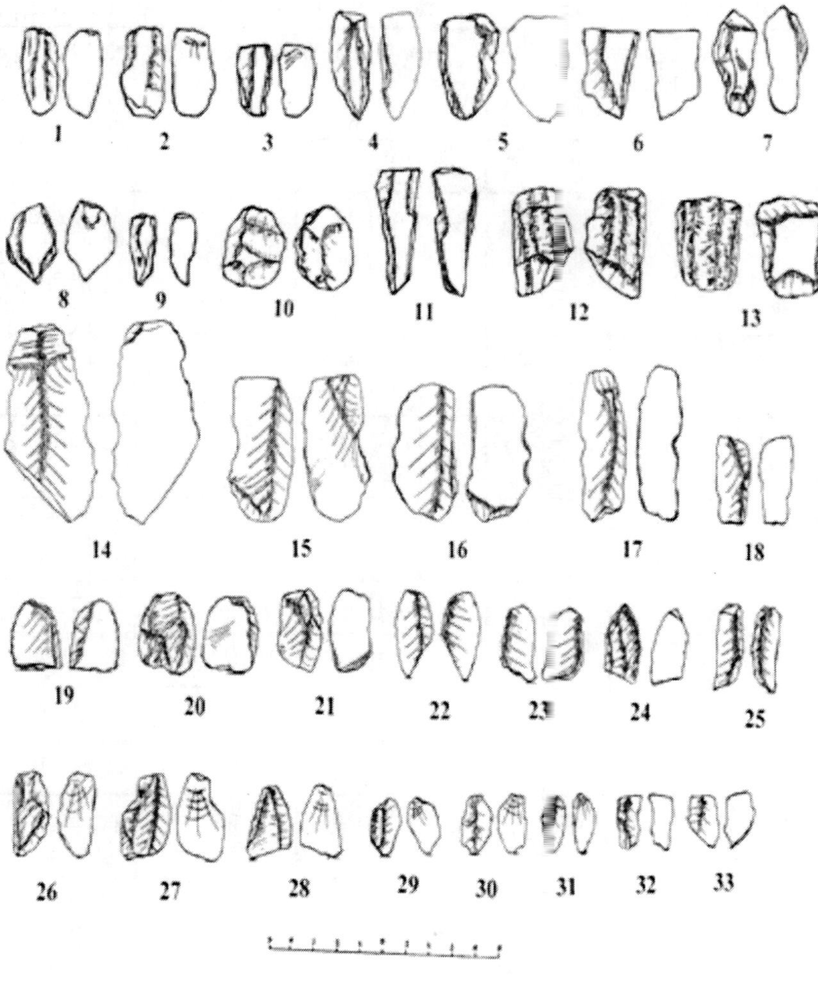

Fig.18: Rajamunda microliths artefacts.
1,3,14,15,25,30,31 & 32-Blade; 2,18-Parallal sided blade; 4, 22-Point; 5,10,16,21,26-Side scraper; 11,12,13-Blade core; 6-Keel blade; 7-End scraper; 8,9,23,29-Borer; 19,20-Thumb nail scraper; 24,27-Utilised flake; 28,33-Blade fragment

Sites on Foot Hill Area

Microliths have been found from only one site on foot hill area. The microlithic recoveries of Jalanda Hatapada are presented in tabular form.

Table No.3.8 Distribution of microliths in Jalanda Hatapada (JHP)

Sl. No.	Typology	Mean measurement (in cm)			Mean ratio			Material	No	Percentage
		L	B	T	T/L	B/L	T/B			
1	Blade	2.4	1.6	0.6	0.25	0.66	0.37	Milky quartz-2, Chert-1 Crystal-1	4	23.52 %
2	Utilized flake	2.4	1.5	0.7	0.29	0.62	0.46	Chert-3	3	17.64 %
3	Parallel sided blade	3.4	2.3	0.9	0.26	0.67	0.39	Milky quart-1	1	5.88 %
4	Pen knife blade	4.3	1.8	0.7	0.16	0.41	0.38	Milky quartz-1	1	5.88 %
5	Borer	4.3	2.2	1.1	0.25	0.51	0.5	Chert-2	2	11.76 %
6	Point	3.2	2.4	1.0	0.31	0.41	0.41	Chert-2	2	11.76 %
7	Scraper	3.6	2.6	0.8	0.22	0.72	0.30	Chert-1	1	5.88 %
8	Blade core	2.4	2.1	1.3	0.54	0.87	0.61	Chert-2	2	11.76 %
9	Rounded core scraper	3.7	3.5	2.4	0.64	0.94	0.68	Chert-1	1	5.88 %
Total									**17**	**99.96%**

The details of blade tool is reported from this site which include blade, utilized flake, parallel sided blade, pen knife blade, borer, point, scraper, blade core, round core scraper. The blade is dominant artefacts in blade tool category. Chert is the main raw material used in the blade industry (Table-3.8, Fig.19).

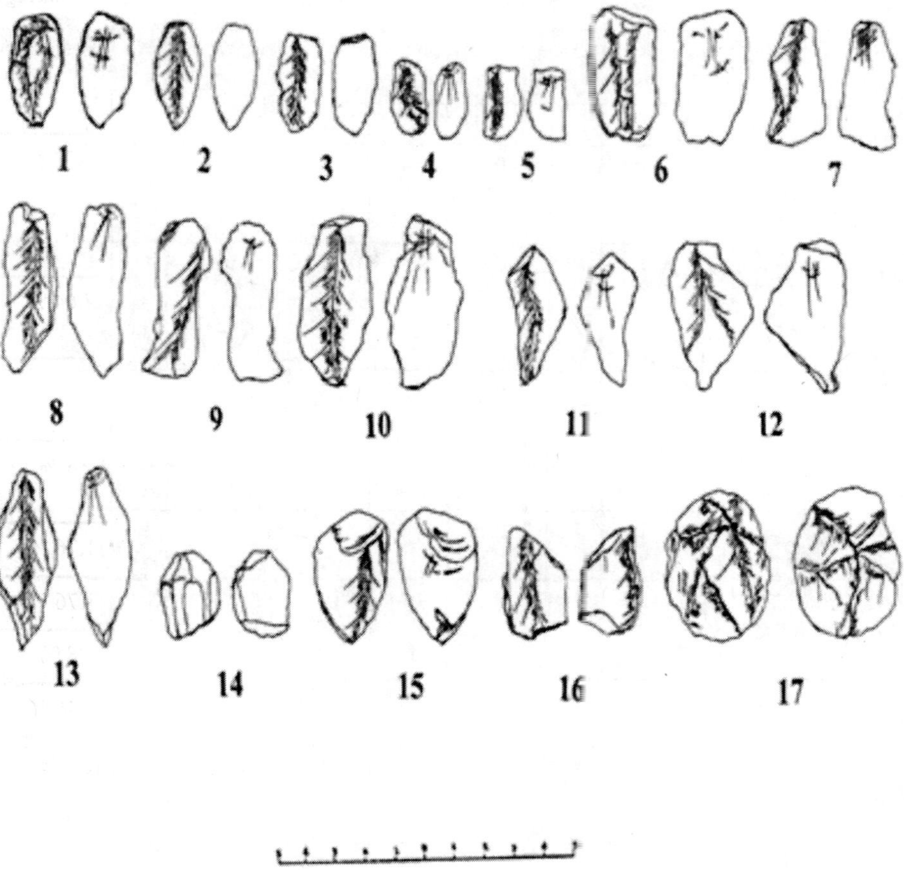

Fig.19: Jalanda Hatapada microliths artefacts.
1,2,3,4-Blade; 5,7,9-Utilised flake; 6-Parallel sided blade; 8-Pen knife blade; 10,13-Borer; 11,15-Point; 12-Scraper; 14,16-Blade core, 17-Round scraper.

Sites on Piedmont Area

Microliths have been found from five sites on Piedmont area. Such sites are located in the undulated and erosional areas. The sites are Atanaka Reserve Forest, Karadapal-I, Rugudidiha, Sorbeda Dautasala and Kadamdiha. The microlithic recoveries are presented in tabular form.

Table No-3.9 Distribution of microliths in north of Atanaka Reserve Forest (ARF).

Sl. No.	Typology	Mean measurement (in cm)			Mean ratio			Materials	No	Percentage
		L	B	T	T/L	B/L	T/B			
1	Parallel sided blade	2.4	1.1	0.5	0.20	0.45	0.45	Iron ore-2, Chert-1	3	18.75%
2	Blade	2.4	1.3	0.5	0.20	0.54	0.38	Quartzite-1, Chert-2, Ash grey chert-1	4	25.00%
3	Burin	2.8	1.6	0.3	0.10	0.57	0.18	Chert-1, Ash grey chert-1	2	12.50%
4	Triangle	2.4	1.6	0.5	0.20	0.66	0.31	Chert-2	2	12.50%
5	Side scraper	2.6	1.7	0.5	0.19	0.65	0.29	Chert-2	2	12.50%
6	Side cum end scraper	3.1	2.3	0.9	0.29	0.74	0.39	Milky quartz-1	1	6.25%
7	Crescent	2.3	0.9	0.9	0.39	0.39	1	Milky quartz-1	1	6.25%
8	Borer	3.2	2.7	0.9	0.28	0.84	0.33	Chert-1	1	6.25%
Total									**16**	**100%**

Table No- 3.10 Distribution of microliths in Karadapal-I site (KDP-I).

Sl. No.	Typology	Mean measurements (in cm)			Mean ratio			Material	No.	Percentage
		L	B	T	T/L	B/L	T/B			
1	Parallel sided blade	3.3	1.2	0.4	0.12	0.36	0.33	Chert-1	1	5.26%
2	Blade	2.6	1.5	0.6	0.23	0.57	0.4	Milky Quartz-4 Chert-2	6	31.57%

contd...

3	Borer	2.6	1.6	0.7	0.26	0.61	0.43	Grey chert-2	2	10.52%
4	Triangle	2.3	1.0	0.4	0.17	0.43	0.4	Chert-1	1	5.26%
5	Scraper	2.4	2.0	0.8	0.33	0.83	0.4	Grey chert-1 Chert-2	3	15.78%
6	Point	3.0	2.2	0.6	0.2	0.73	0.27	Vain chart-1 Chert-1	2	10.52%
7	Blade core	2.3	2.0	1.4	0.60	0.86	0.7	Iron ore-1 Chert-1	2	10.52%
8	Side scraper	3.4	2.5	1.7	0.5	0.73	0.68	Grey chert-1	1	5.26%
Total									**18**	**99.95%**

Table No -3.11 Distribution of microliths in Rugudidiha site (RGD).

Sl. No.	Typology	Mean measurement (in cm)			Mean ratio			Material	No	Percentage
		L	B	T	T/L	B/L	T/B			
1	Blade	2.5	1.3	0.5	0.2	0.52	0.38	Chert-2 Milky quartz-1	3	11.11%
2	Parallel sided blade	2.1	1.0	0.4	0.19	0.47	0.19	Chert-4	4	14.81%
3	Pen knife blade	2.8	1.4	0.6	0.21	0.5	0.42	Chert-2 Cherty quartz-1	3	11.11%
4	Point	2.4	0.8	0.4	0.16	0.33	0.5	Chert-2 Quartz-1	3	11.11%
5	Borer	3.1	1.6	0.7	0.22	0.51	0.43	Chert-3	3	11.11%
6	Crescent	2.7	1.1	0.6	0.22	0.40	0.54	Chert-2	2	7.41%
7	Blade (fragment)	3.3	1.4	0.6	0.18	0.42	0.42	Chert-1	1	3.70%
8	End scraper.	3.7	2.9	1.2	0.32	0.78	0.41	Grey chert-1	1	3.70%
9	Side scraper	2.9	2.3	0.7	0.24	0.79	0.30	Chert-1	1	3.70%
10	Scraper.	2.3	1.7	0.5	0.21	0.73	0.29	Chert-1	1	3.70%
11	Blade core	2.5	1.7	1.0	0.4	0.68	0.58	Chert-5	5	18.52%
Total									**27**	**100%**

Table No-3.12 Distribution of microliths in Sorbeda Dautasala (SBD).

Sl. No.	Typology	Mean measurement (in cm)			Mean ratio			Materials	No	Percentage
		L	B	T	T/L	B/L	T/B			
1	Core rounded scraper	5.3	4.6	2.4	0.45	0.86	0.52	Chert-3	3	12.00%
2	End scraper	4.4	3.3	1.1	0.25	0.75	0.33	Chert-3	3	12.00%
3	Side scraper	4.0	3.0	0.9	0.22	0.75	0.3	Chert-4	4	16.00%
4	Blade core	3.5	2.5	1.6	0.45	0.71	0.64	Banded chert-1 Chert-2	3	12.00%
5	Thumbnail scraper	3.5	2.4	0.6	0.17	0.68	0.25	Chert-1	1	4.00%
6	Concave scraper	4.2	2.8	1.1	0.26	0.66	0.39	Chert-1	1	4.00%
7	Blade	3.1	1.8	0.9	0.29	0.58	0.5	Chert-2 Chert-1	3	12.00%
8	Trapezoid	3.4	3.2	0.6	0.17	0.94	0.18	Quartz-1	1	4.00%
9	Point	3.3	1.3	0.6	0.18	0.39	0.46	Chert-4	4	16.00%
10	Pen knife blade	4.1	2.3	0.9	0.21	0.56	0.39	Banded chert-1	1	4.00%
11	Crescent	2.5	0.9	0.6	0.24	0.36	0.66	Quartz-1	1	4.00%
Total									**25**	**100.00%**

Table No-3.13 Distribution of microliths in Kadamdiha (KDH).

Sl. No.	Typology	Mean measurement (in cm)			Mean ratio			Material	No	Percentage
		L	B	T	T/L	B/L	T/B			
1	Parallel sided blade	4.0	1.8	0.8	0.2	0.45	0.44	Cherty quartz-1, Ash grey chert-1	2	2.70%
2	Blade (Fragmented)	1.6	1.2	0.3	0.18	0.75	0.25	Chert-5, Milky quartz-3	8	10.81%

contd...

3	Blade	3.3	1.4	0.6	0.18	0.42	0.42	Chert-6, Milky quartz-3, Cherty quartz-1, Greenish chert-2	12	16.21%
4	Micro blade	1.9	0.6	0.3	0.15	0.31	0.5	Chert-2	2	2.70%
5	Pen knife blade	3.6	1.7	0.7	0.19	0.47	0.41	Chert-1, Milky quartz-1, Cherty quartz-1	3	4.05%
6	Side scraper	3.4	2.3	1.2	0.35	0.67	0.52	Chert-2, Banded chert-1	3	4.05%
7	Thumb nail scraper	2.3	2.1	0.8	0.34	0.91	0.38	Chert-1, Milky quartz-2, Grey chert-1	4	5.40%
8	Round scraper	2.6	2.6	1.3	0.5	1	0.5	Chert-1, Milky quartz-1	2	2.70%
9	Blade cum end scraper	3.8	2.2	1.2	0.31	0.57	0.54	Chert-1	1	1.35%
10	Concave scraper	3.5	2.1	0.8	0.22	0.6	0.38	Chert-3	3	4.05%
11	Blade cum borer							Chert-1	1	1.35%
12	Point	2.7	1.4	1.0	0.37	0.51	0.71	Chert-3, Cherty quartz-2 , Milky quartz-1, Grey chert-1	7	9.45%
13	Burin	2.7	1.5	0.5	0.18	0.55	0.33	Milky quartz-2	2	2.70%
14	Micro borer	2.0	1.5	0.3	0.15	0.75	0.2	Chert-1	1	1.35%
15	Borer	3.6	1.5	0.8	0.22	0.41	0.53	Chert-2, Milky quartz-2	4	5.40%

contd...

16	Lunate/ crescent	2.5	1.2	0.4	0.16	0.48	0.33	Chert-2, Milky quartz-1	3	4.05%
17	Triangle	3.3	2.7	1.0	0.30	0.81	0.37	Milky quartz-1	1	1.35%
18	Trapezoid	2.9	2.6	1.0	0.34	0.89	0.38	Milky quartz-1	1	1.35%
19	Blade core	3.5	2.7	1.9	0.54	0.77	0.70	Chert-2, Milky quartz-2	4	5.40%
20	Utilised flake	2.5	1.7	0.4	0.16	0.68	0.23	Chert-3	3	4.05%
21	Flake	2.9	1.7	0.7	0.24	0.58	0.41	Chert-3, Cherty quartz-1, Banded chert-1	5	6.75%
22	Scraper	2.7	2.2	0.8	0.29	0.81	0.36	Chert-1, quartz-1	2	2.70%
Total									**74**	**99.92%**

The site Atanaka Reserve Forest is dominated by microlithic tools which include parallel sided blade, blade, burin, triangle, side scraper, side cum end scraper crescent and borer. Blade is the dominant variety of implement and chert is principal raw material (Table-3.9, Fig.20, Pl.7). This Karadapal-I site falls under the category of blade tool industry in which the artefacts are identified as parallel sided blade, blade, borer, triangle, scraper, side scraper, point, blade core etc. The proportion of blade and scraper is high. Chert is the principal raw material used for the artefacts (Table- 3.10, Fig.20, Pl.8). The details of the microliths artefacts of Rugudidiha site is dominated by blade component. The typology includes blade, parallel sided blade, pen knife blade, point, blade core are dominant variety in microliths artefacts. Most of these tools are made on chert. Apart from these the table shows mean measurements of the artefacts as well as the percentage (Table-3.11, Fig.21, Pl.9).

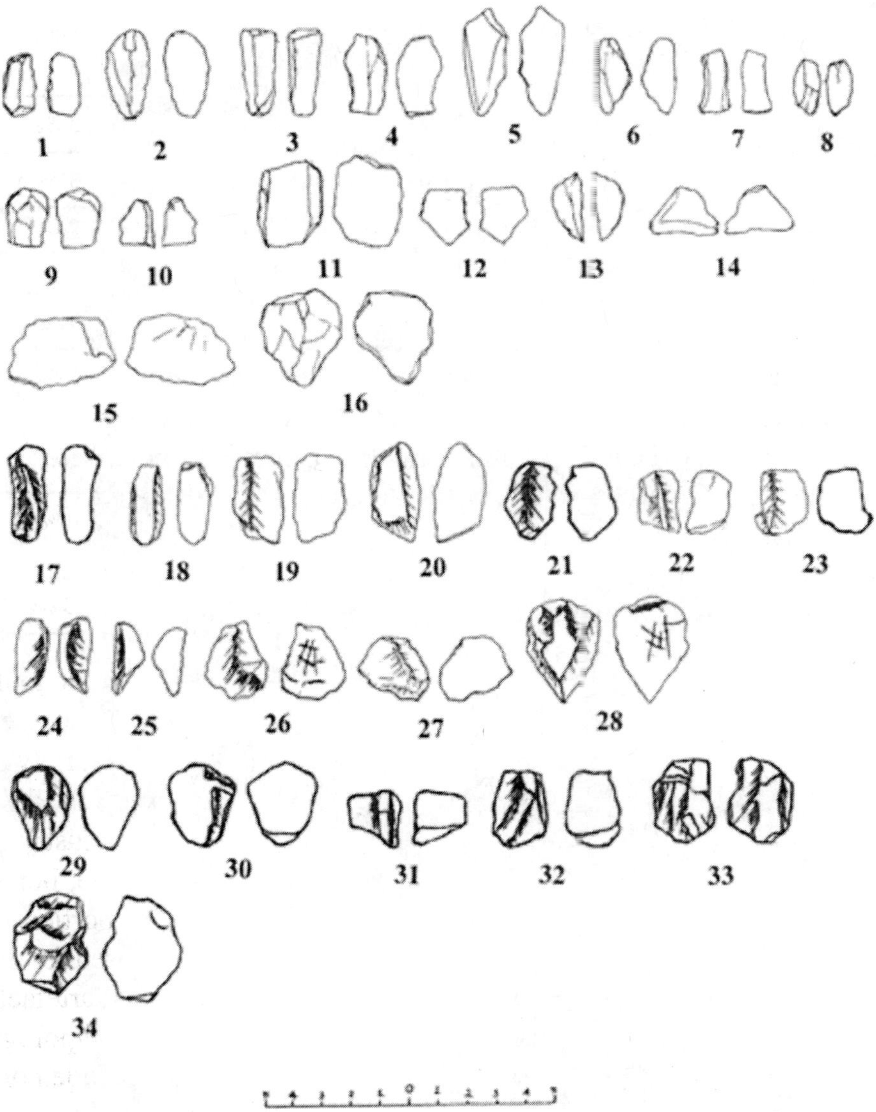

Fig.20: Atanka Reserve Forest microlithic artefacts.
1,3,7-Parallal sided blade; 2,4,8,9-Blade; 5,12-Burin; 6,14-Triangle; 10,15-Side scraper; 11-Side cum end scraper; 13-Cresent; 16-Borer.
Karadapal-I
17-Parallal sided blade; 18 to 23 Blade; 24,30 Borer; 25-Traingle; 26,27 & 32-Scraper; 28,28-Point,31,33-Blade core; 34-Side scraper.

The Sorbeda Dautasala site has yielded fine variety microlithic tools with some small size of axe and adze. Microlithic implements included core rounded scraper, end scraper, side scraper, blade core, thumb nail scraper, concave scraper, blade, trapezoid, point penknife blade and crescent. Variety of a large number of blade core indicates that it could be a factory site. Chert is the dominant variety of raw material for manufacturing the microlithic implement (Table-3.12, Fig.22, Pl.10). The open air site of Kadamdiha yielded 74 microliths which include parallel sided blade (2), blade (12), blade fragment (8), micro blade (2), pen knife blade (3), side scraper (3), thumb nail scraper (4), round scraper (2), blade cum end scraper (1), concave scraper (3), blade cum borer (1), point (7), burin (2), micro borer (1), borer (4), lunate/crescent (3), triangle (1), trapezoid (1), blade core (4), utilized flake (3), flake (5) and scraper (2). It is also interesting to note that again the blade is dominant variety artefacts. Chert, grey cherts, banded chert, cherty quartzite and milky quartz are mainly used for making these artefacts (Table-3.13, Fig.23, Pl.11).

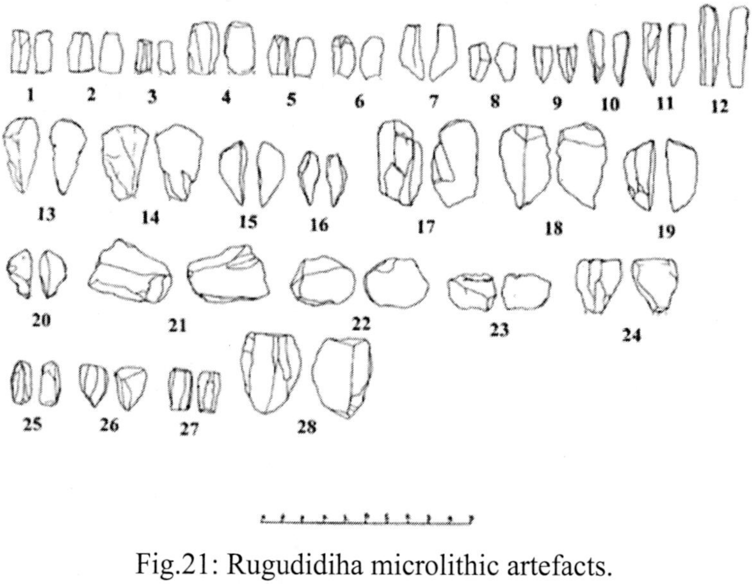

Fig.21: Rugudidiha microlithic artefacts.
1,2,4,5-Parallal sided blade; 3,6,16-Blade; 7,8,17-Penknife blade; 9,10,11-Point 12,13,19-Borer; 14,15-Cresent/Lunate; 18-Blade fragment; 20-End scraper; 21-Side scraper; 22-Scraper; 23 to 28-Blade core.

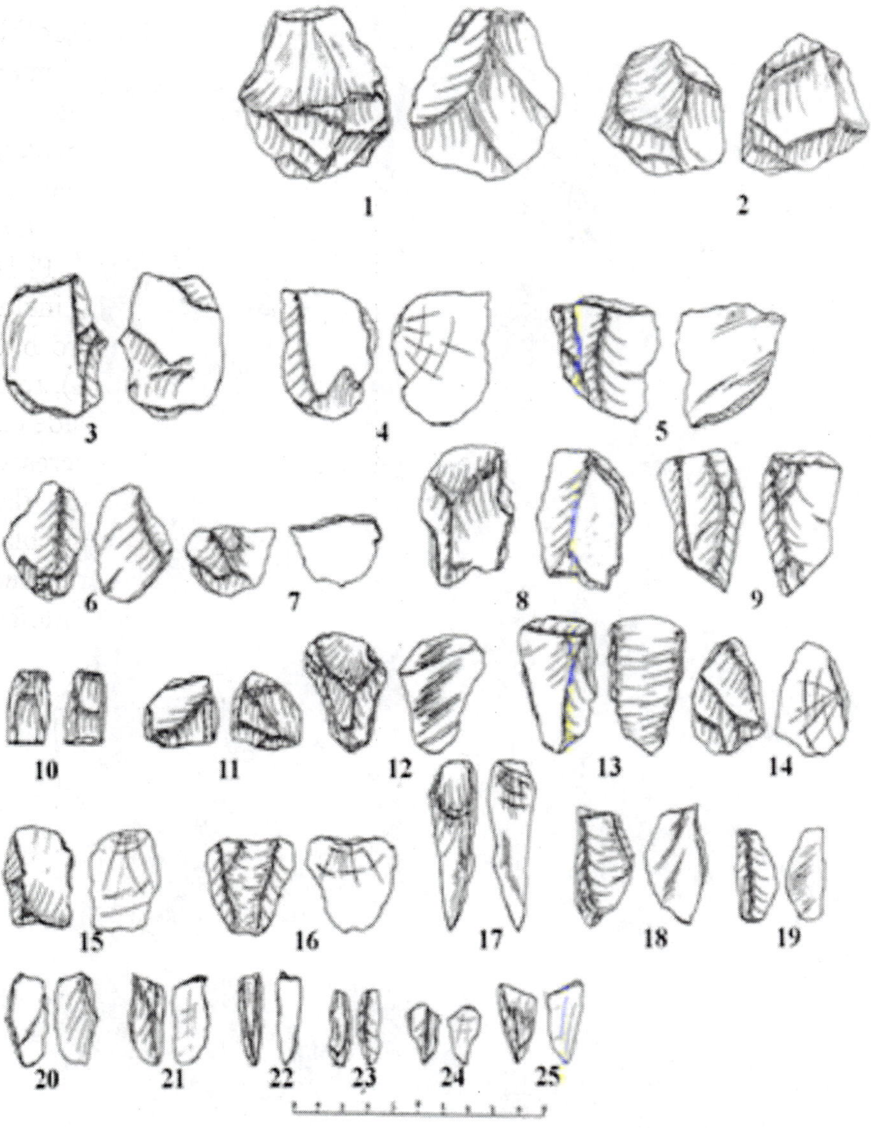

Fig.22: Sorbeda Dautasala microliths artefacts.
1,2,8-Core scraper; 3,6,14-End scraper; 4,5,13-Side scraper, 7-Thumbnail scraper; 9,10,11-Blade core; 12-Concave scraper; 15,19,21-Blade; 16-Trapeze;17,20,22,25-Point;18-Penknife blade; 24-Cresent/Lunate.

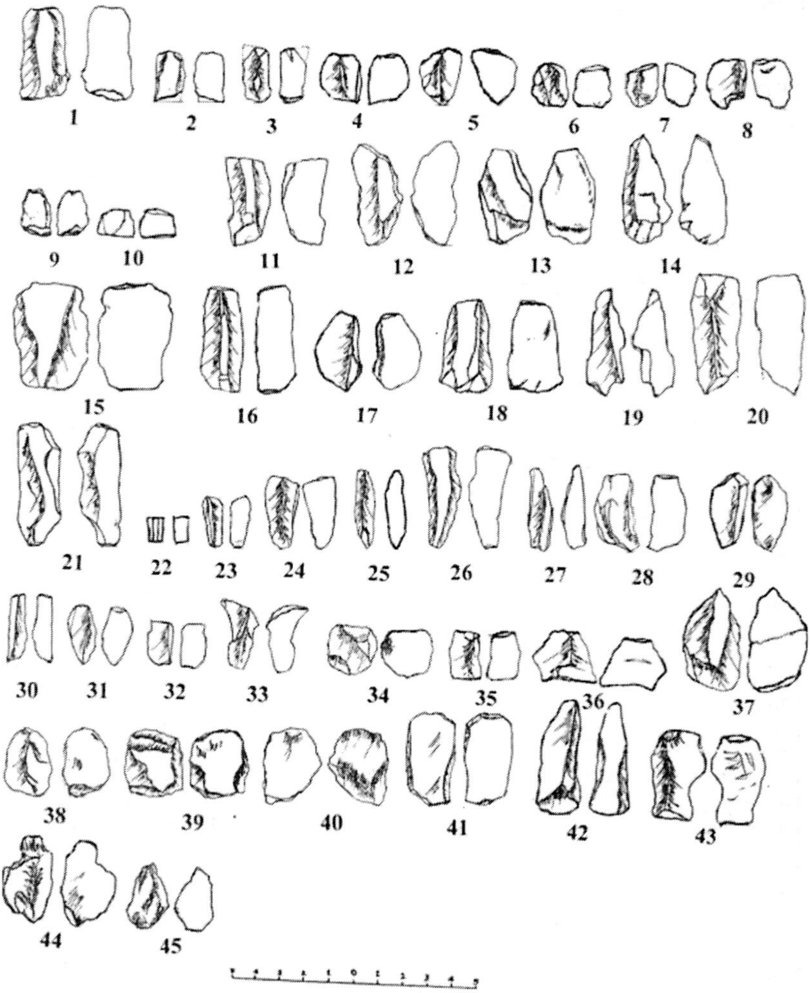

Fig.23: Kadamdiha microlithic artefacts.
1,16-Parallal sided blade; 2,4,7,22,32-Blade fragment; 3,11,10,21,23,26 to 31,39-Blade; 5,14,25,38a- Point; 6,34-Thumbnail scraper; 8,9,13- Utilized flake; 12,38b-Side scraper; 17, 20, 24-Pen knife blade; 18-Blade cum end scraper; 19,36-Flake; 33-Blade cum borer; 38-Scraper; 37,40,43-Borer; 41,42-Concave scraper.

Sites on River Bank cum Foot Hill Area

The river bank cum foot hill sites include the sites of Karadapal-II, Mohanpur Shiva Mandir and Nemliloti. The microlithic recoveries are presented in tabular form.

Table No-3.14 Distribution of microliths in Karadapal II (KDP II).

Sl. No.	Typology	Mean measurement (in cm)			Mean ratio			Materials	No	Percentage
		L	B	T	T/L	B/L	T/B			
1	Parallel sided blade	2.9	1.6	0.5	0.17	0.55	0.31	Ash grey chert-2 Iron ore-1 Chert-2	5	20.83%
2	Pen knife blade	2.6	1.8	0.6	0.23	0.69	0.33	Ash grey chert-2	2	8.33%
3	Blade	2.4	1.3	0.5	0.20	0.54	0.38	Quertz-2 Milky quertz-1 Chert-1	4	16.66%
4	End scraper	3.9	1.2	0.9	0.23	0.30	0.75	Yellow chert-1	1	4.16%
5	Point	2.5	0.7	0.4	0.16	0.28	0.57	Grey chert-2 Quartzite-1	3	12.50%
6	Tang point	2.0	0.9	0.4	0.2	0.45	0.44	Ash grey chert-1	1	4.16%
7	Triangle	1.7	0.8	0.3	0.17	0.47	0.37	Querz-1	1	4.16%
8	Crescent	2.1	0.7	0.4	0.19	0.33	0.57	Quartzite-1	1	4.16%
9	Utilised flake	2.8	1.9	0.6	0.21	0.67	0.31	Quartzite -1	1	4.16%
10	Round scraper	3.2	2.4	1.3	0.40	0.75	0.31	Iron ore-1	1	4.16%
11	Side cum end scraper	3.0	2.4	0.7	0.23	0.8	0.29	Chert-1	1	4.16%
12	Blade core	2.8	2.5	1.7	0.60	0.89	0.68	Chert-3	3	12.50%
Total									**24**	**99.94%**

Table No-3.15 Distribution of microliths from Mohanpur Shiva Mandir site (MSM).

Sl. No.	Typology	Mean measurement (in cm)			Mean ratio			Material	No.	Percentage
		L	B	T	T/L	B/L	T/B			
1	Blade (Fragmented)	1.3	1.2	0.5	0.38	0.92	0.41	Iron ore-1, Chert-5	6	13.04%
2	Blade (Micro)	1.5	0.9	0.2	0.13	0.6	0.22	Banded chert-1	1	2.17%
3	Point	1.7	1.1	0.3	0.17	0.64	0.27	Iron ore-1, Chert-2	3	6.52%
4	Utilized flake	2.0	1.4	0.4	0.2	0.7	0.28	Vain chert-1 Grey chert-1 Chert-1	3	6.52%
5	Parallel sided blade	3.3	1.8	0.6	0.18	0..54	0.33	Vain chert-1 Milky quartz-1 Grey chert-1	3	6.52%
6	Notch scraper	2.0	1.2	0.5	0.25	0.6	0.41	Chert-1	1	2.17%
7	Penknife blade	2.5	1.0	0.5	0.2	0.4	0.5	Chert-1 Quartz-1	2	4.34%
8	Blade	2.4	1.2	0.5	0.20	0.5	0.41	Quartz-1 Milky quartz-2 Ash grey chert-1, Grey quartz-1	8	17.39%
9	Fluted core/ Flake core	2.0	1.1	0.6	0.3	0.55	0.54	Chert-1	1	2.17%
10	Trapezoid	2.5	2.4	1.0	0.4	0.96	0.41	Greenish quartz-1	1	2.17%
11	Lunate	3.0	1.3	0.5	0.16	0.43	0.38	Chert-1, Milky quartz-1	2	4.34%
12	Borer	2.8	1.7	0.7	0.25	0.60	0.41	Chert-2, Agate-1? Banded chert-1	4	8.69%
13	End cum side scraper	2.6	1.6	0.6	0.23	0.61	0.37	Chert-1	1	2.17%
14	Tang point	3.0	1.6	0.5	0.16	0.53	0.31	Chert-1	1	2.17%

contd...

15	Blade core	2.7	2.0	13	0.48	0.74	0.65	Chert-2, Quartz-1 Banded chert-1 Grey chert-1	6	13.04%
16	Scraper	2.3	2.1	0.8	0.34	0.91	0.38	Chert-1	1	2.17%
17	Round scraper	4.1	3.5	2.1	0.51	0.85	0.6	Grey chert-1	1	2.17%
18	Microlith chip	0.9	0.7	0.2	0.22	0.77	0.28	Chert-1	1	2.17%
Total									46	99.93%

Table No-3.16 Distribution of microliths in Nemliloti (NLT).

Sl. No.	**Typology**	**Mean measurement (in cm)**			**Mean ratio**			**Materials**	**No**	**Percentage**
		L	**B**	**T**	**T/L**	**B/L**	**T/B**			
1	Blade	1.7	1.1	0.5	0.29	0.64	0.45	Milky quartz -2 Grey quartz-1	3	30.00%
2	Blade core	2.6	1.9	1.1	0.42	0.73	0.57	Chert-1	1	10.00%
3	Parallel sided Blade	2.2	1.5	0.6	0.27	0.68	0.4	Milky quartz-1	1	10.00%
4	Trapezoid	2.2	2.0	0.7	0.31	0.90	0.35	Milky quartz-1	1	10.00%
5	Crescent	4.8	1.6	1.1	0.22	0.33	0.68	Milky quartz-1	1	10.00%
6	Round scraper	4.8	3.9	2.0	0.41	0.81	0.51	Milky quartz-1	1	10.00%
7	Side scraper	2.5	2.0	0.6	0.24	0.8	0.3	Milky quartz-1	1	10.00%
8	Utilized flake	3.1	2.8	1.0	0.32	0.90	0.35	Milky quartz -1	1	10.00%
Total									**10**	**100%**

From Karadapal-II site, it is clear that microliths are the dominant in this site. The parallel sided blade shares 20.83% of whole microlithic. The other microliths include pen knife blade, end scraper, point, tang point, triangle, crescent, utilized flake, round scraper, side-cum- end scraper and blade core. Chert is the main raw- material used for these artefacts (Table-3.14, Pl.12). The Mohanpur Shiva Mandir site has yielded 46 number of microliths, the dominant varieties are blade, blade fragment and blade core where as the different types of scraper, point, lunate, trapezoid flake etc are of minor variety type. The table also shows mean measurements of the artefacts as well as the percentage and material variety. Chert is the dominant variety of raw material (Table-3.15, Fig.24, Pl.13). The Nemliloti site indicates microlithic tool assemblages which include blade, blade core, parallel sided blade, trapezoid, crescent, round scraper, side scraper, and utilized flake. Blade (30%) is the dominated tool types in this site. Milky quartz is important raw material for manufacturing the implement (Table-3.16).

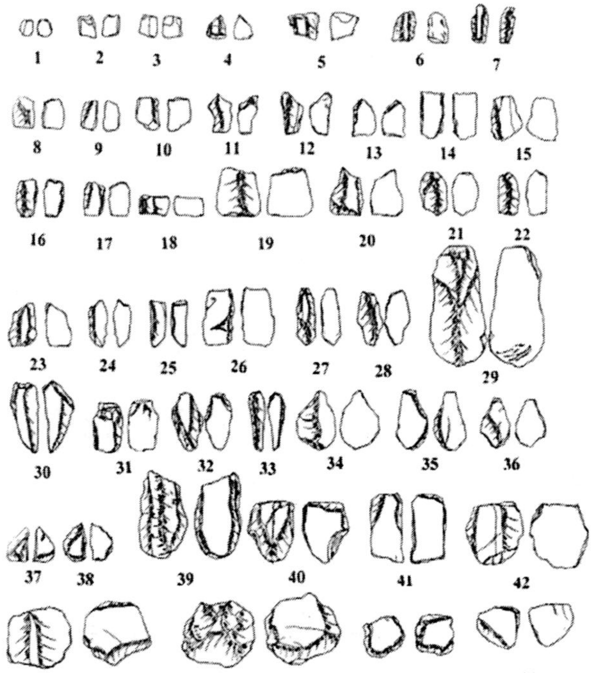

Fig.24: Mohanpur Shiva Mandir site microlithic artefacts.
1-Microlithic chip; 2,3,5,6,8,18-Blade fragment; 7,15,21,22,23,24,26 & 33-Blade; 9-Micro blade; 10,13,20-Utilized flake; 11-Notch scraper; 12,27-Pen knife blade; 14,17,29-Parallel sided blade, 16-Fluted flake; 19-Trapezoid; 25,30-Lunate, 28,34,35 & 36-Borer; 31-End cum side scraper, 32-Tang point; 4,37 & 38,40,41,42,43 & 45-Blade core; 44-Round scraper; 46-Scraper.

Site-wise and Eco-zone wise analysis of Artefacts

Under this sub head the detail studies of the artefacts are arranged Eco-zone wise and site-wise with typologically. As mentioned earlier, the sites are divided under four eco-zones. The following contains site-wise and type-wise distribution of microlithic artefacts of each eco-zone.

Table No-3.17 Site-wise and Type-wise distribution of microlithic artefacts of River bank sites.

Tool type	River bank site						Total No	Percentage
	Bhaluguda .	Dalo Puranadiha	Gopapur gadhuaghta	Kadamdar	Rajamunda	Talabirikala badamsala		
Blade	1	6	7	1	11	1	27	20.00%
Blade fragment	-	-	-	1	-	-	1	0.74%
Parallel sided blade	1	3	-	4	2	1	11	8.14%
Pen knife blade	-	2	1	4	-	-	7	5.18%
Side scraper	2	-	-	3	5	-	10	7.40%
End scraper	-	-	1	-	1	-	2	1.48%
End cum side scraper	-	-	-	1	-	-	1	0.74%
Thumb nail scraper	2	1	-	2	2	-	7	5.18%
Round scraper	-	1	-	3	-	-	4	2.96%
Blade cum scraper	-	-	1	-	-	-	1	0.74%
Borer cum end scraper	-	-	1	-	-	-	1	0.74%
Keel blade	-	-	-	-	1	-	1	0.74%
Blade core cum borer	-	-	-	2	-	-	2	1.48%
Point	3	-	3	3	2	-	11	8.14%

contd...

Tang point	1	1	-	1	-	-	3	2.22%
Burin	-	-	1	1	-	-	2	1.48%
Micro borer	-	-	1	-	-	-	1	0.74%
Borer	3	1	1	6	4	-	15	11.11%
Crescent / lunate	2	2	-	2	-	-	6	4.44%
Trapezoid	-	-	-	2	-	-	2	1.48%
Blade core/ flake core	1	1	-	-	3	-	5	3.70%
Utilized flake	-	1	4	-	2	1	8	5.92%
Point with Deep notch	-	-	1	-	-	-	1	0.74%
Crescent cum borer	-	1	-	-	-	-	1	0.74%
Flake	-	1	-	-	-	1	2	1.48%
Scraper	-	1	-	2	-	-	3	2.22%
Total	**16 (11.85)**	**22 (16.29)**	**22 (16.29)**	**38 (28.14)**	**33 (24.44)**	**4 (2.96)**	**135**	**99.93%**

Table No-3.18 Site-wise and Type-wise distribution of microlithic artefacts of Foot hill site.

Tool type	Foot hill Site	Total No.	Percentage
	Jalanda Hatapata		
Blade	4	4	23.53%
Parallel sided blade	1	1	5.88%
Pen knife blade	1	1	5.88%
Round scraper	1	1	5.88%
Point	2	2	11.76%
Borer	2	2	11.76%
Blade core/ flake core	2	2	11.76%
Utilized flake	3	3	17.65%
scraper	1	1	5.88%
Total	**17**	**17**	**100%**

Table No-3.19 Site-wise and Type-wise distribution of microlithic artefacts of Piedmont site.

Tool type	Piedmont site					Total No.	Percentage
	Atanaka Reserve Forest	Karadapal-I	Rugudidiha	Sorbeda dautasala	Kadamdiha		
Blade	4	6	3	3	12	28	17.5%
Blade (micro)	-	-	-	-	2	2	1.25%
Blade fragment	-	-	1	-	8	9	5.62%
Parallel sided blade	3	1	4	-	2	10	6.25%
Pen knife blade	-	-	3	1	3	7	4.37%
Side scraper	2	1	1	4	3	11	6.87%
End scraper	-	-	1	3	-	4	2.5%
End cum side scraper	1	-	-	-	-	1	0.62%
Thumb nail scraper	-	-	-	1	4	5	3.12%
Round scraper	-	-	-	3	2	5	3.12%
Concave scraper	-	-	-	1	3	4	2.5%
Point	-	2	3	4	7	16	10.00%
Burin	2	-	-	-	2	4	2.5%
Micro borer	-	-	-	-	1	1	0.62%
Borer	1	2	3	-	4	10	6.25%
Crescent / lunate	1	-	2	1	3	7	4.37%
Triangle	2	1	-	-	1	4	2.5%
Trapezoid	-	-	-	1	1	2	1.25%
Blade core/ flake core	-	2	5	3	4	14	8.75%
Utilised flake	-	-	-	-	3	3	1.87%
Flake	-	-	-	-	5	5	3.12%
Blade cum borer		-	-	-	1	1	0.62%
Blade cum end scraper	-	-	-	-	1	1	0.62%
scraper	-	3	1	-	2	6	3.75%
Total	**16 (10.00)**	**18 (11.25)**	**27 (16.87)**	**25 (15.62)**	**74 (46.25)**	**160**	**99.94%**

Table No-3.20 Site-wise and Type-wise distribution of microlithic artefacts of River bank cum Foot hill sites.

Tool type	River bank cum Foot hill Site			Total No.	percentage
	Karadapal-II	Mohanpur shiva mandir	Nemliloti		
Blade	4	8	3	15	18.75%
Blade (micro)	-	1	-	1	1.25%
Blade fragment	-	6	-	6	7.5%
Parallel sided blade	5	3	1	9	11.25%
Pen knife blade	2	2	-	4	5.0%
Side scraper	-	-	1	1	1.25%
End scraper	1	-	-	1	1.25%
End cum side scraper	1	1	-	2	2.5%
Round scraper	1	1	1	3	3.75%
Point	3	3	-	6	7.5%
Tang point	1	1	-	2	2.5%
Borer	-	4	-	4	5.0%
Crescent / lunate	1	2	1	4	5.0%
Triangle	1	-	-	1	1.25%
Trapezoid	-	1	1	2	2.5%
Blade core/ flake core	3	7	1	11	13.75%
Utilized flake	1	3	1	5	6.25%
Microlith chip	-	1	-	1	1.25%
Notch scraper	-	1	-	1	1.25%
scraper	-	1	-	1	1.25%
Total	**24 (30.00)**	**46 (57.5)**	**10 (12.5)**	**80**	**100.00%**

There are total 6 no of sites under river bank category and 135 specimens have been collected for its analytical study, in which blade is the dominant variety and possess total 27 (20.00%) and the minimum number of artefacts are end cum side scraper, blade cum scraper, borer cum end scraper, keel blade, micro borer, point with deep notch, crescent cum borer represent 1 (0,74%) each specimen. The borer specimen is second dominant variety and represents 15 (11.11%). The other dominant varieties are point and parallel sided blade represent 11 each (8.14%)(Table-3.17).

One site comes under the foot hill site and yielded 17 specimens. Out of these 17 no specimen recorded under foot hill site, the blade is dominant variety and possesses 4 specimen (23.52%) and followed to it the Utilized flake 3 specimen (17.69%), the Blade core, Borer, Point represent each 2 specimen (each 11.76%). The other specimens are Parallel sided Blade, Pen Knife Blade, Round scraper and Scraper represent 1specimen (5.88%) (Table-3.18).

There are total 5 no of sites fall under piedmont category and about 160 specimens have been collected for its analytical study. In which blade is dominant variety and possesses total 28 no (17.5%) and the second dominant variety is Point 16 no (10.00). The other dominant variety are Blade core 11 no (6.87). The other important artifacts represented as side scraper 11 no (6.87%) parallel sided blade and borer each 10 (6.25%) etc. The blade cum end scraper, end cum side scraper and micro borer are of rare variety (Table-3.19).

There are total three numbers of sites under the river bank cum foot hill site and from which 80 specimens have been collected. From the river bank cum foot hill sites important tool type is Blade 15 specimen (18.75%) followed by Blade core 11specimen (13.75), Blade 9 specimen (11.25%) and some of less important specimen are Micro blade, Side scraper, end scraper, triangle, Microlith chip, Notch scraper and Scraper represent 1 specimen each (1.25%) (Table-3.20).

Component-wise and Eco-zone wise analysis of Artefacts

Table No-3.21 Component-wise and Eco-zone wise distribution of microlithic artefacts.

Artefacts	Typology	Eco zone wise distribution					
		River bank	**Foot hill**	**Piedmont**	**River bank cum foot hill**	**Total No**	**Percentage**
Flake Component	Side scraper	10	-	11	1	22	12.5%
	End scraper	2	-	4	1	7	3.98%
	Thumb nail scraper	7	-	5	-	12	6.82%
	Borer	15	2	10	4	31	17.62%
	Utilized flake	8	3	3	5	19	10.78%
	Round scraper	5	1	5	2	13	7.38%
	Borer cum scraper	1	-	-	-	1	0.57%
	Blade core/ Flake core	7	2	14	11	34	19.31%
	Concave scraper	-	-	4	-	4	2.27%
	Notch scraper	-	-	-	1	1	0.57%
	Side cum end scraper	1	-	1	2	4	2.27%
	Tanged point	3	-	-	2	5	2.85%
	Scraper	3	1	6	1	11	6.25%
	Flake	2	-	5	-	7	3.98%
	Micro borer	1	-	1	-	2	1.13%
	Blade core cum	2	-	-	-	2	1.13%
	Microlithic chips	-	-	-	1	1	0.57%
	Total	**67**	**9**	**69**	**31**	**176**	**99.98%**
Blade Component	blade	27	4	28	15	74	34.25%
	Parallel sided blade	11	1	10	9	31	14.35%
	Pen knife blade	7	1	7	4	19	8.78%

contd...

	Point	11	2	16	6	35	16.20%
	Crescent	6	-	7	4	17	7.88%
	Triangle	1	-	4	-	5	2.31%
	Trapezoid	-	-	2	2	4	1.86%
	Blade cum scraper	1	-	1	-	2	0.93%
	Crescent cum borer	1	-	-	-	1	0.46%
	Keel blade	1	-	-	-	1	0.46%
	Blade fragment	1	-	9	6	16	7.40%
	Blade (micro)	-	-	2	1	3	1.38%
	Blade cum borer	-	-	1	-	1	0.46%
	Point with deep notch	1	-	-	-	1	0.46%
	Burin	2	-	4	-	6	2.78%
	Total	**70**	**8**	**91**	**47**	**216**	**99.96%**

The broad category is flake component in which, artefacts includes side scraper, end scraper, thumb nail scraper, borer, utilized flakes, round scraper, borer cum scraper, blade core, concave scraper, notch scraper, side cum end scraper, tanged point, scraper, flake, micro borer, blade cum borer and microlithic chips. The second component includes blade, parallel sided blade, pen knife blade, point crescent, triangle, trapezoid, blade cum scraper, crescent cum borer, keel blade, blade fragment, blade (micro), blade cum borer, point with deep notch and burin. In case of flake component, the flake core/black core are dominant variety whereas in the blade component, the blade hold majority i.e. 74 specimens (34.25%). The flake component and blade component occurrence in foot hill are is very less and piedmont site has collected in respect of higher than other eco-zone sites.

Raw Material Distribution of Microlithic Artefacts

Table No-3.22: Raw material distribution of microlithic artefacts.

Tool type	Chert	Cherty quartzite	Ash grey chert	Grey chert	Greenish chert	Vain chert	Iron ore	Banded chert	Quartz	Grey quartz	Crystal	Milky quartz	Agate	Greenish quartz	Yellowish chert
Blade	30	1	2	4	5	1	-	-	5	1	1	24	-	-	-
Blade (micro)	2	-	-	-	-	-	-	1	-	-	-	-	-	-	-
Blade fragment	11	-	-	-	-	-	1	-	-	-	-	4	-	-	-
Pen knife blade	6	2	2	1	-	-	-	2	1	-	-	5	-	-	-
Parallel side Blade	10	1	3	1	-	1	3	-	2	-	-	10	-	-	-
Side scraper	12	-	1	1	-	-	-	1	-	1	-	6	-	-	-
End cum side scraper	2	-	-	-	-	-	-	-	1	-	-	1	-	-	-
Thumb nail scraper	5	-	-	1	-	-	1	-	-	-	-	5	-	-	-
Round scraper	5	-	-	1	-	-	1	1	-	-	-	5	-	-	-
Blade cum end scraper	1	-	-	-	-	-	-	-	-	-	-	1	-	-	-
Borer cum end scraper	-	-	-	-	-	-	-	1	-	-	-	-	-	-	-
Keel blade	-	-	1	-	-	-	-	-	-	-	-	-	-	-	-
Concave scraper	4	-	-	-	-	-	-	-	-	-	-	-	-	-	-
Point	18	2	-	3	-	1	1	-	4	-	-	6	-	-	-
Tanged point	3	-	1	-	-	-	-	-	-	-	-	1	-	-	-
Burin	2	-	1	1	-	-	-	-	-	-	-	2	-	-	-
Micro borer	2	-	-	-	-	-	-	-	-	-	-	-	-	-	-
Borer	17	-	-	3	-	-	1	1	2	-	1	5	1	-	-
Crescent/lunate	6	-	-	-	-	-	-	-	3	-	-	8	-	-	-
Triangle	3	-	-	-	-	-	-	-	1	-	-	1	-	-	-
Trapezoid	-	-	-	-	-	-	-	-	1	-	-	2	-	1	-
Blade core	24	-	-	3	-	-	1	2	2	-	-	2	-	-	-

contd...

Utilized flake	8	-	-	1	-	1	-	2	2	-	-	5	-	-	-
Point with deep notch	-	-	-	-	-	-	-	-	-	-	-	1	-	-	-
Crescent cum borer	1	-	-	-	-	-	-	-	-	-	-	-	-	-	-
Flake	4	1	-	-	-	-	-	1	1	-	-	-	-	-	-
Notch scraper	1	-	-	-	-	-	-	-	-	-	-	-	-	-	-
Scraper	7	-	-	1	-	-	-	-	2	-	-	1	-	-	-
Microlith chip	1	-	-	-	-	-	-	-	-	-	-	-	-	-	-
Blade cum borer	1	-	-	-	-	-	-	1	-	-	-	-	-	-	1
Total	**191**	**7**	**14**	**22**	**2**	**4**	**9**	**13**	**27**	**2**	**2**	**95**	**1**	**1**	**2**
392 (99.95%)	(48.72%)	(1.78%)	(3.57%)	(5.61%)	(0.51%)	(1.02%)	(2.29%)	(3.31%)	(6.88%)	(0.51%)	(0.51%)	(24.23%)	(0.25%)	(0.25%)	(0.51%)

The raw material distribution of microlithic artefacts collected from the widely distributed Kakharua survey sites. The materials are divided into 15 varieties as per colour composition and nature. They are basically of crypto-crystalline and crystalline rocks as the representative assemblage of this culture are also considerably noticed in the region. They are mostly opaque and translucent rocks ranging from medium to fine grained siliceous rock type. But chert is the most common raw material exploited for manufacturing of Mesolithic artefacts. Out of 392 specimens, chert comprises 191 (48.72%), followed by cherty quartzite 7(1.78%), ash-grey chert 14 (3.57%), grey chert 22 (5.61%), greenish chert 2((0.51%), vain chert 4(1.02%), iron ore 9 (2.29%), banded chert 13 (3.31%), quartz 27(6.88%), grey quartz 2(0.51%), crystal 2 (0.51%), milky quartz 95(24.23%), agate 1(0.25%), greenish quartz 1 (0.25%) and yellowish chert 2 (0.87%). All these raw material are locally available (Fig.25).

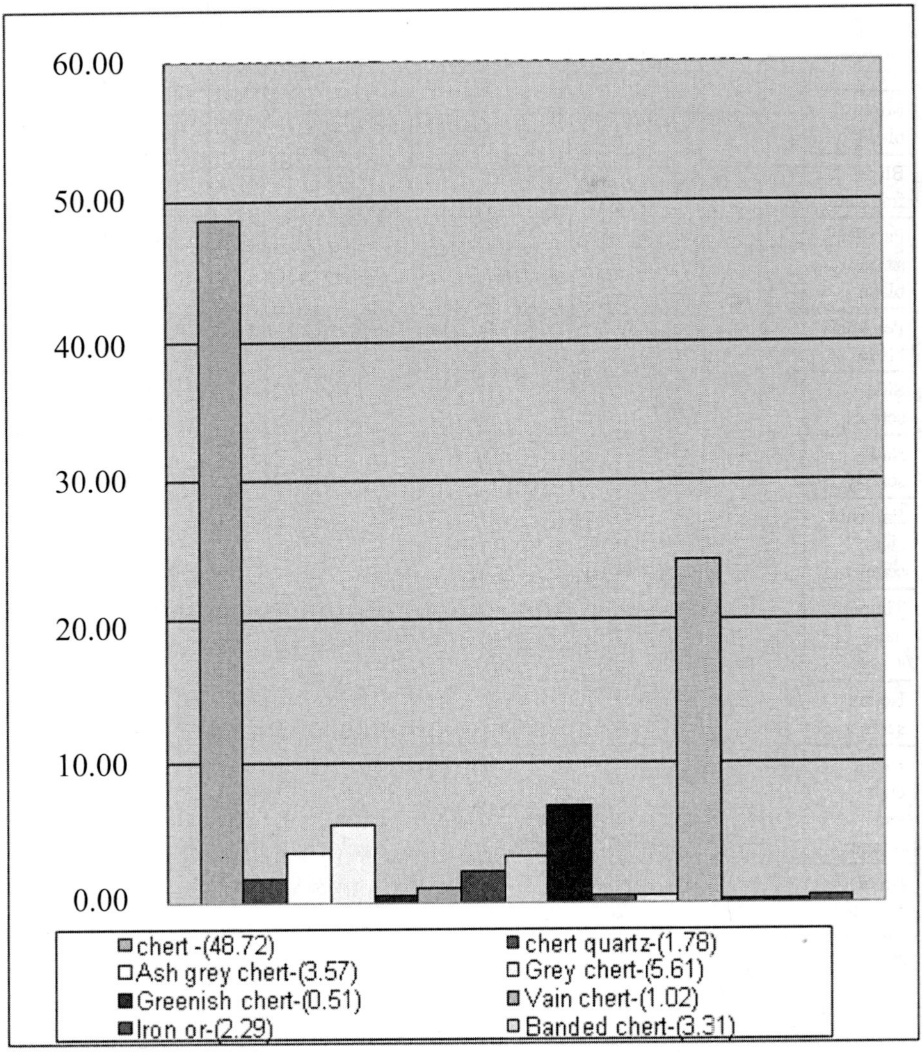

Fig.25: Raw material distribution of Mesolithic artefacts.

Table No-3.23 Site-wise distribution of microlithic artefacts.

Tool type	MSM	RGD	KDPI	JHP	BLG	SBD	GPG	RMD	KDP II	ARF	[illegible]	TBS	DPD	KDD	KDH	Total	percentage
Blade	8	3	6	4	1	3	7	11	4	4	[illegible]	1	6	1	12	74	18.87%
Micro blade	1	-	-	-	-	-	-	-	-	-	-	-	-	-	2	3	0.76%
Blade fragment	6	1	-	-	-	-	-	-	-	-	-	-	-	1	8	16	4.08%
Parallel sided blade	3	4	1	1	1	-	-	2	5	3	1	1	3	4	2	31	7.90%
Pen knife blade	2	3	-	1	-	1	1	-	2	-	-	-	2	4	3	19	4.84%
Side scraper	-	1	1	-	2	4	-	5	-	2	1	-	-	3	3	22	5.61%
End scraper	-	1	-	-	-	3	1	1	1	-	-	-	-	-	-	7	1.78%
End cum side scraper	1	-	-	-	-	-	-	-	1	1	-	-	-	1	-	4	1.02%
Thumb nail scraper	-	-	-	-	2	1	-	2	-	-	-	-	1	2	4	12	3.06%
Round scraper	1	-	-	1	-	3	-	-	1	-	1	-	1	3	2	13	3.31%
Blade cum end scraper	-	-	-	-	-	-	1	-	-	-	-	-	-	-	1	2	0.51%
Borer cum end scraper	-	-	-	-	-	-	1	-	-	-	-	-	-	-	-	1	0.25%
Keel blade	-	-	-	-	-	-	-	1	-	-	-	-	-	-	-	1	0.25%
Concave scraper	-	-	-	-	-	1	-	-	-	-	-	-	-	-	3	4	1.02%
Blade-core cum borer	-	-	-	-	-	-	-	-	-	-	-	-	-	2	-	2	0.51%

contd...

Blade cum borer	-	-	-	-	-	-	-	-	-	-	-	-	-	-	1	1	0.25%
Point	3	3	2	2	3	4	3	2	3	-	-	-	-	3	7	35	8.92%
Tanged point	1	-	-	-	1	-	-	-	1	-	-	-	1	1	-	5	1.27%
Burin	-	-	-	-	-	-	1	-	-	2	-	-	-	1	2	6	1.53%
Micro borer	-	-	-	-	-	-	1	-	-	-	-	-	-	-	1	2	0.51%
Borer	4	3	2	2	3	-	1	4	-	1	-	-	1	6	4	31	7.90%
Crescent/ lunate	2	2	-	-	2	1	-	-	1	1	1	-	2	2	3	17	4.33%
Triangle	-	-	1	-	-	-	-	-	1	2	-	-	-	-	1	5	1.27%
Trapezoid	1	-	-	-	-	1	-	-	-	-	1	-	-	-	1	4	1.02%
Blade core	7	5	2	2	1	3	-	3	3	-	1	-	1	2	4	34	8.67%
Utilised flake	3	-	-	3	-	-	4	2	1	-	1	1	1	-	3	19	4.84%
Point with deep notch	-	-	-	-	-	-	1	-	-	-	-	-	-	-	-	1	0.25%
Crescent cum borer	-	-	-	-	-	-	-	-	-	-	-	-	1	-	-	1	0.25%
Flake	-	-	-	-	-	-	-	-	-	-	-	1	1	-	5	7	1.78%
Notch scraper	1	-	-	-	-	-	-	-	-	-	-	-	-	-	-	1	0.25%
Micro lithic chip	1	-	-	-	-	-	-	-	-	-	-	-	-	-	-	1	0.25%
Scraper	1	1	3	1	-	-	-	-	-	-	-	-	1	2	2	11	2.80%
Total	**46 (11.73%)**	**27 (6.88%)**	**18 (4.59%)**	**17 (4.33%)**	**16 (4.08%)**	**25 (6.37%)**	**22 (5.61%)**	**33 (8.41%)**	**24 (6.12%)**	**16 (4.08%)**	**10 (2.5%)**	**4 (1.02%)**	**22 (5.61%)**	**38 (9.69%)**	**74 (18.87%)**	**392**	**99.10%**

The evidence of microlithic on Kakharua valley comes from 16 sites which are basically located on the foot hill, river bank, piedmont and foot hill cum river bank areas. As the whole area is covered with the jungle, it is very difficult to trace out the large amount of specimen from these sites. However, out of 392 lithic implements collected from the various sites, the maximum i.e. 74 (18.87 %) are collected from

Kadamdiha. On the basis of the number of evidences, the Mohanpur Shiva Mandir site comes next to it having 45 (11.73%) number of artefacts. The minimum i.e. 4 (1.02%) number of artefacts collected from an exposed area of Tala Birikala Badamsala.

In respect of the individual tool typology, the blade comprises of 74 specimens (18.87%), micro blade 3 (0.76%), blade fragment 16 (4.08%), parallel sided blade 31 (7.90%), pen knife blade 19 (4.84%), side scraper 22 (5.61%), end scraper 7 (1.78%), end cum side scraper 4 (1.02%), thumb nail scraper 12 (3.06%), round scraper 13 (3.31%), blade cum end scraper 2 (0.51%), borer cum end scraper 1 (0.25%), keel blade 1 (0.25%), concave scraper 4 (1.02%), blade core cum borer 2 (0.51%), blade cum borer 1 (0.25%), point 35 (8.92%), tang point 5 (1.27%), burin 6 (1.53%), micro borer 2 (0.51%), borer 31 (7.90%), crescent 17 (4.33%), triangle 5 (1.27%), trapezoid 4 (1.02%), blade core 34 (8.67%), utilized flake 19 (4.84%), blade core 34 (8.67%), utilized flake 19 (4.84%), point with deep notch 1 (0.25%), crescent cum borer 1 (0.25%), microlith chip 1 (0.25%), and scraper 11 specimen (2.80%) (Table-3.23, Fig.26).

Considering the above discussion, it is noticed that a well developed blade technology is the most important feature of the microlithic assemblages in Kakharua valley. The artefacts were probably prepared by the soft hammer of bone or wood, by the punch of by pressure techniques.

Recoveries of Microlithic Artefacts

Flake component:- A total of 176 (26.30 % from the total collection) artefacts of this component has been obtained from four eco-zones. Artefacts of this component include side scraper 22 (12.5 %), end scraper 7 (3.98%), thumb nail scraper 12 (6.82%), borer 31 (17.62%), utilized flake 19 (10.78%), round scraper 13 (7.38%), borer cum scraper 1 (0.57%), blade core 34 (19.31%), concave scraper 4 (2.27%), notch scraper 1 (0.57%), side cum end scraper 4 (2.27%), tanged point 5 (2.85%), scraper 11 (6.25%), flake 7 (3.98%), micro borer 2 (1.13%), blade core cum borer 2 (1.13%), chips 1(0.57%). Among these artefacts most of are usually use siliceous rock for manufacturing the component.

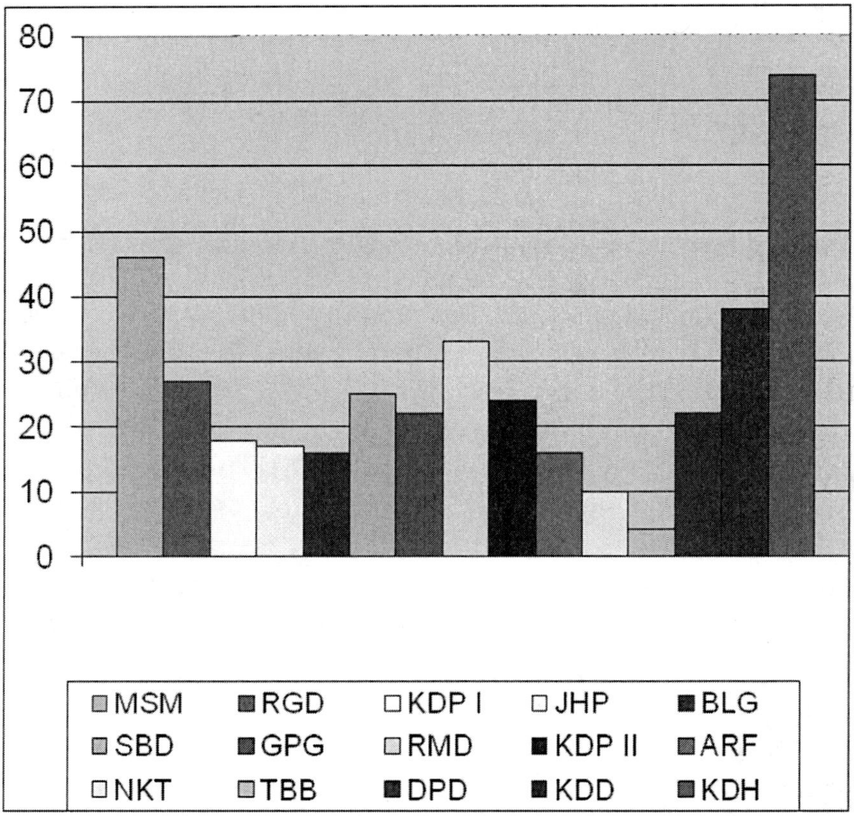

Fig.26: Site-wise distribution of microliths.

Side Scraper

As the name denotes, these tools have a side working edge. These vary from elongated to oval in shape flaking and chipping concentrate in both side with some cases retouching observed on the surface out of 22 side scraper 12(54.54%) of chert, 1(4.54%) of ash grey chert, 1 (4.45%) grey, 1 (4.54%) banded chert, 1(4.54%) grey quartz and 6 (27.27%) made of milky quartz.

1. **KDD** -20, Side scraper, 1.8 x 1.2 x 0.5 cm, this is made out of milky quartz. One side has retouch to shape into side scraper (Pl.5).

2. **KDP-I** -18, Side scraper, 3.4 x 2.5 x 1.7 cm, grey chert. A number of small retouches have been made to make this scraper (Fig.20, Pl.8).
3. **SBD** -16, Side scraper, 4.6 x 2.9 x 1.1 cm, The specimen is made of black chert. One side of the implement has long retouch. (Fig.22, Pl.10).
4. **RMD** -19, Side scraper, 4.9 x 2.7 x 0.9 cm, Made out of ash grey chert. One side of this Specimen has number of retouch. (Fig.18, Pl.6).

End Scraper

There are several end scrapers made on siliceous rock found from the study area. The details of an end scraper is given below.

1. **RGD**-20, End scraper, 3.7 x 2.9 x 1.2 cm, Made out of grey chert. The lower end has been retouched. (Fig.21, Pl.9).
2. **SBD** -17, End scraper, 4.0 x 3.0 x 0.8 cm, Made out of black chert. The working end is retouched. (Fig.22, Pl.10).
3. **GPG** -20, End scraper, 2.8 x 1.5 x 0.9 cm, Made out of black chert. This specimen has beautiful retouch with a notch. .

Borer

Borer is found in the form of crescent cum borer and blade cum borer. It is made on a thick flake of siliceous rock having a long projectile drill head. The drill head is fashioned by removing minute chips and then by retouching. The upper surface is retained with original cortex and flaked- chipped sloppy side. The lower surface is retained with a shallow flake scar. The artefact was probably used for boring or drilling.

1. **JHP** -13, Borer, 4.4 x 2.0 x 1.3 cm, Made out of chert material. The thick pointed end has poly hydra facet. (Fig.19).
2. **JHP** -10, Borer, 4.2 x 2.4 x 1.0 cm, Made out of chert material. The three pointed end has retouch. (Fig.19).

3. **KDD** -12, Borer, 3.0 x 1.2 x 0.8 cm, Made out of chert material. Several retouch make the thick pointed end poly hydra facet. (Fig.17, Pl.5).
4. **RGD** -19, Borer, 2.3 x 1.2 x 0.5 cm, chert material. The working end has retouched to blunt poly hydra facet. (Fig.21, Pl.9).

Blade component

Altogether 216 Blade components have been found from four eco-Zones. The majority of artefacts are made out of crypto-crystalline rocks. These include 74 (34.25%) blade, 31 (14.35%) parallel sided blades, 19 (8.78%) pen knife blade, 35 (16.20%) points, 17 (7.88%) crescent, 5 (2.31%) triangle, 2 (0.93%) blade cum scraper, 1 (0.46%) crescent cum borer, 1 (0.46%) keel blade, 16 (7.40%) blade fragment, 3 (1.38%) blade (micro), 1 (0.46%) blade cum borer, 1 (0.46%) point with deep notch, 6 (2.78%) burin. These artefacts are prepared either by fluting or pressure flaking technique. Retouching is made on some selected pieces of artefacts. The details of these artefacts are described below.

Blade

Blade is the dominant tool type of this component. It is found from all the four eco-zones out of the total collection of 74 Blade 4 (5.40%) are found from foot hill sites, 28 (37.83%) are from piedmont area, 27 (36.48%) are from river bank site and 15 (20.27%) are from river bank cum foot hill sites. Cutting edges of these artefacts are almost straight and occasionally irregular. Among the total collection 30 (40.54%) are on chert, 1 (1.35%) cherty-quartzite, 2 (2.70%) ash grey chert, 4 (5.40%) grey chert, 5 (6.75%) greenish chert, 1(1.35%) vain chert, 5 (6.75%) quartz, 1 (1.35%) grey quartz, 1 (1.35%) grey quartz, 1 (1.35%) crystal and 24 (32.43%) milky quartz, the length, breadth and thickness vary respectively.

1. **MSM** -3, Blade fragment, 1.2 x 1.0 x 0.4cm, made out of chert material trapezoid section, cutting edge is sharp in nature (Fig.24, Pl.13).

2. **RGD** -6, Blade, 1.9 x 1.0 x 0.4 cm, made out of milky quartz. Triangular section, cutting edge sharp in nature (Fig.21, Pl.9).
3. **KDP-I** -2, Blade, 2.7 x 1.1 x 0.6 cm, made out of chert. One side blunt and working edge is sharp. Trapezoidal in cross section (Fig.20, Pl.8).
4. **KDP-I** -6, Blade, 2.1 x 1.3 x 0.6 cm, made out of milky quartz. Both side sharp edge, triangular cross section (broken) (Fig.20, Pl.8).
5. **SBD** -18, Blade (retouched), 3.4 x 2.7 x 0.8 cm made out of quartz. The both ends are retouched (Fig.22, Pl.10).
6. **GPG** -2, Blade, 2.6 x 1.5 x 0.7 cm, milky quartz. Both side sharp edge and one long end is broken.
7. **RMD** -4, Blade, 3.1 x 1.6 x 0.5 cm, grey chert. Two sides have marked sharp edge and trapezoidal cross section (Fig.18, Pl.6).
8. **DPD** -6, Blade, 3.9 x 2.3 x 1.1 cm, made out of milky quartz. Blade with denticulate in one end, where as other end has sharp cutting end (Pl.4).
9. **TBB** -1, Blade, 3.5 x 2.1 x 0.8 cm, grey chert. Both side sharp edge and long end has broken. It is roughly trapezoidal cross section.

Point

There are 35 points collected from the four eco-zones of the study area i-e 2 (5.71%) are from foot hill area, 16 (45.71%) are from piedmont sites, 11 (31.42%) are from river bank sites and 6 (17.14%) are from river bank cum foot hill sites. Out of the total number of collected point specimen 18 (51.42%) are made on chert, 2 (5.71%) are on cherty quartzite, 3 (8.57%) are on grey chert, 1 (2.85%) is of vain chert, 1 (2.85%) of Iron Ore, 4 (11.42%) are of quartz and 6 (17.14%) are on milky quartz. The size of these artefacts varies from specimen to specimen. The length, breadth and thickness measurement show wide range respective to its size.

1. **MSM** -36, Point, 1.9 x 1.1 x 0.5 cm, made out of iron ore. The pointed end has retouch to make more prominent projection. (Fig.24, Pl.13).
2. **KDD** -26, Point, 3.3 x 1.9 x 0.6 cm, milky quartz. The pointed end has retouch. Butt end has a good notch to hold stick or bone for good operation. (Fig.17, Pl.5).
3. **RGD** -9, Point, 2.6 x 0.7 x 0.4 cm, made out of chert material. Typical point with number of retouch. (Fig.21, Pl.9).
4. **KDP-I** -12, Point, 3.4 x 2.5 x 0.6 cm, vain chert. Typical leaf type. And pointed edge. (Fig.20, Pl.8).
5. **BLG** -10, Point, 2.1 x 1.4 x 0.5 cm, milky quartz. This may be used as arrow head. The butt end has also retouched. (Fig.16).
6. **GPG** -6, Point, 2.9 x 1.3 x 0.5 cm, chert (Black). The pointed end has a number of retouches and the butt end has a notch in which one can used in arrow point.
7. **RMD** -7, Point, 3.8 x 1.8 x 0.9 cm, chert (Black). Very thick butt end with three small retouch at pointed edge. (Fig.18, Pl.6).

Parallel Sided Blade

Parallel sided blade is the third dominant (14.35%) tool category of the blade component that comes next to blade and point. These artefacts are found from four eco-zones. Among the total collection 1 (2.85%) is from foot hill sites, 10 (28.57%) are from piedmont area, 11 (31.42%) are from river bank sites and 9 are from riverbank cum foot hill sites. Out of the total collection of the Parallel sided Blade, the maximum i.e. 10 (28.57%) are of chert, 10 (28.57%) of milky quartz, 3 (8.57%) of ash grey chert, 3 (8.57%) from iron ore, 2 (5.71%) on quartz, and each 1 (2.85%) from cherty quartz, grey chert and vain chert respectively. These are basically made out of blade and either end of these specimens are straight and sharp with triangular to trapezoidal cross section.

1. **RGD** -1, Parallel sided blade, 2.0 x 0.8 x 0.3 cm, made out of chert. Triangular cross section and beautiful single ridge with sharp cutting edge (Fig.21, Pl.9).

2. **KDD** - 2, Parallel sided blade, 2.4 x 1.2 x 0.4 cm, milky quartz, triangular cross section, the cutting edge is sharp in nature (Fig.17, Pl.5).
3. **RGD** -5, Parallel sided blade, 1.9 x 1.0 x 0.5 cm, chert. Two ridges make it trapezoid in section; the cutting edge is very sharp (Fig.21, Pl.9).
4. **KDP-I** -1, Parallel sided blade, 3.3 x 1.2 x 0.4 cm, chert. Both side sharp edges, triangular in section (Fig.20, Pl.8).
5. **RMD** - 21, Parallel sided blade, 3.1 x 1.5 x 0.6 cm, milky quartz. The sharp end is retouched (Fig.18, Pl.6).
6. **DPD** -1, Parallel sided blade, 2.5 x 1.5 x 0.5 cm, quartz, edge of the blade is sharp in nature (Pl.4).

Pen Knife Blade

The pen knife blade is the fourth dominant category in the blade component of the study area. These are recovered from the four eco-zones. Out of the total collection of 19 (8.78%) specimens 1 (5.26%) is from foot hill site, 7 (36.84%) each from piedmont as well as river bank sites and 4 (21.05%) from river bank cum foot hill site. The distribution of raw material wise of the specimen are 6 (31.57%) chert, 5 (26.31%) milky quartz, 2 (10.52%) cherty quartzite, 2 (10.52%) ash grey chert, 1 (5.26%) grey chert, 2 (10.52%) banded chert and 1 (5.26%) quartz. The length of the specimens ranges in between 4.3 to 2.6 cm, the breadth varies from 1.8 to1.1 cm and the length range from 0.6 to 0.7 cm.

1. **JHP** -8, Penknife blade, 4.3 x 1.8 x 0.7 cm, made out of chert. It is typical pen knife blade. (Fig.19).
2. **KDD** -3, Penknife blade, 3.1 x 1.4 x 0.7 cm, made out of chert. Trapezoid cross section one end has been retouched to make it. (Fig.17, Pl.5).
3. **KDD**-22, Pen knife blade, 2.6 x 1.[illegible] x 0.6 cm, made out of milky quartz, one end and upper top is very sharp. (Pl.5).

Crescent/Lunate

This type of artefacts is found from the piedmont, river bank and cum foot hill sites. Out of the total collection of 17 (4.44%) crescents, 7 (4.37%) are found from piedmont site, 6 (4.44%) are from the river bank and 4 (50.00%) are from the river bank cum foot hill site. The percentage is calculated in respective to the eco-zone. These specimens are basically made on small flake with deliberate retouch of one end to from the crescent. This geometrical tool is typical microlithic variety. These specimen are made on crypto-crystalline rock, i.e. 6 (35.29%) on chert, 3 (17.64%) on quartz and 8 (47.05%) on milky quartz as per its total collection. The maximum lengths of the crescent range between 4.5 to1.9 cm. similarly the breadth and the thickness 2.0 to 0.8 cm and 1.4 to 0.5 cm respectively.

1. **KDD** -32, Crescent/ lunate, 4.5 x 2.0 x 1.4 cm, made out of chert, roughly crescent form with sharp edge. (Pl.5).
2. **RGD**-14, Crescent/ lunate, 3.0 x 1.2 x 0.6 cm, made out of chert, retouch to make the typical one where as the other end has sharp. (Fig.21, Pl.9).
3. **BLG**-12, Crescent/ lunate , 1.9 x 0.8 x 0.5 cm, made out of milky quartz, The sides of the artefact has retouch to make it. (Fig.16).

Burin

The burin specimens are found from piedmont and river bank sites. These are made on flake of siliceous rock material like different chert variety and milky quartz. The length, breadth and thickness range from 3.7 to 1.9 cm, 1.7 to 1.4cm and 0.5 to 0.3 cm respectively.

1. **ARF** -5, Burin, 3.7 x 1.5 x 0.4 cm, chert (ash grey). The pointed end has been created deliberately by retouch. (Fig.20, Pl.7).
2. **ARF** -12, Burin, 1.9 x 1.7 x 0.3 cm, chert. The implement is retouched from two sides to make burin pointed end. (Fig.20, Pl.7).
3. **KDH** -50, Burin, 2.4 x 1.4 x 0.5 cm, milky quartz. The both ends are retouched to make burin point. (Fig.23, Pl.11).

Triangle

In respect to the geometrical tool implement the triangle is important one collected from piedmont as well as river bank site. Out of the total collection in the study area there are 5 (2.3%) specimen of triangle, in which 4 (80.00%) from piedmont sites and 1 (20.00%) from the river bank site. The length of three triangles ranges from 2.6 to 1.7 cm, the breadth from 1.6 to 0.8 cm and similarly the thickness of triangle range from 0.4 to 0.3cm.

1. **KDP-II**-13, Triangle, 1.7 x 0.8 x 0.3 cm, made out of quartz. The triangle has been retouched to make it deliberately. (Pl.12).
2. **ARF** -6, Triangular, 2.6 x 1.6 x 0.4 cm, made out of chert (black). It is a typical Triangular with retouch. (Fig.20, Pl.7).
3. **KDP-I** -9, Triangle, 2.3 x 1.0 x 0.4 cm, made out of chert. Several retouches have made this as triangle. (Fig.20, Pl.8).

Trapezoid

This is another important microlithic variant of the blade component. There are total 4 (1.02%) number of trapezoid collected from the piedmont and river cum foot hill sites. The measurements ratio show that the length ranging 3.4 to 2.2 cm, breadth 3.2 to 2.0 cm and thickness range in between 0.6 to 0.7 cm. The detailed descriptions of some of the specimen are given below.

1. **NLT** -4, Trapezoid, 2.2 x 2.0 x 0.7 cm, made out of milky quartz. Both long axis ends is Sharp.
2. **SBD** -19, Trapezoid, 3.4 x 3.2 x 0.6 cm, made out of quartz. Most of side has been retouched to make this shape. (Fig.22, Pl.10).

Blade cum Scraper

There are two specimen of blade cum scraper collected from the Gopapur Gadhuaghat river bank site and from Kadamdiha a piedmont site. The measurement of Gapapur Gadhuaghat specimen is 2.8 x 1.4 x 1.0 cm, made out of milky quartz, its both sides are retouched. The Kadamdiha blade cum scraper ratio is 2.8 x 2.0 x1.9 cm and made out of chert raw material (Fig.23, Pl.11).

Crescent cum Borer

The only piece of crescent cum borer is found from a river bank site Dalo Puranadiha. It is made on a flake of black chert. It is crescent shape with one end thick and the same thick part is retouched to form the borer. The length, breadth and thickness of the specimen is 2.2 cm, 0.8 cm and 0.4 cm respectively (Pl.4).

Keel Blade

The only specimen reported from a river bank site Rajamunda. This is made out of ash grey chert. The measurement of the specimen is 3.1 cm, 2.3 cm and 0.8 cm respectively. One end of the specimen possesses the keel. (Fig.18, Pl.6).

Point with Deep Notch

The point with deep notch is only specimen from the Gopapur Gadhuaghat site, which falls in the river bank eco-zone. The artefact is made out of crypto crystalline siliceous material i.e milky quartz. The specimen has pointed end with two deep notches and its length, breadth and thickness is 3.6 cm, 1.6 cm and 0.8 cm respectively.

Blade cum Borer

The blade cum borer comes under the artefacts of blade component. This specimen is found from the river bank site Kadamdiha and made out of the chert. One of its ends is thick slightly pointed for bore or piercing other material. The measurement is 2.7 cm, 1.4 cm. and 1.0 as length, breadth and thickness respectively (Fig.23, Pl.11).

Main features of Palaeolithic and Mesolithic Cultures of Kakharua Valley.

This chapter contains an account of the Palaeolithic and Mesolithic recoveries from my survey in the Kakharua valley. With regard to the Palaeolithic culture, only one site (Barikaguda) has been found with three artefacts. Hence, it may be inferred that the Kakharua valley had not attracted much attention of Palaeolithic people. On the other hand, we come across 15 sites with microlithic artefacts. This implies that during Mesolithic period, the Kakharua valley became an important destination of prehistoric man. Hence, it is relevant to discuss the major characteristics of the Palaeolithic culture and Mesolithic culture of Kakharua valley which are as follows:

1. The Palaeolithic artefacts are very limited in the high land adaptation and only one site represents chopper and cleaver implements.
2. The investigation area receives high rainfall and has tropical deciduous vegetation, surrounded by stretches of thick forest and hill ranges, so the sites may be comparable with forested ecological Mesolithic sites of Keonjhar (Mohanty 2000:115-152).
3. The sites have been discussed under four eco-zones such as river bank sites, foot hill sites, piedmont sites and river bank cum foot hill sites.
4. The microlithic artefacts have been divided into two components- flake and blade. The flake component includes the types of side scraper, end scraper, thumb nail scraper, borer, utilized flakes, round scraper, borer cum scraper, blade core, concave scraper, notch scraper, side cum end scraper, tanged point, scraper, flake, micro borer, blade cum borer and microlithic chips. The blade component includes the types of blade, parallel sided blade, pen knife blade, point crescent, triangle, trapezoid, blade cum scraper, crescent cum borer, keel blade, blade fragment, blade (micro), blade cum borer, point with deep notch and burin. An important feature is that the Kakharua river valley culture has a well-developed blade technology.
5. The different tool types imply their use for different range of activities, such as cutting, piercing, scraping, boring etc.

Hence the Mesolithic sites in the Kakharua valley could have functioned as camp sites with short term occupation. On the basis of available data, it is not possible to identify which was the base camp.

6. In addition to quartz and other siliceous rock, chert is the dominant raw material for manufacturing of tiny sophisticated artefacts. It is also the easily collected rock type in the area. The recovery of a number of blade cores in some sites implies exploitation of local raw materials. However, no mesolithic manufacturing site could be precisely determined.
7. No large site with heavy duty lithic component is reported from the Kakharua survey, therefore the Mesolithic culture is supposed to be used for different subsistence pattern as seasonal food gathering.
8. The piedmont sites represent 160 no of specimens (40.81%) of microliths and occupy the highest range of artefacts where as the foot hill site yielded very low amount of implements such as 17 no of specimens (4.33%). Followed by that the river bank site represents 137 no of specimens (34.94%) and the river bank cum foot hill site yielded 78 no specimens (19.895).
9. In the blade component blade represent highest 74 no specimens (34.24%) and followed by that point 35 no (16.20%), parallel sided Blade 31no (14.35%) besides other minor artefacts. In flake component flake core/blade core is dominant variety with 34 no specimens (19.31%). Next to that borer represent 31 no of specimens (17.62%) and side scraper 22 no specimen (12.5%) apart from the other minor artefacts.

In the next chapter, neolithic remains will be discussed.

CHAPTER 5

Neolithic Culture of Kakharua Valley

During the present survey, emphasis has been given to locate maximum sites from the river valley for which an intensive field exploration has been conducted on the foothills, piedmont area and river basins. On the basis of these locations, these Neolithic sites are divided into four categories, such as the sites of foothill, the sites of piedmont area, the sites of foot hill cum river bank and the sites on river banks in the same way. The sites located near different hills and mountains are categorized as the sites of foothills, whereas the sites present within a distance of about 100 mt from the existing river banks are categorized as the sites on river bank. Similarly, the sites located neither on the foot hills nor close (100 mt) to the river banks are categorized as site of piedmont area.

From this survey 19 Neolithic sites have been discovered from the valley of Kakharua and its small feeder channel, out of which eight are on the river banks, four from foot hill, six on the piedmont area, and one on the foot hill cum river bank area.

Sites on River Bank Area

Neoliths have been represented from eight sites on river bank area. The river bank sites include the river bank or exposed material from reverine action. Such sites are Baisnavadar, Bisriguda, Gopapur Munda Sahi, Khalinala, Kadamdar, Kamparkala, Rajamunda, Tentulimula gaiguthani. The Neolithic recoveries are presented in tabular form with its mean ratio, mean measurement, detail typology, material and percentage.

Table No-4.1 Distribution of Neolithic artefacts in Baisnavadar (Excluding grid Materials) (BND)

Sl. No.	Typology	Mean measurement (in cm)			Mean ratio			Material	No.	Percentage
		L	B	T	T/L	B/L	T/B			
1	Axe	13.1	6.5	3.1	0.23	0.49	0.47	Dolerite-14 Dolerite-2	16	50.00%
2	Axe (broken)	7.8	5.5	2.5	0.32	0.70	0.45	Dolerite-3	3	9.37%
3	Adze	11.5	6.1	3.0	0.26	0.53	0.49	Dolerite-5	5	15.62%
4	Ring stone (Broken)	dia. 9.2	3.9					Quartzite-1 Laterite-1	2	6.25%
5	Neolithic flake	7.6	5.3	1.4	0.18	0.69	0.26	Dolerite-6	6	18.75%
Total									32	99.99%

Table No-4.2 Distribution of Neolithic artefacts in Baisnavadar Grid materials (BND)

Sl. No.	Typology	Mean measurement (in cm)			Mean ratio			Material	No.	Percentage
		L	B	T	T/L	B/L	T/B			
1	Axe	12.2	5.5	2.9	0.23	0.45	0.52	Dolerite-4	4	16.66%
2	Adze	11.0	4.5	3.1	0.28	0.40	0.68	Dolerite-1	1	4.16%
3	Axe (broken)	8.5	5.3	3.0	0.35	0.62	0.56	Dolerite-2	2	8.33%
4	Chisel	9.7	4.3	2.3	0.23	0.44	0.53	Dolerite-1	1	4.16%
5	N. flake	5.1	4.8	1.1	0.21	0.94	0.22	Dolerite-16	16	66.66%
Total									**24**	**99.97%**

Table No-4.3 Distribution of the Neolithic artefacts in Bisriguda (BSG)

Sl. No.	Typology	Mean measurement (in cm)			Mean ratio			Materials	No.	Percentage
		L	B	T	T/L	B/L	T/B			
1	Axe	10.0	5.7	2.8	0.28	0.57	0.49	Dolerite -14 Diorite-5	19	31.14%
2	Adze	10.6	6.6	2.8	0.26	0.62	0.42	Dolerite-6	6	9.83%
3	Axe (broken)	7.2	5.1	2.3	0.31	0.70	0.45	Dolerite-8 Diorite-1	9	14.75%
4	Neolithic blank	5.8	5.9	3.0	0.51	1.01	0.50	Dolerite-1 Diorite-1?	2	3.27%
5	Neolithic flake	5.9	4.6	1.1	0.18	0.77	0.23	Dolerite-25	25	40.98%
Total									**61**	**99.97%**

Table No-4.4 Distribution of Neolithic artefacts in Gopapur Munda Sahi (GMS)

Sl. No.	Typology	Mean measurement (in cm)			Mean ratio			Materials	No.	Percentage
		L	B	T	T/L	B/L	T/B			
1	Unfinished Axe (core)	17.0	8.9	5.8	0.34	0.52	0.65	Dolerite-2	2	15.38%
2	N. flake	6.2	6.1	1.3	0.20	0.98	0.21	Dolerite-11	11	84.61%
Total									**13**	**99.99%**

Table No-4.5 Distribution of Neolithic artefacts in Khalinala (Jamudiha Gaiguthani) (KLN).

Sl. No	Typology	Mean measurement (in cm)			Mean ratio			Material	No.	Percentage
		L	B	T	T/L	B/L	T/B			
1	Axe	11.1	6.5	2.4	0.21	0.58	0.36	Dolerite-1	1	33.33%
2	Shouldered axe	7.9	4.3	2.2	0.27	0.54	0.51	Dolerite-1	1	33.33%
3	Neolithic blank	8.6	6.6	3.7	0.43	0.76	0.56	Dolerite-1	1	33.33%
Total									3	99.99%

Table No-4.6 Distribution of Neolithic artefacts in Kadamdar (KDD)

Sl. No.	Typology	Mean measurement (in cm)			Mean ratio			Material	No	Percentage
		L	B	T	T/L	B/L	T/B			
1	Adze	10.7	8.0	3.0	0.28	0.74	0.37	Dolerite-1	1	100%
Total									**1**	**100%**

Table No-4.7 Distribution of Neolithic artefacts in Kamparkala (KPK)

Sl. No.	Typology	Mean measurement (in cm)			Mean ratio			Materials	No.	Percentage
		L	B	T	T/L	B/L	T/B			
1	Axe	11.3	5.6	2.4	0.21	0.49	0.42	Dolerite? -2	2	50%
2	Dimple marked hammer stone	14.7	9.2	6.4	0.43	0.62	0.69	Quartzite?-2	2	50%
Total									4	100%

Table No-4.8 Distribution of Neolithic artefacts in Rajamunda.(RMD)

Sl. No.	Typology	Mean measurement (in cm)			Mean ratio			Material	No.	Percentage
		L	B	T	T/L	B/L	T/B			
1	Chisel	13.3	3.9	3.2	0.24	0.29	0.82	Dolerite ?-1 Dolerite-1	2	66.66%
2	Axe	7.6	4.7	1.8	0.23	0.61	0.38	Dolerite-1	1	33.33%
Total									**3**	**99.99%**

Table No-4.9 Distribution of Neolithic artefacts in Tentulimula Gaiguthani (TMG)

Sl. No.	Typology	Mean measurement (in cm)			Mean ratio			Materials	No.	Percentage
		L	B	T	T/L	B/L	T/B			
1	Axe	10.5	6.1	2.3	0.21	0.58	0.37	Dolorite-3	3	60%
2	Adze	11.8	5.8	2.4	0.20	0.49	0.41	Dolerite-1	1	20%
3	Chisel	9.8	3.0	2.1	0.21	0.30	0.7	Dolerite-1	1	20%
Total									**5**	**100%**

There are total 32 artefacts collected from Baisnavadar site, which include axe, axe (broken), adze, ring stone and neolithic flake. The axes and adzes are of different range and variety. The mean measurement of axe is 13.1 cm, 6.5 cm and 3.1 cm, the adze is 11.5 cm, 6.1 cm and 3.0 cm, broken axe is 7.8 cm, 5.5 cm and 2.5 cm and neolithic flake is 7.6 cm, 5.3 cm and 1.4 cm as in length, breadth and thickness respectively. The principal raw material is dolerite (Fig.27 & 28, Pl.14). A good number of lithic implements are distributed on the eroded surface, so a heavily exposed area has been selected for grid collection or systematic collection. The collection yielded 24 numbers of tools which include axe, adze, chisel and neolithic flake. These are basically of flaked, chipped, partly flaked and chipped and well grounding variety. The principal raw material is dolerite (Fig.29, Pl.15). The surface collection and the grid materials taken together imply that it was a manufacturing site. Bisriguda is another important primary site, from which 61 neolithic artefacts have been collected from the surface. This is an open air site. Erosional surface has exposed the lithic material from certain pockets. The artefacts comprises of axe (19, 31.14%), adze (6, 9.83%), broken axe (9, 14.75%), neolithic blank (2, 3.27%), neolithic flake (25, 40.98%). The raw material used in the manufacturing of artefacts is mainly dolerite (Fig.30, Pl.16 & 17).The Gopapur Munda Sahi is factory site which is distributed along the main drainage of Kakharua and due to its seasonal and flood activities maximum lithic evidences are washed away. However, out of 13 neolithic artefacts 11 are medium to big size flakes and 2 are unfinished axe core reported from the sites. The raw materials are basically of dolerite variety.

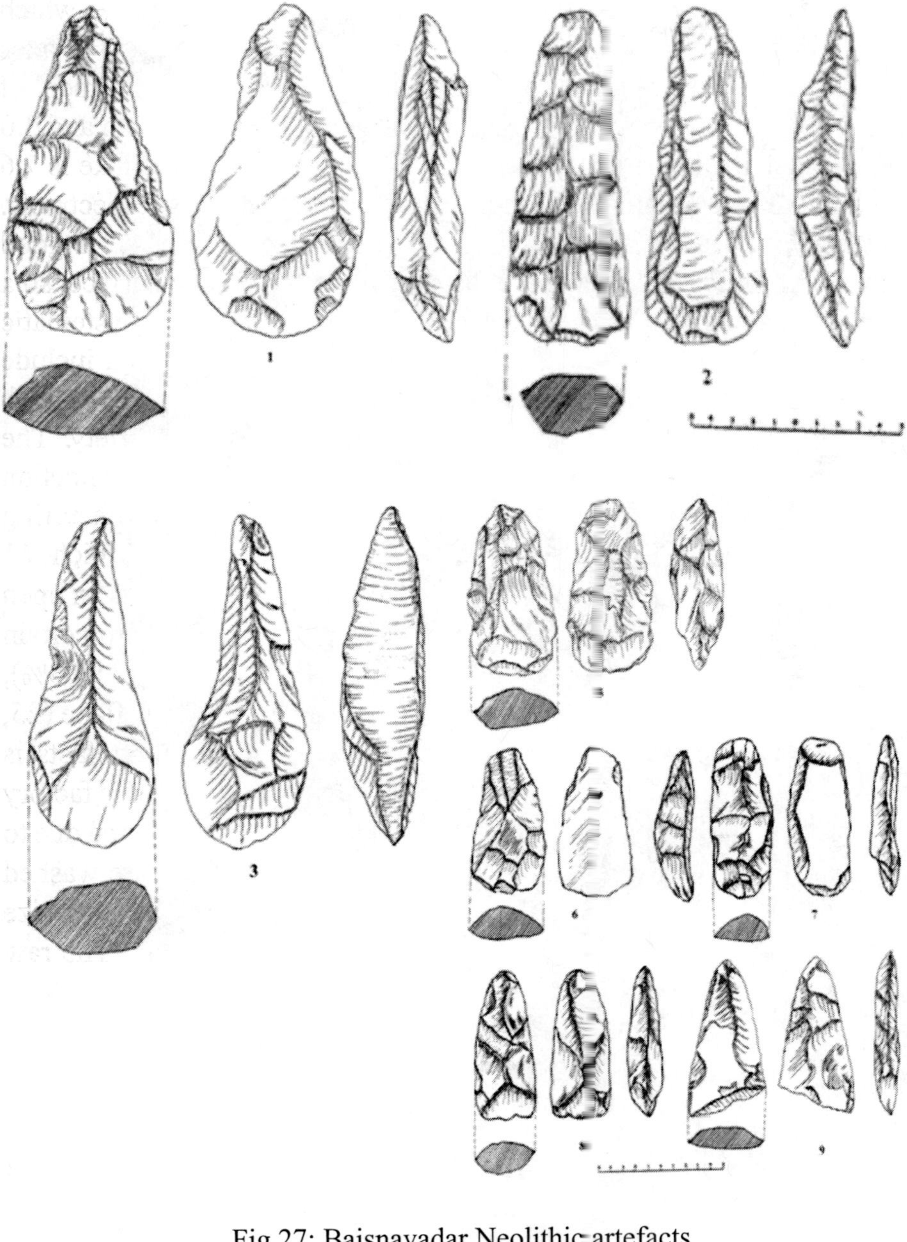

Fig.27: Baisnavadar Neolithic artefacts
1-5 & 7-9 Axe; 6-Adze.

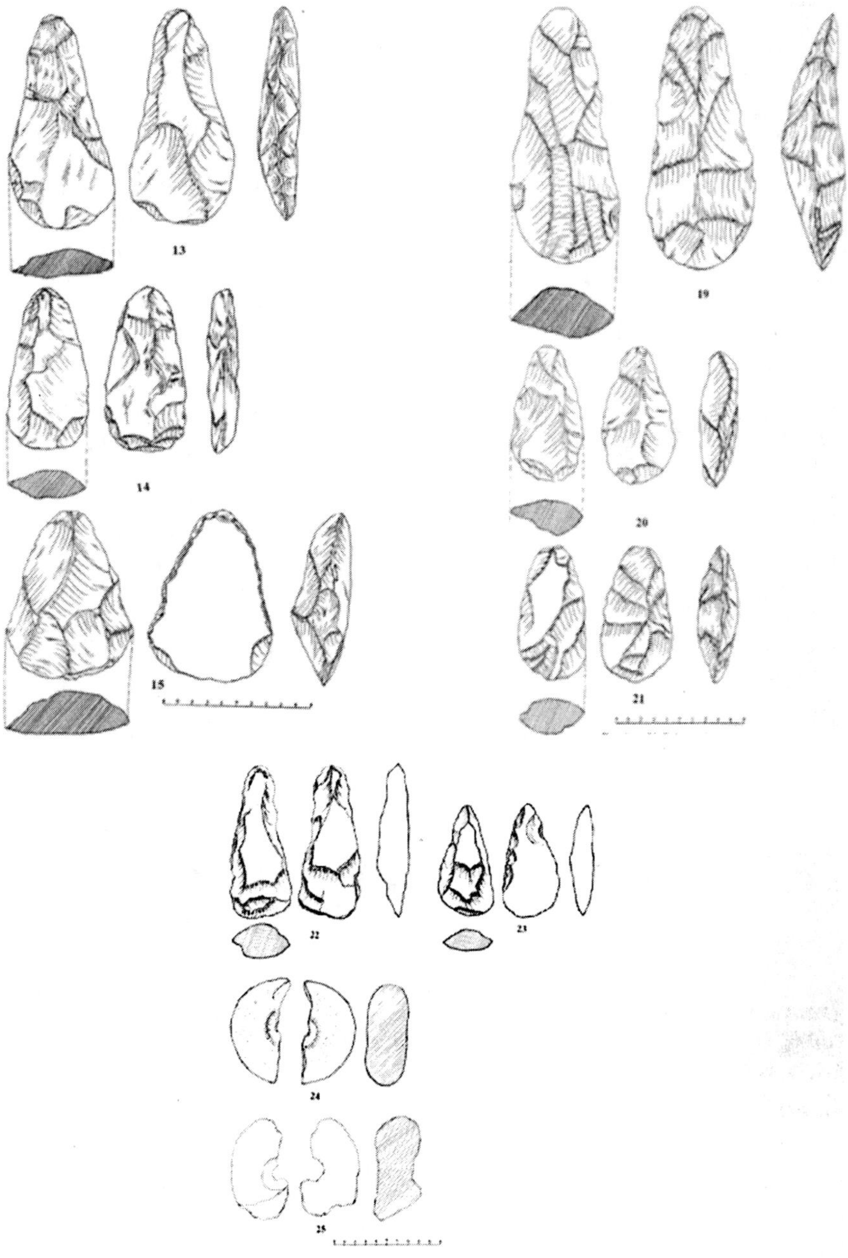

Fig.28: Baisnavadar Neolithic artefacts.
13,14 & 22 - Axe; 15 & 23-Adze; 24-25- Ring Stone

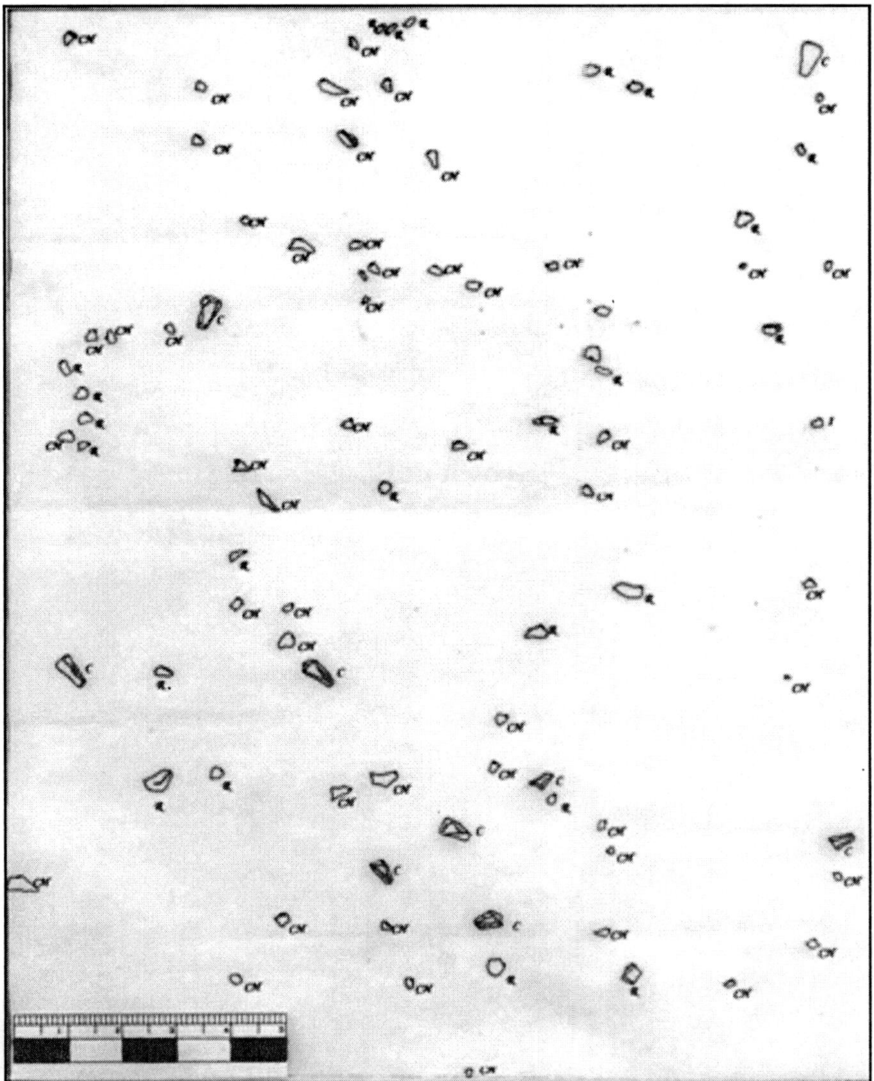

Scale-1m=5 cm.

Index

C- Neolithic Implements
Ch- Neolithic Chip & flakes
R- Rough stone piece
I-Iron ore

Fig.29: Neolithic Implementes at Baisnavadar Grid.

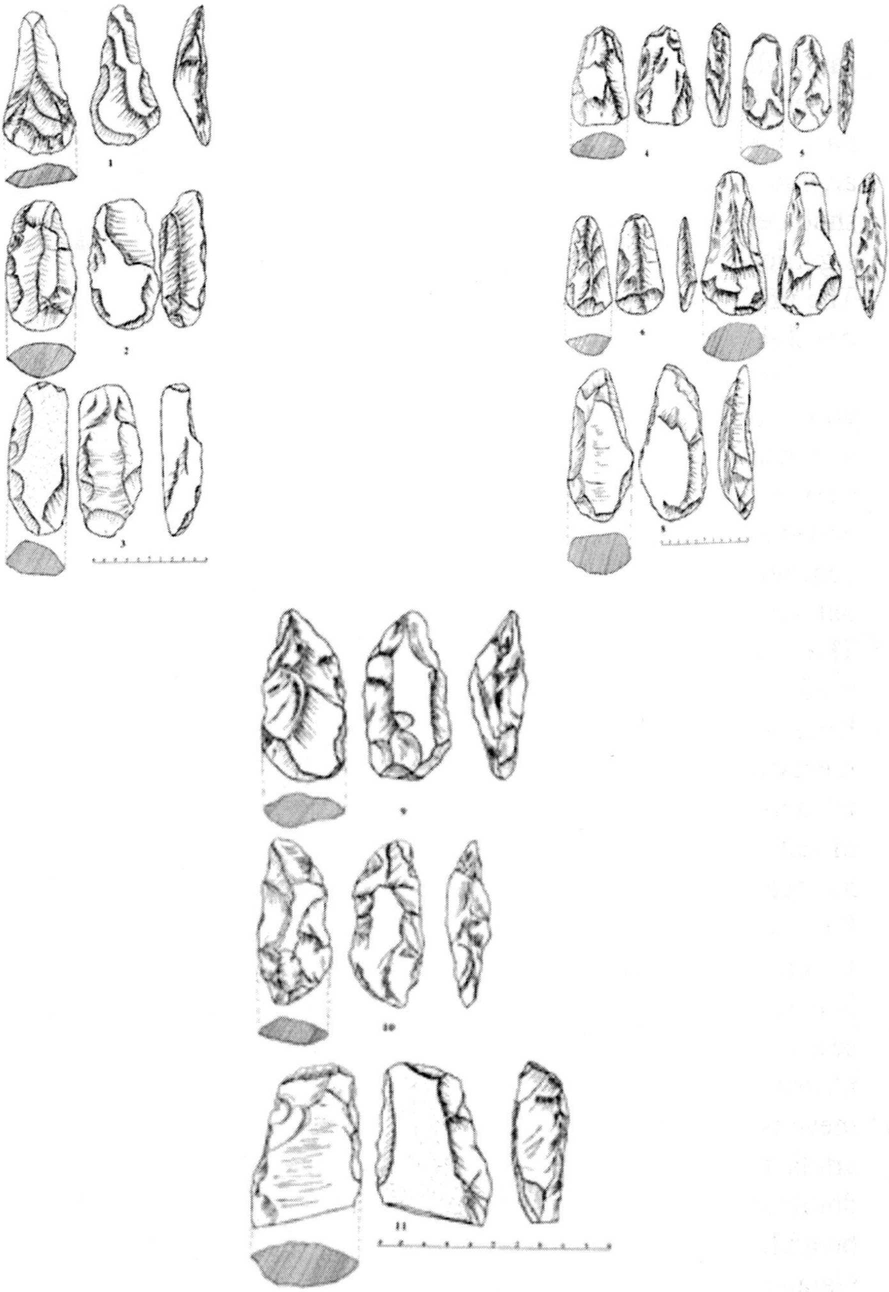

Fig.30: Bisriguda Neolithic artefacts.
1- Adze, 2 to 11- Axe.

The Khalinala site near Jamudiha Gaiguthani comes under the river bank zone and has yielded three neolithic artefacts, out of which one shouldered axe is very much significant in the study region. The implement is fully ground, polished and measuring 7.9 cm, 4.3 cm and 2.2 cm. Along with shoulder axe tool, one axe and a neolithic blank is also reported. All these are collected from a dry channel bed, possibly these are washed out material from nearby site. The principal raw material used is dolerite (Fig.18). The Kadamdar neolithic site has represents, only adze is yielded from the site, which is made out of dolerite material (Pl.5). The Kamparkala site has represent four neolithic artefacts, out of which two are axe and other two are dimple marked hammer stone. It is interesting to note that the hammer stone has more than three dimple scar marks on the obverse, reverse as well as in profile area. The mean measurement of axe is 11.3 x 5.6 x 2.4 cm and that of hammer stone mean is 14.7 x 9.2 x 6.4 cm (Fig.31, Pl.19). The Rajamunda site neolithic artefacts have included chisel and axe. In Neolithic artefacts chisels are dominant one and its mean measurement read as 13.3 cm length, 3.9 cm breadth and 3.2 cm thickness and mean ratio is 0.29 (Pl.20). Tentulimula Gaiguthani is another important neolithic site on the right bank of Kakharua. The erosional surface of the site yielded four artefacts, which

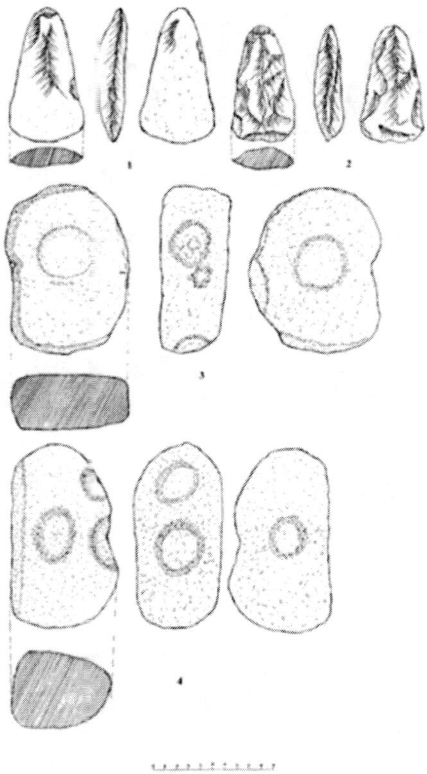

Fig.31: Kamparkala Neolithic artefacts. 1 & 2- Neolithic axe; 3,4-Dimple mark hammer stone.

include axe, adze and chisel. The axe is the dominant variety in the site and followed by that, one adze and one chisel (Fig.32, Pl.22). All these artefacts are of flaked and chipped variety, the mean measurement of axe is 10.5 x 6.1x 2.3 cm, adze is 11.8 x 5.8 x 2.4 cm and chisel 9.8 x 3.0 x 2.1 cm. respectively. The principal raw material is dolerite.

Sites on Foot Hill Area

Neoliths have been represented from four sites on foot hill area. The foot hill sites include the site close or immediate surface of the mountain or small hillock area and names of the site are Jalanda Hatapada, Jalanda Munda Sahi, Kakharua Protection Forest, and Radodiha. The neolithic recoveries are presented in tabular form with its mean ratio, mean measurement, detail typology, material and percentage.

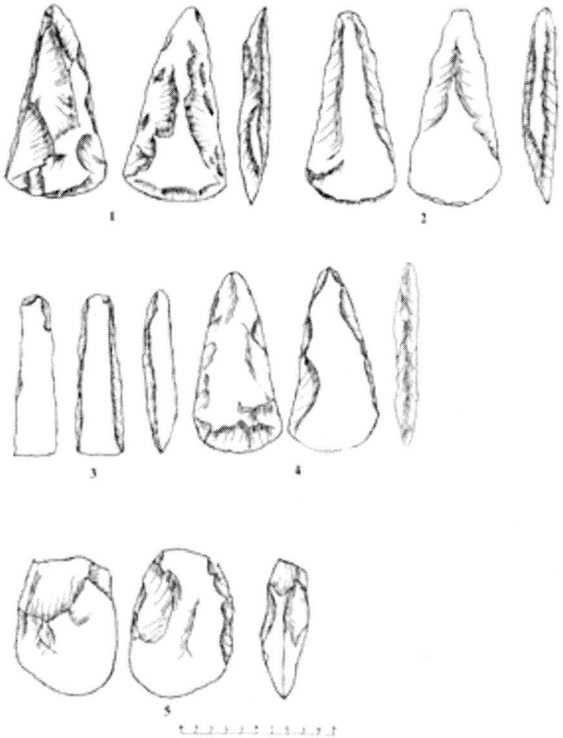

Fig.32: Tentulimula Gaiguthani Neolithic artefacts.
1,2, 4 & 5- Adze; 3- Chisel.

Table No.4.10 Distribution of Neolithic artefacts in Jalanda Hatapada (JHP).

Sl. No.	Typology	Mean measurement (in cm)			Mean ratio			Material	No.	Percentage
		L	B	T	T/L	B/L	T/B			
1	Axe	9.7	5.0	2.0	0.20	0.51	0.4	Dolerite-2, Sandy lime stone-1	3	60.00%
2	Adze	13.7	5.2	2.4	0.17	0.37	0.46	Dolerite-1	1	50.00%
3	Neolithic blank	10.3	9.9	3.3	0.32	0.96	0.33	Dolerite-1	1	50.00%
Total									**5**	**100%**

Table No-4.11 Distribution of the Neolithic artefacts in Jalanda Munda Sahi (JMS)

Sl. No.	Typology	Mean measurement (in cm)			Mean ratio			Material	No.	Percentage
		L	B	T	T/L	B/L	T/B			
1	Chisel	8.4	3.9	2.6	0.30	0.46	0.66	Dolerite-2	2	75%
2	Round scraper	9.8	9.7	3.9	0.39	0.98	0.40	Dolerite	1	25%
Total									3	100%

Table No-4.12 Distribution of Neolithic artefacts in Kakharua Protection forest (KPF)

Sl. No.	Typology	Mean measurement (in cm)			Mean ratio			Material	No.	Percentage
		L	B	T	T/L	B/L	T/B			
1	Neolithic blank	16.5	5.3	3.1	0.18	0.32	0.58	Dolerite-2	2	5.55%
2	Neolithic flake	3.8	3.6	0.8	0.21	0.94	0.22	Dolerite-34	34	94.44%
Total									**36**	**99.99%**

Table No-4.13 Distribution of Neolithic artefacts in Rododiha (RDH)

Sl. No.	Typology	Mean measurement (in cm)			Mean ratio			Material	No.	Percentage
		L	B	T	T/L	B/L	T/B			
1	Axe	16.8	4.8	2.8	0.16	0.28	0.58	Dolerite-1	1	100%
Total									1	**100%**

The Jalanda Hatapada site falls under the foot hill category. The celt component of the site includes axe, adze, neolithic blank etc. The axe is dominant one (60.00 %) in the celt component and dolerite is mainly used for preparing the neolithic artefacts (Pl.23). Another site Jalanda Munda Sahi describes the distribution of neolithic artefacts. A clear examination divided the lithic implement into two types such as chisel and round scraper. The chisels are fully ground and polished type, whereas the scraper is of medium size and big flakes have been detached to make it rounded type. The scraper might also have been used in neolithic period. The mean measurement of chisel is 8.4 x 3.9 x 2.6 cm and the round scraper is 9.8 x 9.7 x 3.9 cm. The principal raw material is dolerite (Fig.33, Pl.24). It is interesting to note that the Kakharua protection forest site has one of the primary dolerite raw material sites. So this site yielded neolithic blank and large variety of neolithic flakes (Pl.26 & 27). The total collection of the artefacts is 36, out of which 34 are neolithic flake and the other two are neolithic blanks. The neolithic blanks measure 16.5 cm, 5.3 cm and 3.1 cm and 3.8 cm, 3.6 cm and 0.8 cm respectively (Pl.25). The Radodiha site falls under foot hill site and yielded one chipped variety. The measurement is 16.8 cm, 4.8 cm and 2.8 cm and made out of dolerite (Pl.28 & 29).

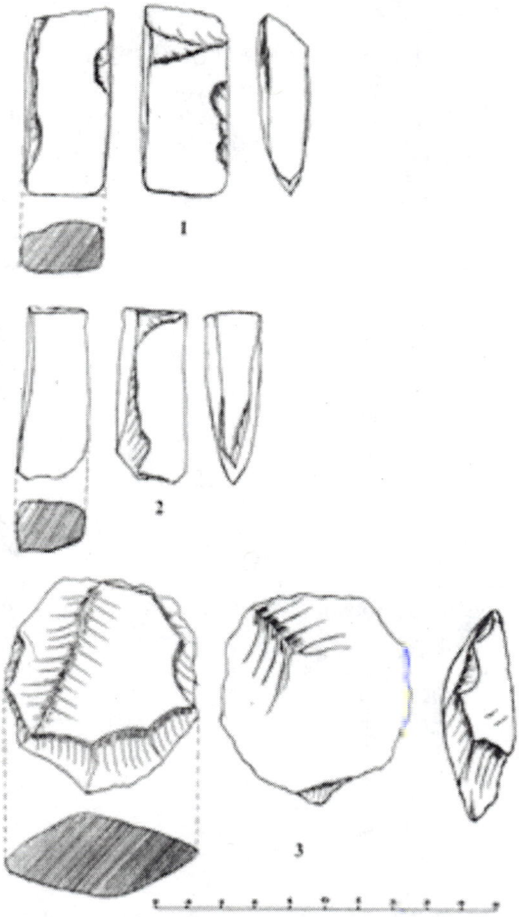

Fig.33: Jalanda Munda Sahi Neolithic artefacts.
1 & 2- Chisel; 3-Scraper.

Sites on Piedmont Area

Neoliths have been represents from six sites on piedmont area. The piedmont sites include the undulated erosional sites and names of the site are Atanaka Reserve Forest, Bankadar, Karadapal-I, Rugudidiha, Sorbeda Dautasala and Sorbeda Kudur. The neolithic recoveries details like mean ratio, mean measurements, typology, materials and percentage are presented in tabular form.

Table No-4.14 Distribution of Neolithic artefacts in Atanaka Reserve Forest (ARF).

Sl. No.	Typology	Mean measurement (in cm)			Mean ratio			Material	No.	Percentage
		L	B	T	T/L	B/L	T/B			
1	Axe (broken)	5.6	4.0	1.9	0.33	0.71	0.47	Dolerite-2	2	66.66%
2	Ring stone (broken)	dia 8.3		4.3				Sand stone-1	1	33.33%
Total									**3**	**99.99%**

Table No-4.15 Distribution of Neolithic artefacts in Bankadar (BKD)

Sl. No.	Typology	Mean measurement (in cm)			Mean ratio			Material	No.	Percentage
		L	B	T	T/L	B/L	T/B			
1	Axe (broken)	8.0	4.9	2.5	0.31	0.61	0.51	Dolerite-2	2	**100%**
Total									2	**100%**

Table No- 4.16 Distribution of Neolithic artefacts in Karadapal-I site (KDP-I).

Sl. No.	Typology	Mean measurements (in cm)			Mean ratio			Material	No.	Percentage
		L	B	T	T/L	B/L	T/B			
1	Ring stone	8.8	4.9	3.7	0.42	0.55	0.75	Sand stone-1	1	100%
Total									**1**	**100%**

Table No -4.17 Distribution of Neolithic artefacts in Rugudidiha site (RGD).

Sl. No.	Typology	Mean measurement (in cm)			Mean ratio			Material	No.	Percentage
		L	B	T	T/L	B/L	T/B			
1	Axe	14.2	5.0	2.6	0.18	0.35	0.52	Dolerite-1	1	16.67%
2	N. Flake	5.2	4.4	0.8	0.15	0.84	0.18	Dolerite-5	5	83.33%
Total									**6**	**100%**

Table No-4.18 Distribution of Neolithic artefacts in Sorbeda Dautasala (SBD)

Sl. No.	Typology	Mean measurement (in cm)			Mean ratio			Materials	No.	Percentage
		L	B	T	T/L	B/L	T/B			
1	Axe	5.9	3.5	1.3	0.22	0.59	0.37	Dolerite-2	2	50.00%
2	Adze	6.2	4.4	2.0	0.32	0.70	0.45	Dilorite-1	1	25.00%
3	Flake (Neolithic)	6.4	2.7	0.9	0.14	0.42	0.33	Dolerite-1	1	25.00%
Total									**4**	**100.00%**

Table No-4.19 Distribution of Neolithic artefacts in Sorbeda Kudur (SBK)

Sl. No.	Typology	Mean measurement (in cm)			Mean ratio			Material	No.	Percentage
		L	B	T	T/L	B/L	T/B			
1	Bar celt	18.8	5.3	3.2	0.17	0.28	0.60	Dolerite-2	2	100%
Total									**2**	**100%**

Apart from microlithic artefacts, the Atanaka Reserve Forest site has yielded three Neolithic artefacts which contain two broken axe, basically flaked and chipped with ridge showing evidence of grinding. The sand stone based ring-stone is well ground and polished. The mean measurement of the axe is 5.6, 4.0 and 1.9 cm length, breadth and thickness respectively. The chief raw material for the axe is dolerite. The

Bankadar site is located near the confluence of Kakharua and Mankara river, one end bounded by Bankadar forest in south and south- eastern part. It is difficult to trace more number of tools in the surrounding due to the bushy forest. However, the site has yielded two broken axes of flaked and chipped variety. The principal raw material of the implements is dolerite. The neolithic artefacts represents 01 specimen of ring stone from Karadapal-I. The Rugudidiha site has yielded 06 specimens in which the neolithic flake is of major variety with 05 specimens (83.33%), followed to it axe is represented by 01 specimen (16.67%). Small axe and adze have been recovered from this Sorbeda Dautsala site (Pl.10). Such types of the neolithic tools were probably used for finishing of wood work. Generally, dolerite was used for making these neoliths artefacts. The Sorbeda Kudur site has important findings of the bar-celt. The mean measurement is 18.8 cm, 5.3 cm and 3.2 cm. in length, breadth and thickness respectively, which is made out of dolerite variety. These two are typically chipped out to be of trapezoidal type and the working end is very sharp. Possibly these artefacts were used as agricultural artefacts, such as plough- share (Fig.34. Pl. 30 & 31).

Sites on River Bank cum Foot Hill Area

Neoliths have been found from only one site on river bank cum foot hill area. The river bank cum foot hill site includes Bijagotha Hatapada. The Neolithic recoveries are presented in tabular form with its mean ratio, mean measurement, detail typology, material and percentage.

Table No-4.20 Distribution of Neolithic artefacts in Bijagatha Hatapada (BHP)

Sl. No.	Typology	Mean measurement (in cm)			Mean ratio			Materials	No.	Percentage
		L	B	T	T/L	B/L	T/B			
1	Chisel	10.1	3.6	2.8	0.27	0.35	0.77	Dolerite-6	6	9.83%
2	Neolithic flake	2.4	2.9	0.7	0.29	1.20	0.24	Dolerite-55	55	90.16%
Total									**61**	**99.99%**

The Bijagatha Hatapada is important river bank cum foot hill site. Out of two heavily exposed areas, 55 small neolithic flakes and 6 chipped chisel have been collected. The heavily concentrated neolithic flakes (mean measurement is 2.4 x 2.9 x 0.7cm.) implies that possibly these flakes were extracted from chipping and pecking technology and hence evidence of a workshop site. The chisels are of flaked and chipped variety. It is only reasonable to presume that the site must have served as a manufacturing centre. The principal raw material is dolerite (Fig.35, Pl.22 & 33).

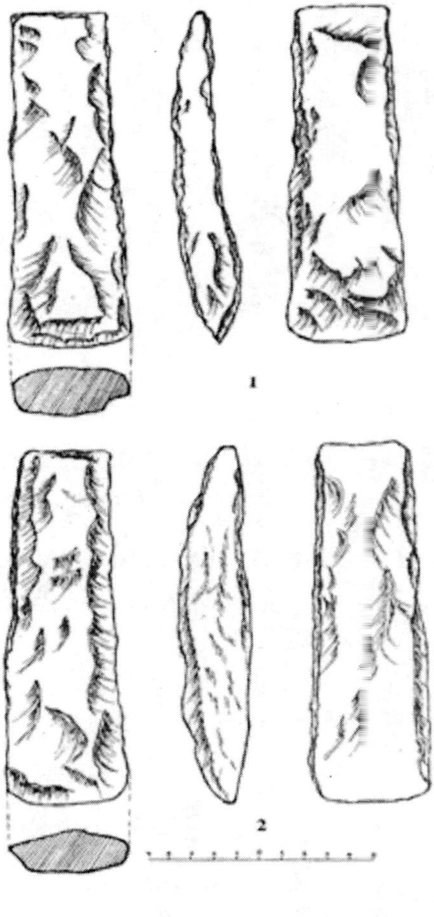

Fig.34: Sorbeda Kudur Neolithic artefacts.
1 & 2-Bar celt.

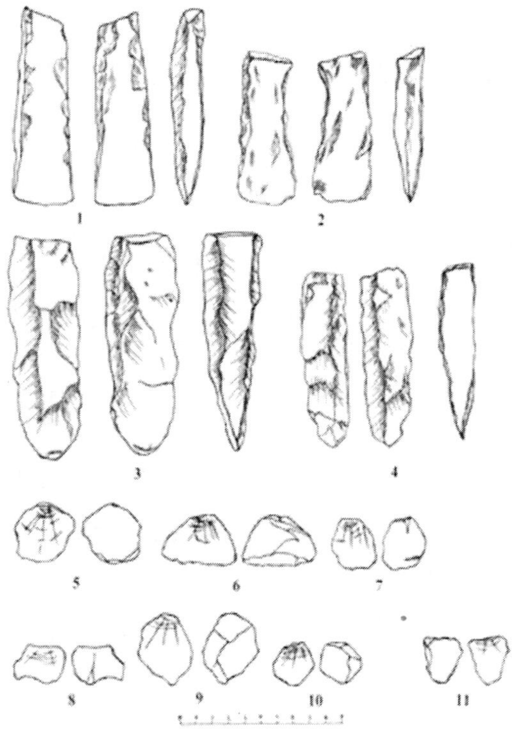

Fig.35: Bijagotha Hatapada Neolithic artefacts
1 to 4- Chisel; 5 to 11- Neolithic flake.

Site-wise and Ecozone-wise Analysis of Artefacts

Table No-4.21 Distribution of artefacts on the river bank sites

Tool type	**Baisnavadar**	**Bisriguda**	**Gapapur Munda Sahi**	**Khalinala**	**Kadamdar**	**Kamparkala**	**Raja munda**	**Tentulimula gaiguthani**	**No.**	**Percentage**
Axe	20	19	-	1	-	2	1	3	46	31.50%
Adze	6	6	-	-	1	-	-	1	14	9.58%
Chisel	1	-	-	-	-	-	2	1	4	2.73%
Shoulder axe	-	-	-	1	-	-	-	-	1	0.68%

contd...

Unfinished/ intermediate axe	-	-	2	-	-	-	-	-	2	1.36%
Broken Axe	5	9	-	-	-	-	-	-	14	9.58%
N. Blank	-	2	-	1	-	-	-	-	3	2.05%
N. Flake	22	25	11	-	-	-	-	-	58	39.72%
Ring stone	2	-	-	-	-	-	-	-	2	1.36%
Dimple mark Hammer stone	-	-	-	-	-	2	-	-	2	1.36%
Total	56(38.35)	61(41.78)	13(8.90)	3(2.05)	1(0.68)	4(2.73)	3(2.05)	5(3.42)	146	99.92%

Table No-4.22 Distribution of artefacts on the foot hill sites

Tool type	**Jalanda Hatapada**	**Jalanda Munda Sahi**	**Kakharua Protection Forest**	**Radodiha**	**No.**	**percentage**
Axe	3	-	-	1	4	9.09%
Adze	1	-	-	-	1	2.27%
Chisel	-	2	-	-	2	4.55%
Neolithic Flake	-	-	34	-	34	77.27%
Neolithic blank	1	-	2	-	3	6.82%
Total	**5(11.36)**	**2(4.54)**	**36(81.81)**	**1(0.05)**	**44**	**100%**

Table No-4.23 Distribution of artefacts on the piedmont site

Tool type	**Atanaka Reserve Forest**	**Bankadar**	**Karadapal-I**	**Rugudidiha**	**Sorbeda Dautasala**	**Sorbeda kudur**	**No.**	**percentage**
Axe	-	-	-	1	2	-	3	16.67%
Adze	-	-	-	-	1	-	1	5.56%
Bar celt	-	-	-	-	-	2	2	11.11%
Broken axe	2	2	-	-	-	-	4	22.22%
N. flake	-	-	-	5	1	-	6	33.33%
Ring stone	1	-	1	-	-	-	2	11.11%
Total	**3(16.67)**	**2(11.11)**	**1(5.56)**	**6(33.33)**	**4(22.22)**	**2(22.22)**	**18**	**100%**

Table No-4.24 Distribution of artefacts on riverbank cum foothill sites

Tool type	Bijagotha Hatapada	No.	Percentage
Chisel	6	6	9.83%
Neolithic flake	55	55	90.16%
Total	**61**	**61**	**99.99%**

All total 8 sites fall under river bank eco-zone category and 145 specimens of Neoliths have been collected. In neolithic artefacts axe is of dominant variety with 46 specimens (31.72%). The sites of Baisnavadar and Bisriguda share the maximum neolithic artefacts with number 56(19.92%) and 61(21.70%) respectively. Gapapur Munda Sahi yielded 13 specimens (8.96%), Khalinala 03 specimens (2.06%), Kamparkala 04 specimens (2.75%), and Tentulimula Gaiguthani 04 specimens (2.75%) respectively (Table - 4.21).

Only 4 sites fall under the foot hill eco-zone namely Jalanda Hatapada with 22 specimens (36.06%), Jalanda Mundasahi with 02 specimens (3.27%), Kakharua Protection Forest with 36 specimens (59.01%) and Radodiha with 01 specimen (1.63%). It is interesting to mention that the site of Kakharua Protection Forest is associated with boulders of dolerite. This was a source of raw material for manufacturing neolithic artefacts. Incidentally, from the survey two neolithic blanks and a good number of large varieties of neolithic flakes have been collected. The Neolithic flakes are spread over an area of 100 mt x 200 mtr. Thus it shows evidence for production of neolithic blanks or semi-finished tools (Table-4.22).

There are total 7 sites under the piedmont eco-zone. They are basically little away from the river bank as well as foot hill site and are flat or uneven surface. In respect of Neolithic implements the axe is of dominant variety. Individually, the site Atanaka Reserve Forest has 16 specimens (8.98%), Bankadar 02 specimens (1.12%), Karadapal-I 19 specimens (10.67%), Rugudidiha 33 (18.53%), Sorbeda Dautasala 29 specimens (16.29%), Sorbeda Kudur 02 specimens (1.12%) and Kadamdiha 74 specimens (41.57%) (Table-4.23).

The river bank cum foot hill eco-zone has yielded 141 specimens from four sites such as Bijagatha Hatapada 61 (43.26%), Karadapal-II 24 (17.02%), Mohanpur Shiva Mandir 46 (32.02%) and Nemliloti 10 (7.09%). Among the neolithic finished artefacts, chisel is dominant and share 06 specimens (4.25%) (Table-4.24).

Eco-zone wise and component-wise distribution of Neolithic artefacts

Table No-4.25 Eco-zone wise and component-wise distribution of Neolithic artefacts

Artefacts	Typology	Eco-zone wise distribution				Total	
		River bank	Foot hill	Piedmont	River bank cum foot hill	No.	Percentage
Celt Component	Axe	46	3	4	-	53	20.15%
	Adze	14	1	1	-	16	6.08%
	Chisel	4	2	-	6	12	4.57%
	Shoulder axe	1	-	-	-	1	0.38%
	Bar celt	-	-	2	-	2	0.76%
	Unfinished/ Intermediate axe	2	-	-	-	2	0.76%
	Broken axe	14	-	4	-	18	6.85%
	Neolithic flank	3	3	-	-	6	2.28%
	Neolithic flake	113	34	6	-	153	58.17%
	Total	**197**	**43**	**17**	**6**	**263**	**100.00%**
Pebble component	Ring stone	2	-	2	-	4	66.67%
	Dimple marked hammer stone	2	-	-	-	2	33.33%
	Total	**4**		**2**		**6**	**100.00%**

The above table shows the Eco-zone wise distribution of lithic artefacts of the Kakharua valley survey. The whole lithics has been divided into four broad categories as per its location such as foothill area, piedmont area, river bank site and river bank cum foothill site. These divisions or categories are represented on the basis of collection i.e. artefacts collected from foot hill area or site designated as foot hill site artefacts collected from river bank site treated as river bank site etc. The whole artefacts are divided into two broad categories as celt component and pebble component. Further, the celt component is divided typologically as axe, adze, chisel, shoulder axe, bar celt, unfinished intermediate axe, broken axe, neolithic blank. The pebble component is divided into ring stone and polisher/dimple mark hammer stone.

Another interesting aspect of these eco-zonal distributions find is that the river bank site has yielded a large number of tools. In case of neolithic, the river bank cum foot hill site has yielded very less amount tools.

Detailed Analysis of Different Range of Artefacts (Axe, Adze and Chisel)

Table No-4.26 A Detail of Typo-Technology of Axe

Attribute	Flake and chipped	flaked chipped and Partially ground	Fully ground and polished	No	Percentage
(A)Cutting Edge shape					
1. Straight	3	1	-	4	7.54%
2. Convex	20	6	1	27	50.95%
3. Splayed	10	2	-	12	22.64%
4. Irregular	9	1	-	10	18.87%
Total	**42**	**10**	**1**	**53**	**100%**

contd...

(B)Butt end					
1. Faceted	9	1	-	10	18.87%
2. Oblique/rounded	18	3	1	22	41.50%
3. Pointed/triangle	10	3		13	24.53%
4. Irregular	3	3	-	6	11.32%
5. Ttrapezoid	2	-	-	2	3.78%
Total	**42**	**10**	**1**	**53**	**100%**
(C) Cross section					
1. Bi- convex	28	9	1	38	71.70%
2. Plano-convex	10	1	-	11	20.76%
3. Rhomdoid	3	-	-	3	5.67%
4. Trapezoidal	1	-	-	1	1.87%
Total	**42(79.24)**	**10(18.86)**	**1(1.88)**	**53**	**100%**

In the typo-technological characteristics, the axe is dominant variety tool type of the Kakharua valley. The site yielded 53 specimens, out of which river bank site has yielded more specimen than other eco-zones. Interestingly, most of artefacts followed flaking and chipping method. The axe has been grouped into three broad categories as per technological point of view such as flaked and chipped type, flaked, chipped and partly ground and the last one is fully ground and polished. A careful observation of these artefacts shows that flaked and chipped variety are mainly collected from workshop site and the flaked, chipped and partly ground type are found both in the workshop site and operational area where as the fully ground and polished axe are noticed in operational area only.

From the technological point of view, it is presumed that the axes generally followed bilateral flaking and chipping techniques and quadrilateral flaking and chipping techniques. Most of the axes are patinated. As per the cutting edge shapes, the convex and splayed variety is of higher frequency. The butt-end traces obliquely rounded, pointed-triangular, faceted, trapezoid and irregular type. The cross sections of axe are divided into bi-convex, plano-convex, rhomboid and trapezoidal shape.

Table No-4.27 Typo-technology of Adze.

Attribute	Flaked and chipped	Flaked chipped and partially ground	Fully ground and polished	No.	Percentage
(A) Cutting edge					
1. Straight	5	1	1	7	43.75%
2. Convex	4	2	-	6	37.5%
3. Splayed	2	-	-	2	12.5%
4. Irregular	1	-	-	1	6.25%
Total	**12**	**3**	**1**	**16**	**100.00%**
(B) Butt end					
1. Facted	2	1	1	4	25.00%
2. Obliqe/rounded	7	1	-	8	50.00%
3. Pointed	1	-	-	1	6.25%
4. Irregular	2	1	-	3	18.75%
Total	**12**	**3**	**1**	**16**	**100.00%**
(C) Cross section					
1. Bi-convex	3	-	1	4	25.00%
2. Plano-convex	7	3	-	10	62.5%
3. Triangular	2	-	-	2	12.5%
Total	**12**	**3**	**1**	**16**	**100.00%**

In comparison to the axe, the proportional occurrence of adze tool type is low. Unlike axe, the adze is also broadly divided into three categories as flaked and chipped, flaked chipped and partly ground and fully ground and polished type. Out of 16 specimens, 12 specimens are of flaked and chipped variety, 03 are of flaked chipped and partly ground and 01 is of fully ground and polished type.

Table No-4.28 Typo- technology of Chisel

Attribute	Flaked and chipped	Flaked chipped and partially ground	Fully ground and polished	No.	Percentage
(A) Cutting edge					
1. Straight	2	3	3	8	66.67%
2. Splayed	1	-	-	1	8.33%
3. Irregular	3	-	-	3	25.00%
Total	**6**	**3**	**3**	**12**	**100.00%**
(B) Butt end					
1. Facted	6	2	1	9	75.00%
2. Oblique/rounded	-	1	-	1	8.33%
3. Irregular	-	-	2	2	16.67%
Total	**6**	**3**	**3**	**12**	**100.00%**
(C) Cross section					
1. Trapezided	3	2	-	5	41.67%
2. Ramdoid	1	-	-	1	8.33%
3. Rectangular	2	1	3	6	50.00%
Total	**6**	**3**	**3**	**12**	**100.00%**

Unlike axe and adze, chisels are represented in a few sites of the Kakharua valley, 12 specimens have been collected which is very low in comparison to axe and adze. On the basis of the surface treatment chisels may also be grouped into three broad categories such as flaked and chipped, flaked chipped and partly ground, and fully ground and polished.

The detailed typo-technological studies show that the cutting edges are straight, splayed and irregular. The butt-end is faceted, obliquely round and of irregular type where as the cross sections are basically of rectangular, trapezoid and rhomboid type. It is noted that flaked and chipped variety cross sections are of trapezoidal and rhomboid type where as the fully ground polished chisels are rectangular in nature.

Table No-4.29 Different range (size) of Neolithic typology

Size range (cm)		Axe	Shouldered axe	Dimple mark stone	Chisel	Adze	Neolithic blank	Bar celt	Neolithic flake	Unfinished axe	Broken axe
LENGTH	<2	-	-	-	-	-	-	-	10	-	-
	2-4	-	-	-	-	-	-	-	77	-	-
	4-6	-	-	-	-	-	1	-	36	-	3
	6-8	9	1	-	-	2	1	-	18	-	7
	8-10	11	-	-	7	2	1	-	7	-	7
	10-12	13	-	-	3	6	1	-	5	-	1
	12-14	11	-	-	1	5	-	-	-	-	-
	14-16	4	-	2	-	1	1	-	-	1	-
	16-18	3	-	-	1	-	1	-	-	-	-
	18-20	1	-	-	-	-	-	2	-	-	-
	20-22	1	-	-	-	-	-	-	-	1	-
Total		**53**	**1**	**2**	**12**	**16**	**6**	**2**	**153**	**2**	**18**
BREADTH	<2	-	-	-	-	-	-	-	8	-	-
	2-4	-	-	-	7	-	-	-	82	-	1
	4-6	36	1	-	5	7	3	2	47	-	16
	6-8	12	-	-	-	5	2	-	12	1	1
	8-10	4	-	1	-	4	1	-	4	-	-
	10-12	1	-	1	-	-	-	-	-	1	-
Total		**53**	**1**	**2**	**12**	**16**	**6**	**2**	**153**	**2**	**18**
THICKNESS	<1	-	-	-	-	-	-	-	101	-	-
	1-2	7	-	-	1	-	-	-	48	-	2
	2-4	41	1	-	10	15	6	2	4	-	16
	4-6	5	-	1	1	1	-	-	-	1	-
	6-8	-	-	1	-	-	-	-	-	1	-
Total		**53**	**1**	**2**	**12**	**16**	**6**	**2**	**153**	**2**	**18**

The size range is an important criterion to understand the tool typology in details, so the different size range of neolithic typology, which includes axe, shoulder axe, chisel, adze, blank, bar celt, unfinished axe, broken axe, neolithic flake and dimple mark stone. The size ranges of axes in respective of length, width and thickness vary widely. In view of the above variation the size ranges in length-wise are grouped into three broad categories viz. small sized (2 cm to 10 cm), medium sized (10.1 cm to 14 cm) and large sized (14.1 cm to 22 cm). Taking into account the axes, out of the 53 nos., 20 specimens are of small size, 28 specimens of medium size and 5 specimens are of large size. The width range also varies from 4 cm to 6 cm, (36 specimens), 6.1 cm to 8 cm (12 specimens), 8.1 cm to 10 cm (4 specimens) and 10.1 cm to 12 cm (1 specimen). In thickness range from 1 cm to 2 cm has 7 specimens, from 2 cm to 4 cm has 41 specimens and 4.1 cm to 6 cm has 5 specimens.

With regard to size range of adze, there are 16 specimens collected from Kakharua survey. In length-wise 4 are of small size, 11 are of medium size and 1 specimen is of large size. In width range, 7 specimens come under 4 cm to 6 cm, range 5 specimens come under 6 cm to 8 cm range and 4 specimens come under 8 cm to 10 cm range. In thickness 15 specimens come under 2 cm to 4 cm range and 1 specimen falls in 4 cm to 6 cm, range 4 of medium sized and 1 no. comes under big size (20 cm to 22 cm).

The bar-celt comes under large size, the unfinished axe is also a large variety, and the broken axes fall under small and medium variety. Apart from these the blank also shows wide variation. All the available specimens are well made and show a wide range of variation in the Kakharua valley.

Table No-4.30 Raw material distribution of Neoliths

No.	Tool type	Dolerite	Diorite	Sand stone	Laterite/ Iron ore	Quartzite?	Sandy lime stone?	Total No.	Percentage
1	Axe	45	7	-	-	-	1	53	19.70%
2	Adze	16	-	-	-	-	-	16	5.94%
3	Chisel	11	1	-	-	-	-	12	4.46%
4	Broken axe	17	1	-	-	-	-	18	6.69%
5	Shoulder axe	1	-	-	-	-	-	1	0.37%
6	Neolithic blank	6	-	-	-	-	-	6	2.23%
7	Neolithic flake	153	-	-	-	-	-	153	56.87%
8	Ring stone	-	-	2	1	1	-	4	1.48%
9	Dimple mark hammer stone	-	-	-	-	2	-	2	0.74%
10	Unfinished axe	2	-	-	-	-		2	0.74%
	Total	**253 (94.05%)**	**9 (3.34%)**	**2 (0.74%)**	**1 (0.37%)**	**3 (1.11%)**	**1 (0.37%)**	**269**	**(99.98%)**

The raw materials of various Neolithic tool types have yielded from the study area. The total collection of 269 artefacts, of which 253 are of dolerite variety, 9 specimens of diorite, 2 specimens of sand stone, 1 specimen of Laterite/iron ore, 3 specimens of quartzite and 1 specimen of sandy lime stone type. The dominant variety of raw material is dolerite. Almost all the artefacts, made on the dolerite show patination of various degrees and colour ranging from reddish brown to yellowish colour (Fig.36).

It is interesting to note that from the survey raw material outcrops are located in the Kakharua Reserve Forest site with a huge amount of large flake and chips. And most of the sites are located about 20 km radius from the raw material epicenter zone. It is also traced that the raw materials were primarily flaked to make blank and then were transported to other localities.

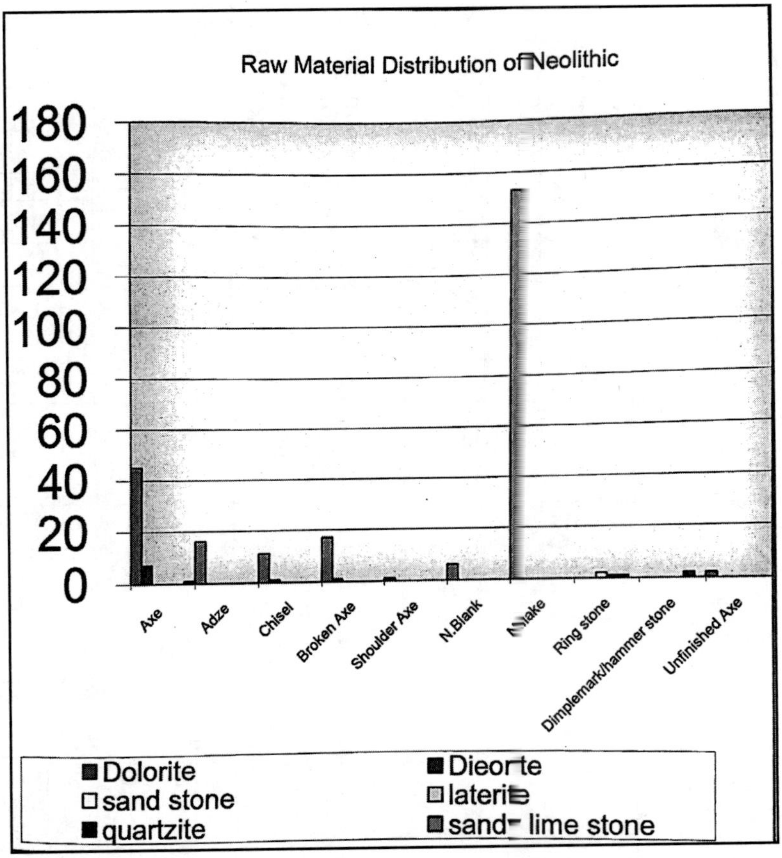

Fig.36: Raw material distribution of Neolithic artefacts.

To know the site-wise and typology-wise occurrence, the distribution pattern of neolithic flake, axe, adze, broken axe and chisel are noticed in high frequency. The sites of Baisnavadar, Bisriguda and Bijagotha Hatapada have yielded a large amount of neolithic flakes along with axe, adze and chisel, which are basically of flaked and chipped variety. In a low frequency Kadamdar, Karadapal-I and Radodiha yielded one artefact each.

Table No-4.31 Site-wise and typology-wise distribution of Neolithic artefacts.

Tool type	Name of the Sites																			Total	percentage
	ARF	**BND**	**BSG**	**BHP**	**BKD**	**GMS**	**JHP**	**JMS**	**KLN**	**KDD**	**KDP-I**	**KPK**	**KPF**	**RGD**	**RMD**	**RDH**	**SBD**	**SBK**	**TMG**		
Axe	-	20	19	-	-	-	3	-	1	-	-	2	-	1	1	1	2	-	3	53	19.70%
Adze	-	6	6	-	-	-	1	-	-	1	-	-	-	-	-	-	1	-	1	16	5.94%
Chisel	-	1	-	6	-	-	-	2	-	-	-	-	-	-	2	-	-	-	1	12	4.46%
Shouldered axe	-	-	-	-	-	-	-	-	1	-	-	-	-	-	-	-	-	-	-	1	0.37%
Bar celt	-	-	-	-	-	-	-	-	-	-	-	-	-	-	-	-	-	2	-	2	0.74%
Unfinished intermediate axe	-	-	-	-	-	2	-	-	-	-	-	-	-	-	-	-	-	-	-	2	0.74%
Broken axe	2	5	9	-	2	-	-	-	-	-	-	-	-	-	-	-	-	-	-	18	6.69%
Neolithic blank	-	-	2	-	-	-	1	-	1	-	-	-	2	-	-	-	-	-	-	6	2.23%
Neolithic flake	-	22	25	55	-	11	-	-	-	-	-	-	34	5	-	-	1	-	-	153	56.87%
Ring stone		2	-	-	-	-	-	-	-	-	1	-	-	-	-	-	-	-	-	4	1.48%
Dimple Mark Stone	-	-	-	-	-	-	-	-	-	-	-	2	-	-	-	-	-	-	-	2	0.74%
Total	**3**	**56**	**61**	**61**	**2**	**13**	**5**	**2**	**3**	**1**	**1**	**4**	**36**	**6**	**3**	**1**	**4**	**2**	**5**	**269**	**99.96%**

It is also interesting that the high frequency occurrence of neolithic flakes has been associated with factory site. The surface of these factory sites has a spread of a large number of neolithic flakes of different size. Flaking and chipping on the entire surface with very little grinding is the main features of the neolithic artefacts. There are 19 sites representing neolithic in nature and 269 specimens have been collected (Fig.37).

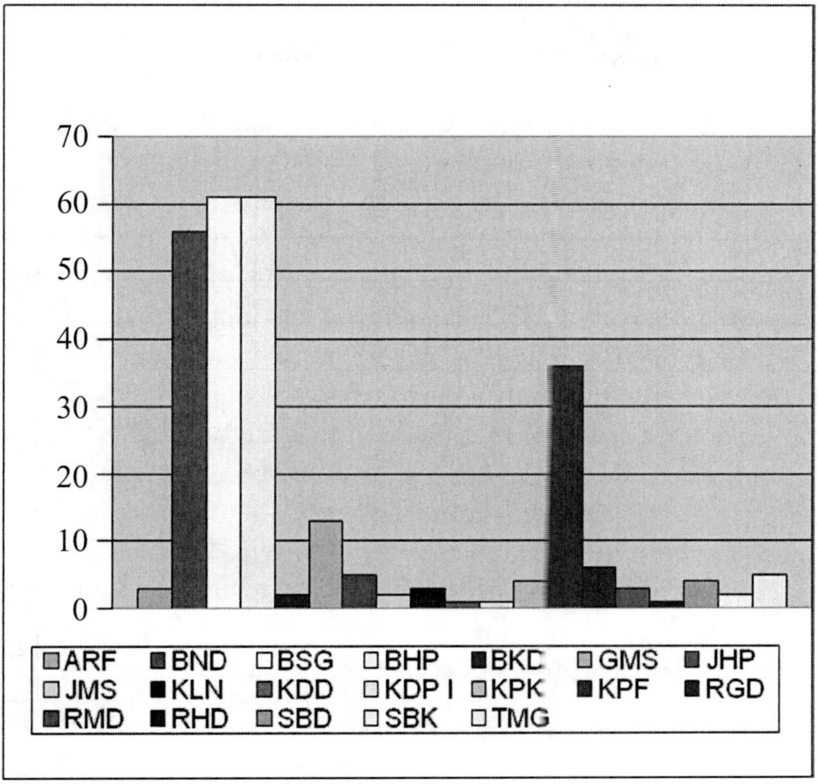

Fig.37: Site-wise distribution of Neolithic artefacts.

Recoveries of Antiquities

While surveying the area, the author had come across some neolithic celt manufacturing centers in different localities. Specimens of this neolithic celt, axe, adze and chisel of various shapes and sizes with chipped, partly chipped fully ground and polished celts have been reported from these localities. All these are found to be made on dolerite, diorite and basalt rock type. Considering the abundance of artefact remains at these sites, it can be inferred that the sites containing the above might have been used for a long period for manufacturing of neolithic artefacts. The neolithic tools are limited under the celt component category as per its general morphological and typo-technological characteristics.

The Celt component

The tool types of the celt component include all the knapped, ground and polished varieties. There are four basic stages of manufacturing; viz- chipping, pecking, grinding and polishing (Bhattacharya 1990, Sahoo 2000; 190). Hence, the celt may be an axe, an adze, a chisel, ring stone with more or less chipped, pecked, ground and polished all over the body and at working edges or ends. The grinding and polishing sometimes is not necessarily done all over the tool surface, sometimes only working edge is found to be ground and polished. The present collection of this component on the basis of technique of manufacturing, typo morphology and probable function may be typified as axe, adze, chisel, unfinished axe, broken axe, shouldered axe, and neolithic blank.

Apart from these the unfinished axe 02 (0.76%) broken axe 18 (6.85%), neolithic blank 06 (2.28%), neolithic flakes 153 (58.17%) are of celt component. The neolithic flakes are highest in number and collected from the four ecozonal distribution. Most of the celt component of this category is made out of dolerite and diorite.

(i) Flaked and Chipped Categories

This category is generally attributed to specimens (axe, adze, chisel and fabricators) of flaked, chipped and un-ground type. Such tools demonstrate only one or two basic stages of manufacturing. In the first stage, preparation of preforms of the above tool type is made by primary flaking of a selected blank. Then resolved flaking of the tool type is done by thorough or sometimes-occasional micro chipping at both the surfaces.

(ii) Flaked, Chipped and Partially Ground

This typology is characterized by axes, adzes, chisels and fabricators which are designed and fashioned by partial chipping of a suitable blank only to develop its working edge in its first stage and subsequently grinding and polishing is done at the same end to have an effective working edge.

This category of specimen is basically made with the completely chipped and partially ground tools. These specimens exhibit the basic technological stages of manufacturing process. At first instance, the desired shape is obtained probably by flaking and micro chipping. Then pecking is done over the flaked and chipped surface of the specimens and subsequently partial grinding adopted thoroughly at the working ends and occasionally at the surfaces. Because of this, the typologies of celt component show well ground working edge and comparatively less ground and insignificant ridge of flaking and chipping.

(iii) Fully Ground and Polished

The specimens of this category include primarily well ground and polished varieties of axe, adze, chisel and fabricator which are probably fashioned by following all the four basic stages of techniques of manufacture. Firstly, the suitable blank (nodule/pebble/flake) for the desired typology is dressed upto its preforms by flaking and then micro-chipping are done to give appropriate shape to it. Secondly, pecking is done to remove or to make smooth the prominent ridges of flakes and chips on it. Thirdly, grinding is done to provide smooth or even surfaces to the tool type and finally polishing is applied to develop the sharpness of the working edge. So in-case of the fully ground and polished celt category there is no trace of flaking, chipping and pecking.

Axe

These are 53 (20.15%) of the total celt component) axes found from the study area. From this collection 46 (31.50 %) are found from the river bank, 03 (16.66 %) from piedmont and 04 (9.09 %) from foot hill site in respective to the eco-zones. The entire collection of this category includes 42 (79.24%) flaked and chipped axes, 10 (18.86 %) flaked, chipped and partly ground axes, 01 (1.88 %) fully ground and polished. They are basically made on sizable prepared blanks, nodules and thick flakes of dolerite, diorite and sandy lime stone. But the use of suitable pebble blanks could not be ruled out. From the entire collection it has been observed that almost all the sub types (flaked and chipped axes, completely chipped and partially ground axes) are manufactured by involving two types of flaking techniques- bilateral flaking or chipping and quadrilateral flaking or chipping. Hence, the axes fabricated by the said flaking techniques possess generally an oval to biconvex, plano-convex, and rhomboid to trapezoidal cross section. According to the cutting edge shape, it is divided as straight, convex, splayed and irregular type, The butt end are generally characterized on faceted, oblique or rounded, pointed or triangle, trapezoid and irregular. Their length, breadth and thickness vary from 6.9 cm to 20.4 cm, from 4.1 cm to 10.4 cm, from 1.9 cm to 4.8 cm. Some of the representative samples of each category are described below.

1. **BND-1 (20.4 x 10.4 x 4.6 cm).** This specimen is a flaked and chipped axe made on a big lump of dolerite having triangular in general shape with pointed butt end. It has a Bi-convex medial cross section. Large to medium type flakes are detached to prepare the axe (Fig.27, Pl.14).
2. **BSG-18 (7.9 x 5.5 x 2.3 cm).** It is an axe of chipped and flaked variety having sub-triangular in general shape with a plano-convex cross-section. The working edge is broken probably due to use.
3. **KPK-1 (12.1 x 6.0 x 2.3 cm).** The axe specimen is partly chipped, ground and of polished variety having triangular shape and convex cross-section. It is made on sizable flake. The flaking and chipping scar marked as the butt end as well as side edge is prominent due to ground and polished on the working end. The working edge is sharp and oblique (Fig.31, Pl.19).
4. **KLN-2 (7.9 x 4.3 x 2.2 cm).** This is the only specimen of shoulder axe in this survey area. It is made on dolerite with the working end sharp and small projection of shoulder. The butt end is faceted and straight, the cross section is rectangular in nature (Pl.18).

Adze

Adze forms the next category of artefacts of celt component. Altogether 16 (5.94%) adzes have been found from the studied area, from which 14 (9.58 %) are from river bank sites, 01 (5.55 %) is from piedmont and 01 (2.27 %) is from the foot hill site in respective to its eco-zones. As compared to the axes and chisels, the percentage of occurrence of adze is very low. Similar to the axe, this category includes 12 (75.00 %) of flake and chipped, 03 (18.75 %) of flake, chipped and partially ground and 01 (6.25%) of fully ground and polished type adze. These adzes are found to be prepared on a sizeable lump of stone or thick flakes of dolerite and diorite. Their length, breadth and thickness vary from 7.2 to 14 cm, from 4.5 to 8.3 cm. and from 2.0 to 3.3 cm respectively. The flaked, chipped and ungrounded adzes are generally longer and thicker than the adzes of partially chipped, grounded and polished and fully ground, polished adze varieties. The shape of the implement is triangular to oblique rounded shapes, Bi-convex to triangular cross section. These are mainly fashioned by flaking, chipping and by grinding too. Some of the representative samples are discussed below

1. **BSG-1 (12.8 x 6.2 x 2.9 cm).** This specimen is made out of dolerite piece. It is basically flaked chipped with ground and polished mark on some part of it. The working end is convex with oblique butt end and the cross section is plano-convex (Fig.30).
2. **BSG-4 (8.9 x 6.3 x 2.6 cm).** It is made out of a dolerite of large flake with partly flaked, chipped and ground type. The flaked and chipped marks are on the middle part as well as at the butt end area where as the working end is well ground. Its working end is straight and the cross section is plano-convex type. Its shape is trapezoidal (Fig.30).
3. **TMG-2 (11.8 x 5.8 x 2.4 cm).** A complete specimen of an ungrounded but fully flaked and chipped variety of trapezoidal in shape. It is made out of dolerite with flat faced butt-end,

convex working end and bi-convex in medial cross-section (Fig.32, Pl.22).

4. **BND-17 (10.8 x 6.1 x 3.4 cm).** It is flaked, chipped and ground on the edge. The butt end is faceted and straight. Working end is convex and cross section is plano-convex (Pl.14).
5. **BND-22 (14.0 x 5.7 x 3.2 cm).** This specimen is made out of dolerite. In order to manufacture the artefacts a good amount of medium to small flakes have been detached. It is generally of sub-triangular type, the butt end is oblique rounded, working end is splayed and the cross section is bi-convex in nature (Fig.27, Pl.14).
6. **BND-G8 (11 x 4.5 x 3.1 cm).** It is basically flaked and chipped. However by one side of the working edge is ground to make it sharp. This specimen is characterized by oblique and rounded butt end, straight and sharp cutting edge, plano-convex cross-section and generally of sub triangular shape.

Chisel

Chisel is the third dominant typology of the celt component collected from the different eco-zones. There are 12 (4.57%) of the total celt component) chisels and out of which 02 (16.66%) are from foot hill area, 04 (33.33%) are from river bank sites and 06 (50.00 %) are collected from the river bank cum foot hill site. The entire collection of this category can be classified into the sub-types such as flaked and chipped 06 (50.00 %), flaked, chipped and partly ground, 03 (25.00 %) fully ground and polished, 03 (25.00 %), (Table-4.28). These are generally made of dolerite rock. It has been observed that typo technologically almost all the chisel variants in the study area have the cutting edge ranging from straight to irregular type, the butt end faceted to irregular type, and the cross section from trapezoidal to rectangular. The flaked and chipped chisel is generally made on suitable natural blocks of dolerite and diorite with minimum flaking and chipping. Most of the chisels possessed the general shape from trapezoidal to quadrilateral. In order to achieve the shape, most of chisels are fabricated. In addition to quadrilateral flaking and chipping the grinding is also marked on lateral margins. The length, breadth and thickness of these tools type are varied and range from 8.3 to 15.5 cm., 3.0 to 5.8 cm and 1.9 to 3.3 cm. respectively. Some of the representative samples are discussed below.

1. **RMD-1 (15.4 x 3.8 x 3.1 cm).** A complete specimen of fully grounded and polished chisel having trapezoidal general shape, faceted butt end, straight but one end little chipped. The medial cross section is rectangular (Pl.20).
2. **JMS-2 (8.1 x 3.6 x 2.7 cm).** The specimen is made out of dolerite with fully ground and polished. Its butt end is broken but working edge is straight and sharp and rectangular cross section (Fig.33, Pl.24).
3. **TMG-3 (9.8 x 3.0 x 2.1 cm).** It is heavily patinated dolerite and working end is marked with ground and polished. This chisel is characterized as straight faceted butt end, straight and sharp and the medial cross section is rectangular (Fig.32, Pl.22).
4. **BHP-1 (8.3 x 3.7 x 2.9 cm).** This is a complete specimen of flaked and chipped variety of chisel. The working end is thinner than the butt end. It is characterized as faceted butt end, splayed working end and trapezoidal cross section (Fig.35, Pl.33).
5. **BND G-2 (9.7 x 4.3 x 2.3 cm).** The chisel is made out of dolerite and flaked, chipped and partly ground polished. It is fabricated as oblique butt end, straight working end trapezoidal cross section.

Shouldered Axe

The shouldered axe is a typical character of the north-eastern neolithic (Krisnaswami-1960). There is a single artefact of this type found from the survey area. The artefact is made out of dolerite. The detail of the specimen is given below.

1. **KLN- 2 (7.9 x mx-4.3 mi-3.4 x 2.2 cm)** Made out of dolerite with grinding and polishing. The working end has sharp end and the shoulder has small projection. Butt end-faceted straight, working end-straight, cross section-rectangular (Pl.18).

Bar Celt

It is a long rectangular or trapezoidal celt. This artefact was probably used for agricultural purpose. There are only 02 (0.76% of the total collection of celt component) artefacts of this type found from the piedmont site. Both of these artefacts are made of dolerite. Two specimens have been described below.

1. **SBK-1(18.5 x mx-5.4 mi-4.2 x 3.2 cm)** Made out of dolerite. It is too long with typical chipping form. Overall it is of long rectangular type. No grinding and polishing mark is noticed on artefact surface. Butt end is straight faceted. Working end is convex type and its cross section is rectangular (Fig.34, Pl.31).
2. **SBK-2 (19.2 x mx-5.2 mi-3.9 x 3.2 cm)** Made out of dolerite. It is long with typical chipping form. Overall it is long rectangular type. No grinding and polishing mark noticed on artefact surface. Butt end is straight faceted. Working end is of convex type and its cross section is rectangular (Fig.34, Pl.31).

Flake

There are total 153 flakes (58.17%) from the total collection of flake component of which 58 (37.90%) are from river bank sites, 34 (22.22%) from foot hills sites, 06 (3.92%) from piedmont sites, and 55 (35.94%) are from the river bank cum foothill sites. Almost all collected flakes are made of dolerite raw material.

1. **GMS-5 (5.6 x 5.4 x 1.3 cm)** made out of dolerite, flaking, fan shaped, secondary flaking.
2. **GMS-8 (7.2 x 4.6 x 1.2 cm)** made out of dolerite, flaking, oblong type shaped, secondary flaking.

3. **BSG-26 (11.3 x 4.4 x 1.4 cm)** made out of dolerite, flaking, this is a large and elongated one.

Neolithic Blank

There are 06 (2.28%) blanks for manufacturing of celt component that are usually large flakes with primary work done to give a preform shape of a celt. Out of these, 03 (50.00) are found from the foot hill site and 03 (50.00%) are found from the river bank sites. All these are detached from dolerite nodules.

1. **BSG-25 (5.2 x 5.6 x 2.9cm)** Made out of diorite, primary and secondary flaking have been detached it is very initial in stage, the working end is broken.
2. **KLN-3 (8.6x 6.6 x 3.7cm)** Made out of dolerite, flaking and chipping all over the surface but it could not give the final shape. The working end is partially prepared and it is straight type, its cross section is convex (Pl.18).

Pebble Component

This component includes both artefacts assemblages made from core or river pebbles and flake- basically large flakes. The detailed typologies are described below.

Ring Stone

This category of pebble tool component is represented by 04 specimens having oval to circular shapes. These were made of locally available raw-materials such as sand stones 02 (50%), laterite 01 (25%), and quartzite 01 (25%). Almost all the specimens possess completely or partly bored central hole having a hour-glass shaped cross section. The central hole of these artefacts was probably done by pecking with pointed stone tools from both of the surfaces. Hence, the central holes have broad mouths at their outer surface that narrows towards the centre.

Ring stones are used sometime for religious- medicinal practices. At the time of stomach pain of cows and bulls, even sometime in case of human being also, they grind a portion of this ring stone on their saddle-quern and prepare a paste from it which is given to the said patient. They believe that the patient gets relief after having this traditional medicine. Because of this important medicinal value the local tribes as well as some non-tribes of the region also collect this stone from different places and keep it carefully at their cow-shed for their future use.

A few representatives of such samples are described below.

1. **BND-24** (dia-9.3 cm) A broken ring stone of quartzite with central hole. It was probably used as mace head or husking stone (Fig.28, Pl.14).
2. **ARF-3** (dia- 8.3 cm) The specimen is partly broken. It is well perforated and grounded. It was used as mace-head or husking stone.

Hammer Stone With Dimple Mark

This category of artefacts is reported from the river bank site and made out of quartzite block. The specimens are roughly rounded in shape with battery mark or dimple mark on the flat surface as well as profile. Description of such specimens is made below.

1. **KPK.** -4 (14.6 x 8.0 x 6.9 cm) This is made out of quartzite rolled pebble and roughly roundish in shape. Three dimple marks on the cross section and each one on the obverse and reverse side are marked (Fig.31, Pl.19).

Main Features of the Neolithic Culture of Kakharua Valley.

From the intensive exploration along with the Kakharua valley specifically in Keonjhar and Angul districts of North-Central Odisha, it is revealed that this geographical region has much potential for the evidence of neolithic culture. The intensive survey in both side of the river in and around Bansapal Block, Nagira panchayat, Jolanda panchayat, Jamardiha panchayat and Dalo panchayat areas resulted in the discovery of 19 neolithic sites. On the geo-morphological location, these sites have been classified into four broad types, viz. river bank site, foot hill site, piedmont site and river bank cum foot hill sites.

Hence, from the survey numerous finished and semi-finished artefacts of the neolithic culture have been collected. The following important characteristic features of neolithic culture of north-central Odisha are inferred from my survey.

1. On the basis of general characteristics of morphological and typo-technological features, the neolithic collection has been classified into two broad categories such as celt component and pebble component.
2. The celt component includes the celt variants classified and characterized by (i) flaked and chipped,(ii) flaked, chipped and partly ground, and (iii) fully ground and polished like axe, adze, chisels etc. Besides, some broken celts of flaked and chipped as well as fully ground and polished varieties have also been recovered from the survey. These types are preferably made on dolerite, diorite and basalt.
3. The pebble component comprises the artefacts assemblages made both on nodules and river pebbles characterized by the types of ring stone, dimple marked hammer stone and blank etc. All these assemblages are of sand stone, dolerite and diorite.
4. The shouldered axe is more widely reported from the coastal Odisha, where as shouldered axe in the present study, probably in north Odisha and north-central Odisha is very rare. The present finding of Kakharua shouldered axe could be compared with shouldered stone axe from Singhbhum in present Jharkhand reported by Valentine Ball.
5. Another important feature is a large boulder rock with shallow polishing mark in Kamparkala, which suggests that the neolithic people might have been grinding and polishing their respective stone tools.
6. A large number of semi-finished tools including innumerable flakes and chips have been recovered from the survey which implies manufacturing or factory site etc. in the region. Being a

part of the same locality the Bonaigarh neolithic culture could broadly be compared with the Kakharua neolithic remains. The neolithic artefacts of Baisnavadar, Bisriguda and Kakharua Protection Forest site have large production unit with semi-finished celts, from where neolithic artefacts could have been manufactured.

7. In the earlier study it has been reported that the raw materials were obtained from nearby site but unfortunately there was no reporting of dolerite outcrop. It is interesting to note that the Kakharua Protection Forest Site has evidence of such out crop and implies that there are two phases of workmanship. The first phase involved the big blank extracted from the outcrop without any evidence of any finished or semi-finished artefacts. However, there are flakes of large size. The second phase of manufacturing shows sites having small flakes and chips along with semi-finished and finished tool.
8. On the functionary aspect and compared with South-east Asia and China, the central Orissan stone bar specifically from Sankerjang have been considered as lithophone (Yule et al 2000). So the stone celt recovered from Sorbeda kudur site is comparable with the type II variety of Sankerjang lithophone.
9. In respect of study of ceramics in north-central Odisha, the Neolithic culture of Pallahara was associated with pottery such as coarse red ware and black and red ware (Basa, et al 2000). Besides pot sherds of red ware were found in Telkoi in Keonjhar district (Dehuri 1998). Hence, their types could not be reconstructed. However, the survey did not yield a single pot sherd. Further work is necessary in this regard for intensive exploration and collection of Neolithic ceramics remains from north-central Odisha.
10. As per finished and semi-finished artefacts, axe and adze are the two dominant types of artefacts of the celt component. Of these two types axes and adzes of flaked and chipped, flaked chipped and partially ground and fully ground are generally

characterized by convex to straight working edge, faceted to pointed and oblique butt-end, bi-convex to trapezoidal cross section. They are generally fashioned adopting the bilateral to quadrilateral flaking and chipping as well as grinding and polishing.

11. Typo-technologically, the celt of Kakharua valley are quite similar to the Bonaigarh neolithic of north-western Orissa (Behera 1991-92, 1992-2000), neolithic of Pallahara region basically the lower part of the Mankara river (Basa et al 2000); and the Telkoi region of Keonjhar (Dehuri 1998).

Moreover, such similarities on typo-technological ground are also observed on the neolithic artefacts reported from southern India (Krishnaswami 1960, Raju 1985), Central Eastern India including Bihar, Jharkhand and West Bengal (Sharma 1952; 14-6; Sen and Chaturvedi 1958:176; Krishnaswami 1960: 56-7, Dani 1960; Ghosh et al 1984: 24-8; Bhattarcharya 1999-170), North Eastern India (Sharma 1980; 41-52, and south-east Asia (Dani 1960; Dulf 1970).

In the next chapter, archaeological recoveries from the historical period will be discussed.

CHAPTER 6

Historical Archaeology of Kakharua Valley

In this chapter, archaeological evidence of the historical period of North Central Odisha is discussed. In this context, inscription in the cave shelter of Sitabinji is an eye opener to the north-central and north Orissa, in which there is reference to Maharaja Sri Disabhanja in Brahmi script belonging to 5th century A.D. (Senapati et.al. 1986:42). A natural rock shelter locally known as 'Ravanachhaya' contains an ancient rock painting depicting a royal procession where a king riding on an elephant holding water lily in his left hand and a goad in right hand along with well decorated attendant, horse man, dress of the soldiers, ornaments and floral motifs are important. Apart from these, the other reported archaeological finds of the site include female figurines, bronze ornaments, beads, ear studs, terracotta, copper cast Puri-Kushana coins, lamp stand, elephant figures and brunt bricks. Another important evidence of the site is the Chaturmukha Sivalinga that shows the ancient Shiva shrine at the site (Ramachandran 1951:5-25; Panigrahi 1981:369, Mohanti 1988; Senapati 1986: 42 and 433-434; Mohapatra 1986: 173-174).

In recent years an early historical site has been reported at Telkoi on the left bank of river Somakoi, a tributary of the river Brahmani. The mound covered an area of 150 x 100 mts. and height is about 6 meter from the water level. It is undisturbed and scattered with a large quantity of potsherds, a few iron artefacts, a dimple scar rubber, spout, dish on stand and flake of deprival fine grained granite (Dehuri 1997).

From present survey in the Kakharua Valley, some sites belonging to historical period are brought to light. These sites are Katiragarh, Rado MIP, Dalo Puruna diha and Nemliloti.

Data Analysis of Historical Artefacts

From present survey, four sites such as Katiragarh, Rado MIP, Dalo Puranadiha and Nemloti are reported Historical artefacts. These findings of Historical period are discussed under different sub heads.

Analysis of Finding of Katiragarh Sculptural Remains

From the mixed sal forest two sculptural remains and two miniature temple (*Urushriga* type) have been located along with large quantity of potsherds. Apart from these a few beads and a terracotta figurine are also found. The site has yielded lateritic platform with one dressed lateritic pillar dismantled. This sheds some light on in building/monument construction. It is interesting to note that in Odisha during early historic and medieval period laterite was profusely used in religious and secular structures.

Sculpture No. 1

The sculpture is made out of black stone. The image is seated on his vehicle (*Vahana*) dog and its upper part is missing. The *vahana* is clearly identified as dog from its anatomic feature. As per the iconographic representation this image is identified as Bhairava. As a sculptural representation, it is quite well in plasticity. Its measurement is 23.2 cm. height and 20.1 cm. width respectively (Pl.35).

Sculpture No. 2

This sculpture was buried little inside the ground. However after scraping of the loose ground earth the detailed features are noticed. This image is also made out of black stone and not in iconometric standard. It is broken into two pieces and has been defaced due to weathering of the stone. The image is standing in posture and have four arms, the right upper arm holding Chakra, the left upper arm holding lotus, whereas the lower two hands are broken from the palm part. The *Karna Kundalas* are very prominent. He wears *Kirita Mukuta* and to the hallo is carved out as that rays franked out from hallo. The garland is also clearly visible in lower part. Because of all these iconographic features, the image is identified as Lord Vishnu and it measures 26.4 x 14.2 x 7.3 cms (Pl.35).

Miniature temples

Two miniature temples have been found which are quite small and show similarly with the *Rekha deul* type. Out of these two architectural fragments, one is partly buried inside the earth upto its *Sikhara* part, so its *beki* and *Amlaka* are clearly visible, whereas another has been noticed quite close to the earlier one. One surface has carved out image in Yogic posture. Both of these architectural parts are made out of laterite. As per the nature of stone and low craftsmanship the Yogic posture is not clearly marked in plan. These two miniature temples are of *triratha* plan. The measurement of the exposed one is 76.4 x 26.6 x 26.6 cms (Pl.36).

Apart from these, an Amlaka of laterite is found in the nearby area implying a temple structure in the locality.

Lateritic Structure

A little away from the sculptural site, a low height podium with a pillar is noticed which is made out of laterite. The measurement of the structure is 2.60 x 2.30 x 0.30 mts. and the pillars base part is 50 x 50 cm. Its upper part represents octagonal facet (Pl.37). It is presumed that this structure is datable to medieval period and possibly meant for religious function. Some local people told that this was the Abhishek Mandap of Raja and was used during the coronation of Bhanja King of Keonjhar.

Terracotta Figurine

A terracotta human figurine is found from a section which is exposed through cutting of an agriculture field. This human figurine is identified through its face and nose and its decorations are prepared by the pinching technique. This is handmade, well fired and measured as maximum length-4.5 cm. maximum/breadth-3.4 cm. & maximum thickness-1.5cm. The hands are extended and of blunt type and the legs are not prepared. So the details of the figure are uncertain (Pl.38 & 40).

Beads

Beads are generally considered as small finds in archaeological literature and because of this; these are not as much emphasized as pottery, coins, metallic and other art historic remains (Basa 1990-91). Beads were probably the first durable ornaments of human being (Dubin 1987:9) and the study of beads has resulted in reconstruction of technology and ancient trade on a more secure basis (Basa 2001:413). There is one bead collected from the erosional surface of the historical mound of Katiragarh. This bead is made of terracotta. It is partly fragment, short cylindrical shaped and circular cross section. The maximum diameter of the bead at its outer surface is 0.8 cm. and length is 2.2 cm.(Pl.38).

Glass Bangle

The Glass bangles are mostly fragmented, black in colour and convex in cross section. The maximum thickness range from 0.4 cm. to 0.5 cm. and length 1 cm.to 4.7 cm. respectively (Pl.38).

Stone Objects

Apart from these objects, the site yielded nine stone objects and most of these were collected from the nearby river beds. Out of nine, two might have been used as hammer due to dimple mark on both the surfaces. Three stones could have been used as muller, out of which one is deliberately made in oblong circular type (fragment from both end). Another is also intensively dressed in rectangular form with square section and the rest one in this series is roughly oblong natural boulder which could have been used as muller. Rest four number of stones are basically river pebble most probably used as pestle. (Fig.38, Pl.41)

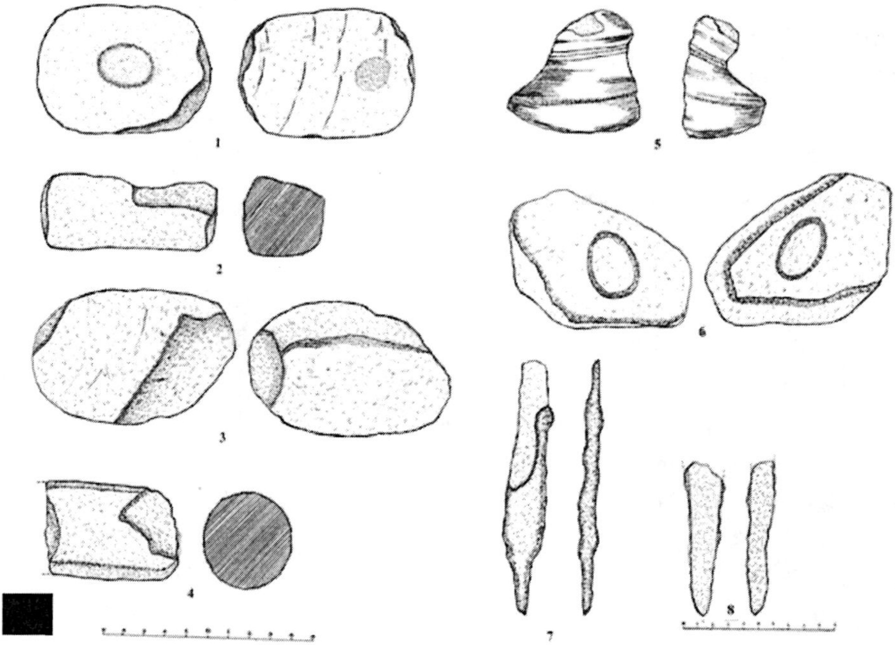

Fig.38: Katiragarh stone artefacts.
1-dimple mark stone; 2-muller fragment; 3-pestle; 4-muller fragment.
5-dabbar;6-dimple mark stone;7-iron arrow head; 8-iron nail fragment.

Potter's Dabber

This artefacts is an ordinary hammer made of brunt clay. It is used for hardening of newly made pottery in the leather hard condition. There is one such type of artefact found from Katiragarh. It is partly fragmented and has round flat bulbous body with small thick knob. Two deep incised marks are also noticed on the knob portion. It is 5 cm in diameter and 8 cm. in height (Fig.38, Pl.41)

Iron Objects

In the historical period the role of iron has been emphasized by scholars (Sahu, B.P.) From the exposed erosion at Katiragarh a few iron implements have been collected.

Implement -1

This specimen is identified as spearhead, whose pointed end is broken. It is heavily patinated and corrosion has made it brittle. The metric measurement of the specimen is 16 x 2.7 x 1.2 cms. in length, breadth and thickness respectively (Fig.38).

Implement -2

It is identified as fragment of a nail, the bottom part is damaged whereas its pointed end is intact. The length, breadth and thickness measure 4.4 x 2.6 x 1.8 cms respectively (Fig.38).

Iron Slag

The site has yielded a good amount of iron slags from surface. It is also interesting to note that a few areas have concentration of such slags. However, during survey the author has picked up few iron slags for laboratory study.

Shivalinga

About 200 mtr. east to the site another sacred place is located from where a small Shivalinga carved out of stone was installed by a local villager. This carved Shivalinga was collected from the nearby area which is tentatively datable to 12th – 13th century A.D. This Shiva linga is installed on a square Yonipitha, the corner has incised mark whereas linga is carved in circular way. Its measurement is 8.1 x 5.9 x 2 cms. in length, breadth & thickness (Pl.39).

Potsherds

Description of Potsherds (Fig.39 to 41, Pl.42)

1. Pot (Handi), grey ware, wheel made, out turned triangular rim, fine to medium fabric, the cross section is thick, core is light grey.

2. Pot with relatively narrow mouth (water pot), grey ware, and wheel made, fine to medium fabric, the upper surface has groove and incised decoration, the core is dull red.
3. Dish, externally projecting rim, black and red ware, medium to coarse fabric, wheel made, the core is dull red.
4. Dish/ Bowl, black slipped ware, externally projecting rim, fine to medium coarse fabric, wheel made, the core is dark grey.
5. Pot (Handi), grey ware, out turned rim, wheel made, fine to medium fabric, the core is dark grey and cross section is thin.
6. Pot (water pot), medium fabric, dull red ware, out turned triangular rim, wheel made, fine to medium fabric, the core is dull red.
7. Pot (Handi), black slipped ware, out turned ledge rim, wheel made, the upper surface has two grooves, the core is dull red, fine to medium fabric.
8. Bowl, black slipped ware, inverted with featureless rim, wheel made, core is dark grey, fine to medium fabric.
9. Pot, black slipped ware, everted triangular rim, narrow mouth, possible high neck, wheel made, fine to medium fabric, the core is dark grey, medium mouth.
10. Pot (Handi), black slipped ware, medium mouth everted rim with inward ledge rim, wheel made, fine to medium fabric, the core is dark grey.
11. Pot (Handi), red ware, everted rim, wheel made, medium to coarse fabric, the core has sandy particle.
12. Pot (Handi), with wide mouth, grey ware, out turned loop rim, low neck, medium to coarse fabric, the core has sandy particle, grey in color.
13. Pot (Handi) with wide mouth, black slipped ware, out turned ledge rim, the ledge is very small, low neck, wheel made, fine to medium fabric, carination marked, and the core is dark grey.
14. Pot (Handi), medium mouth, black slipped ware, out turned rim, wheel made, fine to medium fabric, the core is dark grey.
15. Pot (water pot), narrow mouth, black slipped ware, out turned ledge rim, medium to coarse fabric, the core is dark grey.

16. Pot (water pot), narrow mouth, out turned ledge rim, wheel made, fine to medium fabric, core is grey, deep groove on upper surface.
17. Pot (water pot), black slipped ware, out turned rim, medium to coarse fabric, the core is dull red, the upper surface of the rim are two groove mark. The neck portion has beaded design due to the symmetrical press by the ledge portion.
18. Dish, black slipped ware, out-turn flat rim, the upper surface of the rim is decorated with incised design, in two segment the inner one are long type and outer one small in nature, medium to coarse fabric, the core is dull red.
19. Dish, red ware, everted flat rim, the upper surface is decorated with incised design, fine to medium fabric.
20. Spout, dull red ware, slow wheel made, it is used in a big pot, the joint portion has decorated with incised design in asymmetrical.
21. Handle, red ware, hand made, in the upper part of the joint shows design as two circular appliqué dot looks like circular eyes, fine to medium fabric; the cross section is thick.
22. Spout, red slipped ware, wheel made fine fabric, the outer surface has concentric groove design, and cross section is thin.
23. Spout, red slipped ware, wheel made, fine fabric, the outer surface has concentric groove design, and cross section is thin.
24. Knob of a lid, black polished ware, wheel made, and fine to medium fabric.
25. Pot (water pot), black polished ware, out turned ledge rim, low neck narrow mouth fine to medium fabric, the upper surface has deep concentric grooves.
26. Pot (water pot), grey ware, wheel made out turned ledge rim, narrow mouth, the upper surface has concentric grooves; core is grey, fine to medium fabric.
27. Basin, grey ware, wheel made, out turned rim, wide mouth, core is grey and has sandy particle, medium to coarse fabric.
28. Dish/Bowl, wheel made, the section is very thick ash grey in color.
29. Lamp with flat base, wheel made, and the string cutting marks observed at the base, Red ware, pentagonal cross section showing

one end small channel and decorated with circular appliqué design in the shape of eyes. Fine to medium fabric.

30. Lamp, red ware, wheel made, bi-convex in cross section, decorated with channel in one end and appliqué design on both sides show eyes on lamp, where as the channel shows as mouth, medium to coarse fabric.
31. Base, flat, black polished ware, medium to coarse fabric.

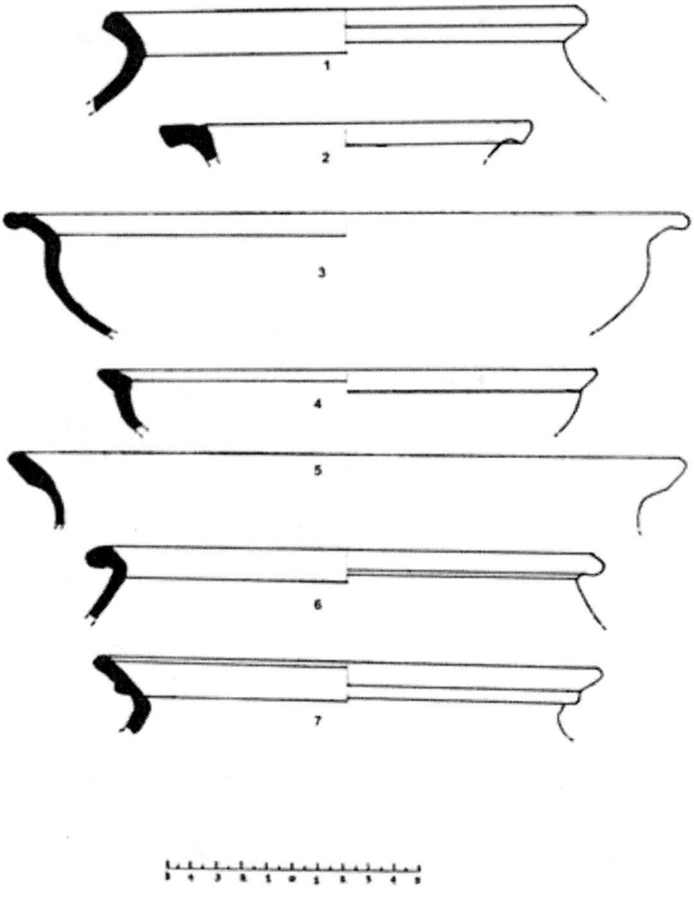

Fig.39: Pottery drawing of Katiragarh 1-7

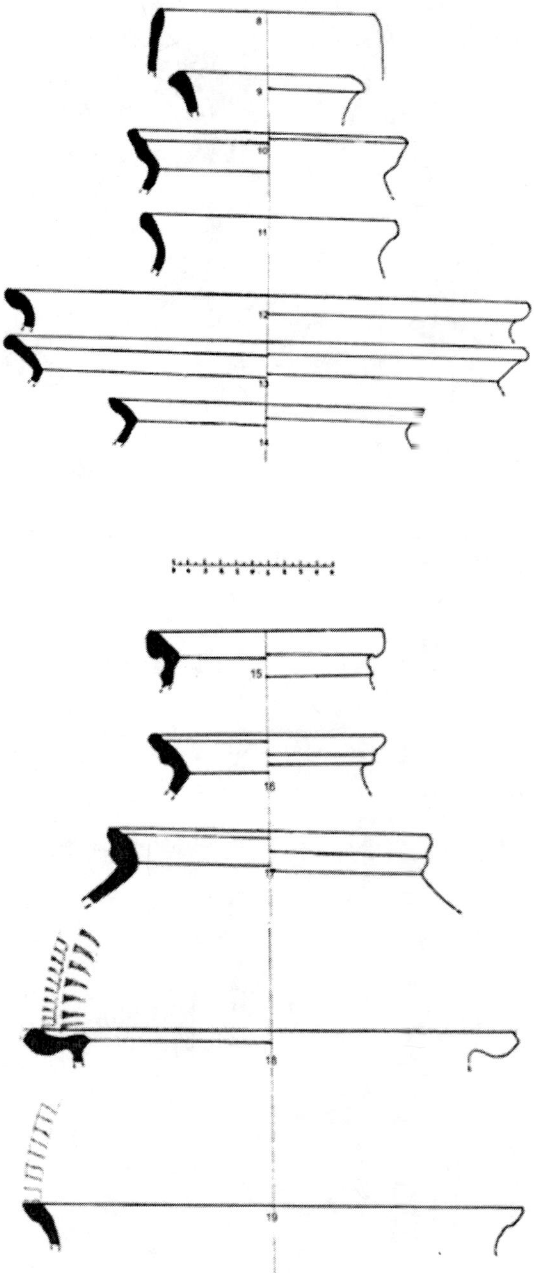

Fig.40: Pottery drawing of Kati agarh 8-19.

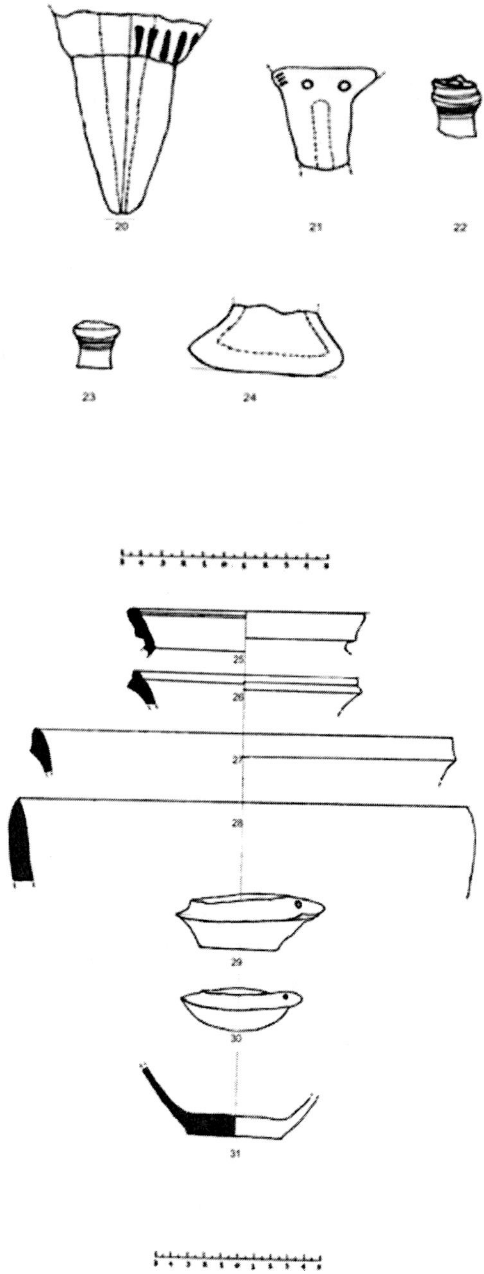

Fig.41: Pottery drawing of Katiragarh 20-31.

Nemliloti Shiva linga

It is another significant discovery of the survey. The site is located in the boarder land of Keonjhar and Angul district on the confluence of Kakharua and Badanadi. The site is locally known as Budha Mahadev. There are two Shiva lingas located close to each other, out of which one is beautifully carved and polished where as the other one is natural rolled rock with rough surface. These two are free standing without any Yonipitha and temple remains. The measurements of two Shiv lingas are dia-12 cm, length-16 cm and dia- 20 cm, length-24 cm, respectively (Pl.43).

Iron Implements from Rado MIP

From the Minor Irrigation Project Rado and its exposed section, three iron implements have been collected. These implements have heavy patina and are in brittle condition.

Implement No. 1

The specimen is identified as small chisel type for carving. The working end is sharp whereas its butt end is thick and tri-angular. The measurement of the specimen is 8.7 × 2.2 × 0.9 cms. in length, breadth and thickness respectively.

Implement No. 2

This is identified as nail, in which one end is pointed and butt end is thick. The matric measurement of the specimen is 4.6 × 1.0 × 0.7 cms. in length, breadth and thickness respectively.

Implement No. 3

This is also identified as nail, but a little bigger than the specimen No.2. The metric measurement of the specimen is 3.5 × 1.4 × 0.9 cms. in length, breadth and thickness respectively.

Bead

There are two beads collected from the erosional surface of the Rado MIP Irrigation project. These beads are made of terracotta. These two beads are described as short cylindrical and bi-conical type. The details of the collected beads are as follows.

Bead No. 1

Terracotta bead, Long barrel shaped. The maximum diameter and the length of the bead is 0.9 cm. and 3.1 cm. respectively (Pl.38).

Bead No. 2

This is bi-conical terracotta bead. The diameter and length of the bead is 0.9 cm. 3.2 cm respectively. (Pl.38)

Description of Potsherds (Fig. 42, Pl. 44)

1. Pot (Handi), wheel made, out turned rim, dull red ware, medium fabric, the core is dull red colour.
2. Pot (Water pot), wheel made, out turned beaded rim, narrow mouth, dull red ware, coarse to medium fabric, the core is dull red.
3. Pot (Water pot), wheel made, out turned beaded rim, narrow mouth, black ware, medium fabric, the core is dark grey in colour.
4. Pot, (Water pot), wheel made, out turned rim, narrow mouth, dull red ware, medium to coarse fabric, the core is dull red in colour.
5. Pot (Handi), wheel made, out turned rim, narrow mouth, black ware, medium fabric, the core is dark grey in colour.
6. Pot (Handi), wheel made, out turned rectangular rim, wide mouth, black ware, medium fabric, the core is dark grey in colour.
7. Pot (Handi), wheel made, out turned loop rim, black ware, medium fabric, the core is dark grey in colour.

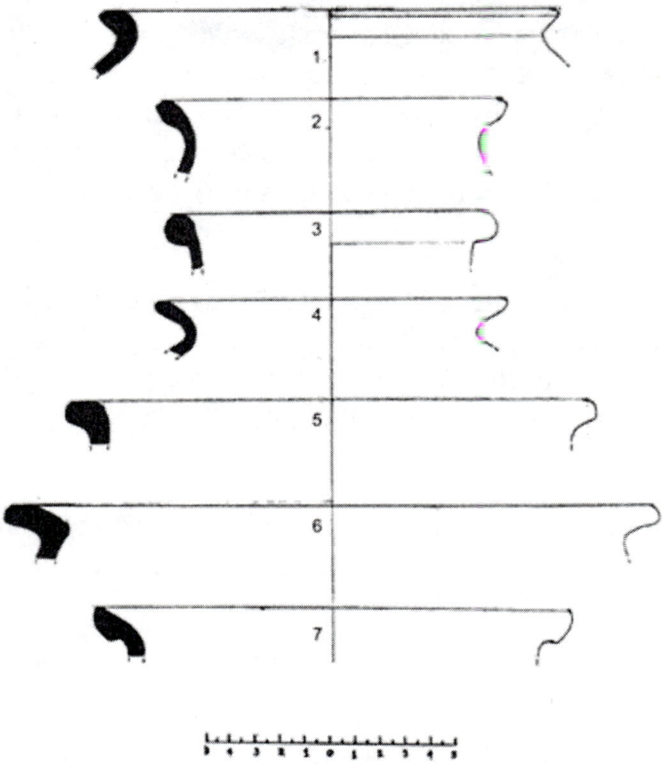

Fig.42: Pottery drawing of Radodiha MIP. 1-7

Dalo Purana Diha (Jamardiha)

Unlike the Katiragarh, in the site Dalo Puruna diha a number of stone implements of historical period has been collected. These stone objects include saddle quern and muller. Almost all stone objects are made on locally available raw materials like cherty quartzite, sand stone, etc. The details of these stone objects are described below.

Saddle Quern

(DPD-1)

The site yielded a fragment of saddle quern. This is irregular in shape and made on sand stone. The present length, breadth and thickness of the object is 16.7 x 10.1 x 9.8 cms. This is of flat base with use mark noticed on both surface. Due to prolonged use of the object, one side of the surface has swallow surface (Fig.43, Pl. 45). However, it is also noticed that the tribal people of the area also used flat based irregular shaped local stone for saddle quern for preparing rice paste and curry paste.

DPD-2

A fragment of muller with a circular cross-section and oblong shape, made out of sand stone has been collected. The metric measurement of the specimen is 6.5 x 5.5 cms. in length and thickness respectively (Fig.43, Pl. 45).

DPD-3

A broken muller is triangular in cross section. Made out of sand stone, it measures 6.0 x 5.7 cms. in length and thickness respectively (Fig.43, Pl. 45).

DPD-4

A fragment of muller, it is roughly oval in cross section made out of sand stone. The metric measurement is 11.1 x 7.2 cms. in length and breadth respectively (Fig.43, Pl. 45).

DPD-5

Fragment of muller oblong variety, circular cross section, and measurement of the specimen is 6.5 x 7.1 cms. length & breadth respectively (Fig.43, Pl. 45).

Description of Potsherds (Fig.43 & 44, Pl. 46)

1. Pot (Handi), black and red ware, wheel made, medium to coarse fabric, out-turned rim, cross section is dark grey. The rim has deep groove.
2. Pot (Handi), black and red ware, wheel made, fine to medium fabric, out-turned rim, cross section is dark grey, the rim has two deep grooves.

3. Pot (Handi), black and red ware, medium to fine fabric out turned rim, cross section is thin and dark grey in color, deep groove marked on rim.
4. Pot, black and red ware, wheel made, medium to fine fabric, out turned rim, the end portion is sharp, cross section is thick and dark grey in colour possibly used as storage jar because of the medium mouth.
5. Basin, red ware, roughly rectangular rim with groove on it, medium fabric, cross section is medium and red in color.
6. Pot (Handi) black and red ware, wheel made, medium to fine fabric, out turned rim. The cross section is dark grey in color.
7. Pot (Handi), red slipped ware, wheel made medium to fine fabric, out turned rim, the slip is applied in some part of the outer rim.
8. Pot (Handi), out turned rim, black and red ware, fine to medium fabric, wheel made, cross section is dark grey and two grooves mark on the rim.
9. Pot (Handi), out turned rim, wheel made, dull red ware, fine to medium fabric, the cross section is dull red.
10. Pot (Handi), out turned loop rim, wheel made, dull red ware, fine to medium fabric, the core is dull red, cross section is thin.
11. Pot (Handi), out turned beaded rim, wheel made, medium to coarse fabric, dull red ware, core is ill fired, the cross section is thin.
12. Pot (Handi), out turned loop rim, black and red ware, wheel made, core is red, two grooves marked on rim, the cross section is thin, fine to medium fabric. This pot is large in size.
13. Pot with medium mouth (water pot), out turned with loop rim, wheel made, dull red ware, the core is grey whereas its outer area is red, the upper part of rim showing concentric groove mark, medium to coarse fabric.
14. Pot with medium mouth, everted pointed rim, black and red ware, wheel made, fine to medium fabric, the cross section is thin, the core is dark grey.

15. Pot with small mouth (water pot), everted rim, dull red ware, fine to medium fabric, the cross section is medium, core is dull red, three concentric groove marks in the upper surface of rim.

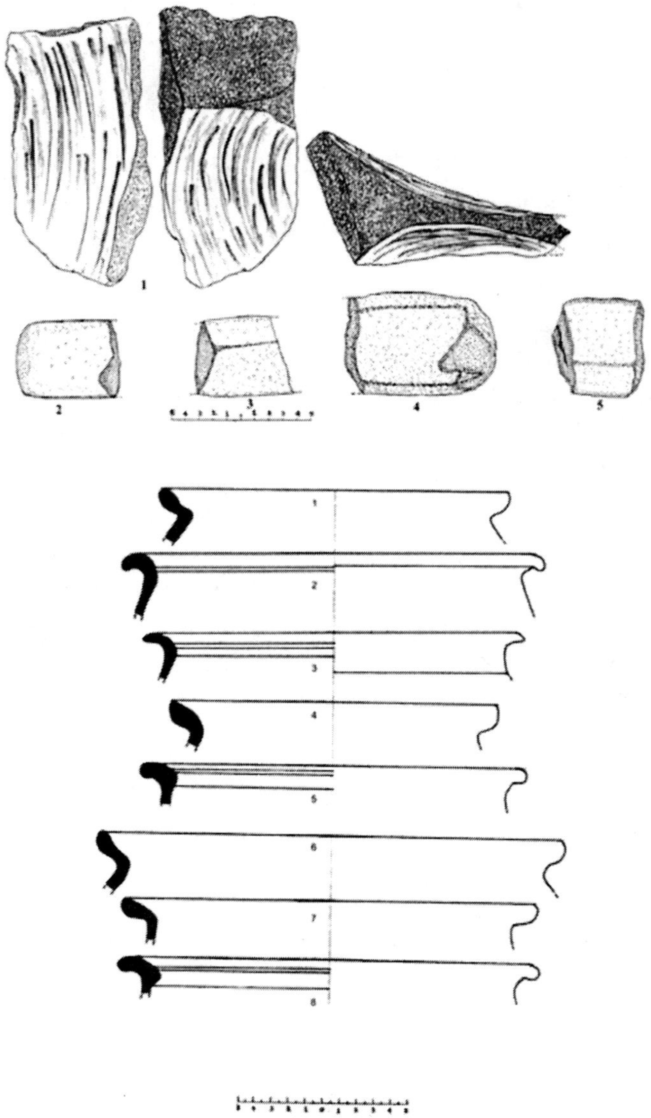

Fig.43: Dalo Puruna diha; stone artefacts; 1-saddle queen, 2, 3, 4, 5 pestle/muller fragments, pottery; 1-8

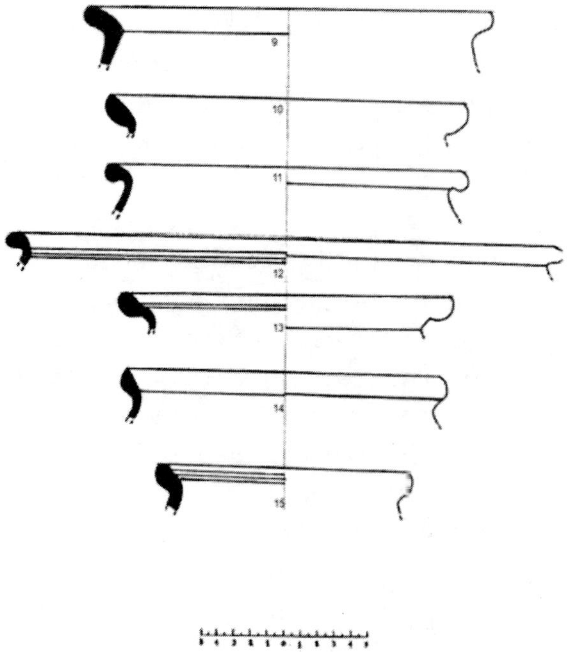

Fig.44: Pottery drawing of Dalo Puruna diha 9-15

Discussion on Historical Archaeology

After careful observation of the historical sites in the Kakharua valley it is noticed that the river valley has small but significant sites relating to the historical period bearing antiquity on either bank of river. These are basically located in long interval due to the natural setup of the region. However, the three sites Nemliloti, Rado MIP and Katiragarh fall in the Keonjhar district, where as the Dalo Puruna diha (Jamar diha) is in Angul district. The Rado MIP and Nemliloti are small in size where as the Katiragarh and Dalo Puruna diha (Jamar diha) is relatively large. Besides, the suffix garh reflects fort in the region or a city where the royal family inhabited. Similarly, Jamar diha reflects the land or area of Jamar family of Jama or Yama; the death God.

Presently, the whole region is inhabited by tribal people such as Pahuri Bhuiyan with other general caste people. Katiragarh has good number of archaeological edifices which signify it as an important site in the hinter land. However, after a study of the Keonjhar's Bhanja dynasty and other important places, it is found that the first Bhanja ruler of Keonjhar, Jyoti Bhanja ruled from a place named "Kanea garh" or "Karua garh" situated nearby Banspal village in a difficult terrain. This is also reflected in Pahuri Bhuiyan song (Das 1989 :200-208). The present antiquities and structural remains like the sculpture of different deities, *Amlaka* of temple, *Urusrunga*, Shiva linga and lateritic structure, lateritic pillar imply that it was an important place. The name Karua garh is Katiragarh because of the name of the Kanea garh or Karua garh is changed in phonetic and presently known as Katiragarh. Secondly, the large number of Brahmanical deities and the structural edifices similar with the Khiching and Benisagar antiquities (Dehuri 2012:68-73) which flourished in the same time period.

The Rado MIP site is close to the Katiragarh site and the antiquities recovered from the site like potsherds, beads, iron implements are quite similar to the Katiragarh site which might be a satellite settlement of the said site.

Another site, Dalo Puruna diha, is located left side of the river Kakharua near the iron crusher of Jamar diha village. The site is extended upto Dalo Puruna diha village. A huge amount of potsherds have been collected from the site but unfortunately the site does not have any structural remains due to heavy destruction of the site such as the construction of two metallic road, iron ore crusher with a staging yard, and digging canal in the nearly area. However, the site is represented by a very thin cultural deposit, which is noticed nearby at, the newly constructed canal region. There is a literary evidence of Jamagarta mandala, a medieval settlement developed in the region whose identification could not be established so far by historian or archaeologist. One may say that the site of Dalo Puruna diha (Jamar diha) could be the Jamagarta mandala of the Medieval period. However, more evidence is required to substantiate it further.

The site Nemliloti yielded a Shiva linga, which is again an interesting aspect because the site is under a dense forest and the local inhabitants are tribal people. So from this finding we could conclude that the site represents an example of incorporation of Brahmanical traits in tribal culture.

The detailed analysis of the finding of potsherds in this chapter provides that the proliferation of shapes, standardized cognitive types, surface features and decorative features represent a considerable advancement in the ceramic tradition. The surface (earth) behaviour of the sites presumes that the potsherds were imported most probably from satellite sites. Due to single culture assemblages, the associated antiquarian remains have provided much information of the culture assemblages. The pottery recovered from the Katiragarh is dominated by red ware and black ware, fabric ranging from medium to coarse. Dalo Puruna diha (Jamar diha) is another important settlement which yielded a good number of potsherds. The red wares are of dominant variety and spread over vast patch of area with minor variety of grey wares. In the Rado diha MIP site the red ware is of dominant variety. Over all the stylistic features such as form and decoration are also significant indicators of social and cultural organization. The recovery of spouted pottery and associated with the sculptural remains ware used for ritual purpose. Many of lamps with pointed wicked channel with soot mark refer to increased proliferation of ritual purposes. Images of Bhairava and Vishnu have been noticed inside the jungle is a significant discovery for this region. The iconographic study of the two specimens represents a highly balanced style of execution. The Bhairava image and his vehicle dog is broken (since their heads are missing) where as the bejewelled Vishnu image is standing and well depicted with demi God at either side.

Main Features of the Historical Archaeology

Some historical sites were discovered as a result of the present exploration. These sites are Katiragarh, Rado MIP Nemliloti and Dalo Puruna diha. The material evidences are basically the household items, iron implements, potsherds, ornamental objects, art and sculptural remains.

1. The discoveries of quern, muller and pestles in these historical sites show that the people used these implements for grinding purpose of food grain and other food staple implying a technological continuity.
2. The sculptural and structural remains highlight the religious behaviour of the people. The presence of sculptures implies the prevalence of Brahmanism in the area.
3. Identified images of Bhairava and Vishnu from Katiragarh site is a significant discovery for this region. The iconographic study of the two specimens represent a highly balanced style of execution
4. Ceramics is a good index of cultural continuity and change. Study of pottery has been utterly neglected in medieval archaeology of Odissa. However, the study has yielded a good amount of ceramics from the historical site Katiragarh, Rado MIP and Dalo Puruna diha.
5. A number of glass bangles and terracotta beads have been found from the site of Katiragarh which highlight, the ornamental aspects. The opaque glass bangle with superior workmanship is an important recovery. Besides, terracotta bead of short cylindrical shape might have been used as necklace. In this connection these bangles and beads demonstrate that the people of the area used them as ornaments.
6. The recovery of the iron implements from Katiragarh and Rado MIP along with iron slags imply that iron smelting technology in the area work was prevalent.
7. The finding of Shiva linga and worship by the local Bhuiyan tribe in the area implies that apart from nature worship of the Bhuiyan the area had evidence of the belief in Hindu aspect of thought and belief. Both the Shiva linga at Nemlitoli and one at the Katiragarh are datable to the medieval period.

Summary and Conclusion

In spite of the progress made in different aspects of archaeology in Odisha, the north central part had not received the required attention it deserves. The present investigation is a modest attempt to fill up that inadequacy. In this section, a summary is provided for all the chapters. In order to provide a background, prior to the Chapter 1, a general introduction was given with the author's interest in this region and potentiality of the sites. The surface exploration with a micro area approach yielded good evidence of lithic remains. With this view, the aims and objectives of the present study are highlighted. These include studying the valley of the Kakharua- a major tributary to the Brahmani - and its surrounding hilly landscape to locate archaeological sites relating to Prehistoric as well as Historical period. Earlier there was no comprehensive work on north central Odisha hence the present attempt. The methods adopted include study of maps and topo-sheets, intensive surface exploration, section scraping, grid, mapping, plotting, drawing, photography and scientific analysis etc. The following would contain a summary of different chapter.

Chapter-1 is basically a review of literature on Indian archaeology as well as a brief note on Odishan archaeology. In particular the limitations of the study on archaeology of Odisha are pointed out. This is succeeded by the review of literature on the archaeological work of north central Odisha.

Chapter -2 describes the study area and the present environment. The description of the region of north central Odisha includes the location, the administrative background, and present environment, such as physiographic features, forest, hill, drainage, system, geology, climate, rain fall and population. The river systems include the Baitarani and the Brahmani river system along with small streamlets.

The Chapter-3 contains descriptions of 30 sites discovered in the Kakharua valley from my surface exploration and an account of the stratigraphy of the area. The total number of 664 artefacts recovered from various sites is presented in a tabular form.

The Chapter-4 contains an account of the palaeolithic and mesolithic recoveries from present survey in the Kakharua valley. With regard to the palaeolithic culture, only one site (Barikaguda) has been found with three artefacts. Hence, it may be inferred that the Kakharua valley had not attracted much attention of palaeolithic people. On the other hand, we come across 15 sites with microlithic artefacts. This implies that during mesolithic period, the Kakharua valley became an important destination of prehistoric man. This chapter is devoted to the distribution and analysis of artefacts of palaeolithic and microlithic in tabular forms, in which the mean metric measurements, mean ratio and their percentage with raw material is discussed. The sites were discussed under four eco-zones: riverbank, foothill, piedmont and foothill-cum river bank. The detailed studies of the artefacts are arranged eco-zone wise and site-wise typologically with total and its percentage.

The microlithic artefacts have been divided into two components i.e flake and blade. The flake component includes the types of side scraper, end scraper, thumb nail scraper, borer, utilized flakes, round scraper, borer cum scraper, blade core, concave scraper, notch scraper, side cum end scraper, tanged point, scraper, flake, micro borer, blade cum borer and microlithic chips. The blade component includes the types of blade, parallel sided blade, pen knife blade, point, crescent, triangle, trapezoid, blade cum scraper, crescent cum borer, keel blade, blade fragment, blade (micro), blade cum borer, point with deep notch and burin. An important feature is that the Kakharua river valley culture has a well-developed blade technology.

The different tool types imply their use for different range of activities, such as cutting, piercing, scraping, boring etc. Hence, the mesolithic sites in the Kakharua valley could have functioned as camp sites with short term occupation. On the basis of available data, it is not possible to identify which was the base camp. In addition to quartz and other siliceous rock, chert is the dominant raw material for manufacturing of tiny sophisticated artefacts. It is also the easily collected/available rock type in the area. The recovery of a number of blade cores in some sites implies exploitation of local raw materials. However, no mesolithic manufacturing site could be precisely determined. No large site with heavy duty lithic component is reported from the Kakharua survey, therefore, the mesolithic culture is supposed to be used for different subsistence pattern as seasonal food gathering. The piedmont sites represent 160 no of specimens (40.81%) of microliths of mesolithic period and occupy the highest range of artefacts where as the foot hill site yielded very low amount of implements such as 17 no of specimens (4.33%). Followed by that, the river bank site was represented by 137 no of specimens (34.94%) and the river bank cum foot hill site yielded 78 specimens (19.89%). In the blade component, blade represent highest 74 specimens (34.24%) and followed to that point 35 (16.20%), parallel sided blade 31 (14.35%) besides other minor artefacts. In flake component flake core/blade core is dominant variety representing 34 specimens (19.31%). Next to that borer represent 31 specimens (17.62%) and side scraper 22 specimens (12.5%) apart from the other minor artefacts.

In Chapter-5 the relics of neolithic culture and the distribution of neolithic sites were discussed. It is very much significant that a number of neolithic sites have been reported from this region. For example Basa, Das and Mohanta have reported neolithic remains in Pallahara region (2000), While Behera (2000) did so in Bonaigarh region. Like microlithic sites, the sites are also divided into four eco-zones such as river bank site, foot hill site, piedmont site and river bank cum foothill site. The site-wise distribution and analysis of artefacts of the neolithic culture are represented in tabular form, in which the mean metric measurements, mean ratio and its percentage with raw material are discussed. Again the whole neolithic remains were discussed under two components such as celt component and pebble component. Further, the celt component is divided typologically as axe, adze, chisel, shouldered axe, bar celt, unfinished intermediate axe, broken axe and neolithic blank. The pebble component is divided into ring stone and polisher/dimple mark hammer stone. Another interesting aspect of these eco-zonal distributions find is that the river bank site has yielded a large number of tools. In case of neolithic, the river bank-cum-foot hill site has yielded very less amount of tools. This is followed by a typo-technological discussion on axe, adze, chisel. These are represented in tabular form. The artefacts have been grouped into three broad categories as per technological point of view such as flaked and chipped type, flaked-chipped and partly ground and the last one is fully ground and polished type. A careful observation of these artefacts shows that flaked and chipped variety are mainly collected from workshop site and the flaked-chipped and partly ground type are found both in the workshop site and operational area where as the fully ground and polished axe are noticed in operational area only. The different size range of neolithic typology is represented in a tabular form. Raw material distribution is also presented in tabular form and with a bar diagram. The dominant variety of raw material is dolerite. Almost all the artefacts, made on the dolerite show patination of various degrees and colour ranging from reddish brown to yellowish colour. It is interesting to note that from the survey raw material outcrops are located in the Kakharua Protection Forest site with a huge amount of large flake and chips. The recoveries of artefacts are discussed under the celt component and pebble component under the category of flaked and chipped variety, partially chipped and partially ground and the fully ground polished tool. Besides, the selected artefacts are discussed briefly with photograph and drawings. The main features are also discussed including the general characteristics of morphological and typo-technological features. The celt component includes the celt variants. The pebble component comprises the artefacts assemblages made both on nodules and river pebbles characterized by the types such as ring stone, dimple marked hammer stone and blank etc. shouldered axe is more widely reported from coastal Odisha, where as shouldered axe in the present study, north-central Odisha is very rare. The neolithic artefacts of Baisnavadar, Bisriguda and Kakharua Protection Forest site have large production unit with semi-finished celts, from where neolithic artefacts were manufactured. The Kakharua Protection site has evidence of raw material outcrops. The evidence implies that there are two phases of workmanship. The first phase involved the big blank extracted from the outcrop without any evidence of any finished or semi-finished artefacts. However, there are flakes of large size. The second phase of manufacturing shows sites having small flakes and chips along with semi-finished and finished tool. On the functionary aspect and compared with South-east Asia and China, the central Odishan stone bars specifically from Sankerjang have been considered as lithophone (Yule et al 2000). So the stone celt recovered from Sorbeda kudur site is comparable with the type-II variety of Sankarjang lithophone. As per finished and semi-finished artefacts, axe and adze are the two dominant types of artefacts of the celt component. Of these two types axes and adzes of flaked and chipped, flaked chipped and partially ground and fully ground are generally characterized by convex to straight working edge, faceted to pointed and oblique butt-end, bi-convex to trapezoidal cross section

The north Odisha has yielded potsherds with neolithic remains but it is interesting to note that no pottery was recovered from the present investigation. The neolithic cultural assemblages, as revealed is very rich in quantity and having flaked and chipped type with very little ground form in working area. The materials are closely similar to those of Bajpur, Telkoi, Bonaigarh cultural assemblages because these sites fall in the same region.

There is very limited excavation in this region, so it is difficult to determine the chronology. However, the Barudih cultural complex is dated around 1100 BC (Agrawal 1984) and the metal age site

Sankerjang, which is close to Kakharua valley is dated to early 1st millennium BC. In view of these two sites the Kakharua neolithic settlements are ascribed to latter half of the second millennium BC. In respect to typological aspect, the fully ground celt is very few and the shouldered celt is restricted to one specimen only. Techno-typologically the celt constitutes a number of variations particularly the convex to straight type working edge, convex to-pointed butt end and rectangular to trapezoidal cross-section.

The neolithic settlements site follow-up linear pattern and are located along with the water source of the river which suggest that the prehistoric people might have exploited the water source as well as the nearby land. The evidence of large quantity of neolithic flakes and chips noticed with semi-finished or chipped variety of stone implements in Baisnavadar, Bisriguda and Bijagotha Hatapada sites imply workshop area for neolithic manufacturing. It has also been reported that the raw material site in this nearby hilly region support the view of manufacturing activities in the region which was also noticed in the Bonaigarh region by Behera.

In Chapter-6 site of historical periods and their material culture were discussed. To begin with the historical recoveries, the sculptural remains from Katiragarh were unique finding in the locality. The sculptural remains and other antiquities are briefly discussed under this broad head line of the analysis of findings. A good quality of ceramic remains is also discussed and reported different type water pot, dish, lamp etc. Followed to the site Nemliloti Shiva linga, Rado MIP iron implements, potsherds are discussed briefly. The material of Dalo Puruna diha site is also discussed. The chapter also contains a note on the discoveries of quern, muller and pestles in these historical sites showing that the people used these implements for grinding purpose of food grain and other food staple. The sculptural remains and structural edifices highlight the religious behaviour of the people and presence of such sculptures implies the prevalence of Brahminism in the area. The finding of Shiva linga and worship by the local Bhuiyan tribe in the area implies that the incorporation of Brahmanical elements in their culture. Both the Shiva lingas at Nemlitoli and one at the Katiragarh are datable to the medieval period. Ceramics are good index of cultural continuity and change. Study of pottery has been utterly neglected in medieval archaeology of Odisha. However, the study has yielded a good amount of ceramics from the historical site Katiragarh, Rado MIP and Dalo Puruna diha which would provide data, with implications for chronology. A number of small antiquities like glass bangles and terracotta beads have been found from the site of Katiragarh highlights, the ornamental aspects. In this connection these bangles and beads demonstrate that the people of the area used them as ornaments. The recovery of the iron implements from Katiragarh and Rado MIP along with iron slags focus that iron smelting technology in the area was prevalent. Broadly, the remains of the historical artefacts possibly belonged to the medieval period.

However, the survey could not locate any chalcolithic site where as chalcolithic site of Kuanr is close to the study area. Before one concludes, one could humbly state that this is quite a modest attempt to reconstruct the archaeological prospect of north-central Odisha. The archaeological remains clearly imply that the area shows a sequence from palaeolithic to historical period, in which sites with the microliths and neolithic or ground stone tools are more numerous. But we could not found chalcolithic and early historical remains from our survey. However, some more work has to be done, which in my opinion, should engage the attention of scholars.

Scope for future work:-

1. Very few number of Palaeolithic tools have been reported from this survey. More survey in relation of other streams and channels may yield more evidence.
2. No ceramic is associated with ground and polishing stone culture (Neolithic Culture) from the present study area.
3. No Chalcolithic site has been located. Hence, more survey should be conducted, to bridge the cultural gaps of area.

4. No major excavation has been conducted in north central Odisha. Problem oriented excavation of sites belonging to different period is the need of the hour.
5. Attempt should be made for recovery of Iron age sites.
6. Although the present survey identifying has resulted is the few historical sites they are considered to be belonging medieval period. So attempt of should also be made for the recovery of early historical as well as iron age site.
7. The study area has been inhabited by tribal people like Pahari Bhuiyan, Juang, Munda etc. So further study with an ethno-archaeological prospective could help interpret the archaeological data more meaningfully.
8. The scientific analysis and inter disciplinary approach should be followed to focus the question of provenance of various artefacts.

In a true sense, it is holistic approach towards the reconstruction of the cultural pattern of north central Odisha.

Bibliography

Acharya, P. 1923-29 *Annual Report of the Archaeological Survey of India*. pp. 100-101.

Acharya. P. and R.P. Chanda, 1930 Exploration in Orissa. *Memories of Archaeological Survey of India.* Calcutta.

Acharya, P. 1934 Monuments of Khiching. *The Mayurbhanj Gazette*, January: 1934:10 - 15.

Acharya, P. 1969 *Odisara Pratnatatwa O Anyanya Prabandha* (In Oriya) part-I, Bhubaneswar, Odisa Sahitya Academy.

Agrawal, D.P. 1969 *The Copper and Bronze Age in India*. Delhi; Munshiram Manoharlal.

Agrawal, D.P. 1984 *Archaeology of India*. New Delhi: Select Book Service Syndicate.

Agrawal, D.P. 1982 *The Archaeology of India*. London: Curzon Press.

Agrawal, D.P. 1984 Origin of Metallurgy in Asia: Myth and Reality. In Bayard, D. (edited) *South Asian Archaeology*. Dunedin, pp. 261-269.

Allchin, Bridget & Raymond Allchin 1968 *The Birth of Indian Civilization*. Middlesex (England): Penguin Books Ltd. Harmendsworth.

Allchin, F.R. 1984 *Archaeology of India*. New Delhi: Select Book Service Syndicate.

Allchin, F.R. 1989a City and State Formation in Early History South Asia. *South Asian Studies* 5:1-16.

Allchin, F.R. 1989b Patterns of City Formation in Early History South Asia. *South Asian Studies* 6:163-73.

Allchin, B and F.R Allchin 1982 *The Rise of Civilization in India and Pakistan*. Cambridge: Cambridge University Press.

Ball, V. 1876 On stone implements found in the tributary states of Orissa. *Proceeding of the Asiatic Society of Bengal* (1876), pp.120-121.

Banarjee, N.R. 1965a *The Iron Age in India*. New Delhi: Munshiram Monharlal.

Banerjee. N.R. 1965b The Iron Age in India. In (pp.177-199) V.N. Misra and M.S. Mate (edited) *Indian prehistory: 1964*, Pune: Deccan College.

Banerji, M.N. 1927 On Metals and Metallurgy in Ancient India. *Indian Historical Quarterly*, III: 121-33, 793-802.

Banerji, R.D. 1930 *History of Orissa*, Vol.-I, Vol.-II, Calcutta. R. Chattarjee.

Banarji, C. S. 1870 Notes on the antiquities of the Nalti, the Asia, and the Mahabinayaka hills of Cuttack. *Journal of the Asiatic Society of Bengal* 39 (part-I):158-171.

Banarji, C.S. 1871 An account of the antiquities of Jajpur in Orissa. *Journal of the Asiatic Society of Bengal,* 40:151-159.

Basa, K.K. 1994 *Problems and Perspectives in Archaeology of Orissa*, Occasional Paper, DSA in Anthropology, Utkal University, Bhubaneswar, India.

Basa, K.K. 1997 Archaeological Heritage In (pp.18-45) P.K. Mishra and J.K. Samal (edited) *Comprehensive History and Culture of Orissa*. Vol-1 (I), New Delhi, Karen Books.

Basa, K.K. 2000 History of Archaeology in Orissa. In (pp.16-61) K.K. Basa and P. Mohanty (edited) *Archaeology of Orissa*.

Basa, K.K., T.K. Das and B.K. Mohanta 2000 Neolithic Culture of Pallahara, Central Orissa. In (pp. 264-84) K.K. Basa and P. Mohanty (edited) *Archaeology of Orissa*.

Behera, P.K. 1989 *Archaeology of Sundergarh District with special reference to the Brahmani Valley, Orissa*. Unpublished Ph.D Thesis, Banaras Hindu University, Varanasi.

Behera, P.K. 1991-92 Sulabhdihi: A Neolithic Celt Manufacturing Centre in Orissa. *Puratattava* 22: 124-132.

Behera, P.K. 1992 The Pebble Tool Component of the Bonaigarh Neolithic Complex, Orissa. *Man and Environment*, 18(2):57-63.

Behera, P.K. 2000 Neolithic Culture Complex of Bonaigarh Orissa. In (pp. 222-263) Basa, K.K. and P. Mohanty edited *Archaeology of Orissa*, Vol-I, New Delhi: Pratibha Prakashan.

Behera, P.K. 2000-01a Investigations into the newly discovered rock art sites of Deulga hills, Orissa. *Pragdhara*, 2:1-11.

Behera, P.K. 2000-01b Excavations at Khambeswaripali – A proto historic Settlement in the middle Mahanadi Valley, Orissa: A Preliminary Report. *Pragdhara*, 2:13-34.

Behera, P.K. 2002 Khambeswaripali- A Protohistoric settlement in the middle Mahanadi valley, Orissa; Result of first seasons (1996-97). In (pp.493-532) G. Sengupta and Sheena Panja (edited) *Archaeology of Eastern India New Perspectives*. Kolkata: Centre for Archaeological Studies and Training, Eastern India.

Behera, K.S. 1993 *Temples of Orissa*. Bhubaneswar: Sahitya Academy Orissa.

Bose, N.K. and D. Sen. 1948 *Excavation in Mayurbhanj*. Calcutta: University of Calcutta.

Brown, P. 1971 *Indian Architecture (Hindu and Buddhist Period)*. Bombay.

Bradthner, M. 1994 Archaeology of Western Orissa; Finds from Nehana. In (pp. 101-14) A. Parpola and P. koskikallio (edited) *South Asian Archaeology 1993*, Helsinki: Southmalainen Tiedeakatemia,Vol-1.

Burkit, M.C.1955 *The Old Stone Age Tools* (3rd edition), Cambridge.

Chakrabarti, D.K. 1976 The Beginning of Iron in India. *Antiquity* L:114-124.

Chakrabarti, D.K. 1988 *A History of Indian Archaeology, From the Beginning to 1947*. New Delhi: Munsiram Monoharlal Publishers Pvt. Ltd.

Chakrabarti, D.K. 1992 *The Early Use of Iron in India.* Delhi; Oxford University Press.

Chakrabarti, D. K. 1999 *India: An Archaeological History (Palaeolithic Beginnings to Early Historic foundations)* New Delhi: Oxford University Press.

Chakraborti, S. 2000 Recent Advances in Prehistory of Mayurbhanj. In (pp. 77-101) K. K. Basa and P. Mohanty (edited) *Archaeology of Orissa*, Vol.1.

Chanda, R.P. 1927 Notes on the Ancient Monuments of Mayurbhanj. *Journal of Bihar Orissa Research Society*, 13(2):131-136.

Chanda, R.P. 1929 *Bhanja Dynasty of Mayurbhanj and Their Ancient Capital Khiching*. Mayurbhanj Archaeological Department.

Chanda, R.P. 1949 *History of Mayurbhanj* 1761-1861, Part- I. Calcutta: Baptist Mission Press.

Chhotray, P.K. 2000 Asurgarh, the mysteries mound in Mahanadi Valley. In *Orissa Review* (in oriya), October. pp. 24-26.

Childe, V.G. 1951 *Social Evolution*. New York: Schumann.

Commiade, L.A. and Burkitt, M.C. 1930. Fresh light on the Stone ages of South east India, *Antiquity* 4.

Dahejia, V. 1979 *Early stone temples of Orissa*. New Delhi: Vikas Publication.

Daniel, G.1968 *The First Civilizatio: The Archaeology of their Origin.* New York: Thomas Y. Crowell (Apollo- Edition).

Daniel, G. 1971 *The Idea of Prehistory.* Edinburg: Edinburg University Press.

Das, T.K. 1995 *Surface Exploration Around Pallahara*, Unpublished M.A. dissertation, Department of Anthropology, Utkal University.

Das, Bipin Bihari 1989 *Shri Bhanja Bhumi Kendujhari* (In Oriya), Barbil: Neelachal Prakashani.

Dash, R.N. 1986 Sankerjang – A Chalcolithic site in Orissa. *The Orissa Historical Research Journal*. 32 (1-2):99-105.

Dash, R.N. 1987-88 *Neoliths of Orissa*. Unpublished Ph.D. Thesis, Utkal University, Bhubaneswar.

Dash, R.N. 1989 Chalcolithic and Copper Bronze Age Cultures in Orissa, *Proceedings of the X Annual Session of the Orissa History Congress*. Bhubaneswar; Rajdhani College. pp. 22-25.

Dash, R.N. 1990-93 Orissa Neoliths: A Typo-technological Study. *Manav* 4:127-147.

Dash, R.N. 2000 The Neolithic Culture of Orissa: A Typo-technological Analysis. In (pp. 201-21) K. K. Basa and P. Mohanty (edited) *Archaeology of Orissa*.

De Terra, H. and T.T. Paterson. 1939 *Studies on The Ice Age in India and Associated Human Cultures*, Washington.

Dehuri, R. 1997 *Archaeological Excavation at Kamparkala, Central Orissa*. Unpublished M.A. dissertation, Department of Anthropology, Utkal University. Bhubaneswar.

Dehuri, R. 1998 *Prehistoric Culture Around Telkoi, District: Keonjhar, Orissa*. Unpublished M.Phil. dissertation, Department of Anthropology, Utkal University, Bhubaneswar.

Dehuri, R. 2004 Paleo Relics around Telkoi, Dist- Keonjhar. *In Orissa Historical Research Journal*, Orissa State Museum, Bhubaneswar. Vol-XLVII, 4: 68-71.

Dehuri, R. 2011 Microlithic culture around Kakharua Valley, North Central Orissa. *Kosala* 4:100-106.

Dehuri, R. 2012 Some evidences of Neolithic remains around Kakharua valley in North Central Orissa, A preliminary study. *Kosala* 5:71-78.

Dehuri, R. n.d. Archaeology of Kakharua Valley, North Central Odisha. Paper selected for *Karuna Shree*, (A volume for Professor Karuna Sagar Behara).

Dehuri, R. 2012 New light on Art and Architectural Tradition of Benisagar, West Singhbum, Jharkhand. In *Central India Journal of Historical And Archaeological Research*, Vol-I (4): 68-73.

Deo, S.B. and M.K. Dhavilkar.1967 *Paunar Excavations*. Nagpur.

Deo, S.B. and J. P. Joshi 1972 *Pauni Excavations*. Nagpur.

Deo, S.B. and Gupta R.S. 1974 *Excavations at Bhokardan*. Nagpur.

Deo, S.B. 1985 Historical Archaeology; Review and perspective. In (pp.87-96) K.N Dikshit (edited) *Archaeological perspective of India since Independence*. New Delhi: Books & Books.

Deva, K. and V.K. Mishra. 1950 *Vaisali Excavation*. Vaishali.

Foote, R. B. 1916, The Foote Collection of Indian Prehistoric and Protohistoric Antiquities, Notes on their ages and distribution, Government Museum, Madras.

Foote, R.B. 1866 On the occurence of stone implements in the lateritic formation in various parts of Madras and north Arcot Districts, *Madras Journal of Literature and Science* 2 , reproduced in Studies in Prehistory, D. Sen and A Ghosh edited firma K.L Mukhapadhyay, Calcutta.

Foote, R.B. 1987 Notes on Some Recent Neolithic and Palaeolithic in South India. *Journal of the Asiatic Society of Bengal*, Vol. LV: 92:259-282.

Ganguly, M.M. 1916 *Orissa and Her Remains*. Calcutta: Thacker Spink and Co.

Ghosh, A. 1973 *The City in Early Historical India*. Simla: Indian Institute of Advanced Studies.

Ghosh, A.K. 1961 Prehistoric Studies in Eastern India. *Science and Culture*, 27 (8):36-75.

Ghosh, A.K. and P.K. Chattopadhyay 1982 An early steel implement from Barudih, Bihar province, India: Metallurgical studies. *MASCA Journal*. University of Pennsylvania, 2(2):63-64.

Ghosh, Asok, K. Ranjana Ray, & P.G. Chatterjee. 1984a On Barudih; A Neolithic site in Bihar. *Bulletin of Indo Pacific Prehistory Association* 5:24-28.

Ghosh, Asok, K. Ranjana Ray, Panchu Chatterjee, Paresh Nanda & Peter Bellowood. 1984b Archaeological Reconnaissance in the Sanjai

Valley, Singhbhum District, Bihar. *Bulletin of the Indo-Pacific Prehistory Association* 5:29-37.

Gopinath Rao, T.A. 1914-16 *Elements of Hindu Iconography*, Madras, Vol-II, part-1. pp.55-63.

Government of Orissa 1971 *Census of India* 1971. Ser.16. Orissa, part-X, Dhenkanal, District Census Hand book 8 (Cuttack 6:1972). pp.264-265.

Hegde, K.T.M. 1981 Scientific basis and technology of ancient Indian copper and iron metallurgy. *Indian Journal of History of Science*, 16:189-201.

Hunter, G.R. 1935 *Interim Report on the Excavation in the Mahadeo hills*, NJ, 1.

Indian Archaeological Review: 1953-54.

Indian Archaeological Review: 1954-55.

Indian Archaeological Review: 1956-57, pp. 20-28.

Indian Archaeological Review: 1961-62, pp. 59-62.

Indian Archaeological Review: 1963-64, pp. 23- 27, 46-48.

Indian Archaeological Review: 1965-66.

Indian Archaeological Review: 1973-74, pp. 6, 25,48-50.

Indian Archaeological Review: 1974-75, pp. 7, 30-31.

Indian Archaeological Review: 1975-76, pp. 2-3,33-35,45,51-52.

Indian Archaeological Review: 1976-77, pp. 3-10,53-55.

Indian Archaeological Review: 1977-78, pp.3-11,27-29,50.

Indian Archaeological Review: 1981-82.

Indian Archaeological Review: 1983-84.

Issac, N. 1960 *The Stone Age Cultures of Kurnool*. Unpublished Ph.D. Thesis, Poona University, Pune.

Joshi, A. 1983 *History and Culture of Khijingakotta Under the Bhanjas*. New Delhi; Vikas Publishing House Pvt. Ltd.

Kar, S. K., K.K. Basa, and P.P Joglekar. 1998 Explorations at Gopalpur, District Nayagarh, Coastal Orissa. *Man and Environment*, 23 (I):107-114.

Kar, S.K. 1995-96 Further Exploration at Gopalpur. *Puratattva* 26:105-106.

Kar, S.K. With an appendix by P.P. Joglekar. 2000 Gopalpur: A Neolithic-Chalcolithic site in Coastal Orissa. In (pp. 368-91) K.K. Basa, and P. Mohanty (edited) *Archaeology of Orissa*.

Kejariwal, O. P. 1988 *The Asiatic Society of Bengal and the Discovery of India's Past*. Delhi: Oxford University Press.

Khilar, B. K. 1997-99 Lithic Cultures around Deo River Basin, Orissa. *Manav*, (Paleo-culture special), 6:73-76.

Kosambi, D.D. 1963 The Beginning of Iron Age in India. *Journal of the Economic and Social History of The Orient,* Vol-VI.

Kramrisch, Stella 1976 *The Hindu Temple*, (Two Volume), Motilal Banarasidas (Reprint).

Lal, B.B. 1949 Sisupalgarh 1948: An Early Historic Fort in Eastern India, *Ancient India.* 5: 62-105.

Lal, B.B. 1954-55 Excavations at Hastinapur and other Explorations in the upper Ganga and Sutlej Basin. *Ancient India*. 10-11.

Lal, B.B. 1981 The two Indian epics vis-à-vis archaeology. *Antiquity* LV. No.213. Durham: Durham University.

Lal, B.B. 1993 Excavation at Sringaverapura 1977-86. *Memoir of the Archaeological Survey of India*, No-88, New Delhi.

Lamberg-Karlovsky, C.C. 1967 Archaeological Metallurgical Technology in Prehistoric Afghanistan, India and Pakistan, *American Anthropologist* 69:145-165.

Leshnik, Lawrence S. 1968 Prehistoric Exploration in North Gujarat and Parts of Rajasthan, *East and West* 18:295-310.

Mehta, R.N. 1968 *Excavation at Nagara*. Baroda: M.S. University of Baroda.

Mehta, R.N. 1968 Nagarkhanda- A study. *Journal of the M.S. University of Baroda*, Vol- XVII (I).

Mehta, R.N. 1971-72 Puranic Archaeology. *Journal of the M.S University of Baroda*, XX-XXI.

Mehta, R.N. and S.G. Kantawala 1975 Patala Vivara myth in the Prabhaskhand - A study. *Journal of the Oriental Institute*, Baroda, XXV, 2.

Mishra, Jitu 2000 Radhanagar: Early Historic Buddhism, Urban Structure and Trade. In (pp. 507-550) K. K. Basa and P. Mohanty edited *Archaeology of Orissa.*

Mishra, P.K. 1998 *Archaeology of Mayurbhanj*. New Delhi: D.K. Printworld (P) Ltd.

Mishra, S.K. 1987-88 Stone Age Antiquities of Joshipur, Orissa – A Survey. *Man in Society*, 3:81-88.

Mishra, S. 1997 *Surface Exploration around Kantala, Angul District, Orissa*. Unpublished M.A. dissertation, Department of Anthropology, Utkal University.

Mishra, C.R. And S. Pradhan. 1990 *Manmunda Excavation; A Preliminary Report*. Sambalpur University, Jyoti Vihar.

Misra, V.N. 1962, Problems of terminology in Indian Prehistory. *Eastern Anthropologist,* XV(2):112-124.

Misra, V.N. 1973 Bagor A Late Mesolithic Settlement in North West India, *World Archaeology* 5, Issue-1: 92-100. London: Routledge Taylor and Francis group.

Mitra, D. and Chakravarti, D.K. 1958-59 Exploration in District Mayurbhanj, *Indian Antiquary*, p. 38.

Mitra, R.L. 1980 *The Vayu Purana*. Anand Sharma Sanskrit Series. Poona.

Morgan, L.H. 1877 *Ancient Society*. New York: Henry Holt and Company.

Mohanta, B.K. 1993 *Lithic Cultural Sequence around Manda*. Unpublished B.A. (Hons) dissertation, Department of Anthropology, Rairangpur College, Rairangpur.

Mohanta, B.K. 1995 *Archaeological Excavation at Bajpur (Pallahara), Orissa*. Unpublished M.A. dissertation, Department of Anthropology, Utkal University, Bhubaneswar.

Mohanta, B.K. 1997 *Surface Survey and Excavation of Muganali, Angul, Orissa.* Unpublished M.Phil dissertation, Department of Anthropology, Utkal University, Bhubaneswar.

Mohanta, B.K. 2000, Neolithic and post-Neolithic Cultures of Northern Orissa (with special reference to Mayur Bhanj and keonjhar district). ph.D. Thesis. Utkal University, Bhubaneswar, India.

Mohanty, P. 1985 The Mesolithic culture of Keonjhar District, Orissa : a preliminary report. *Bulletin of the Deccan College Post Graduate and Research Institute*, 44:103-112.

Mohanty, P. 1988 A Note on Sitabinji. *Indica* 25 (1):11-14.

Mohanty, P. 1989 *Mesolithic Settlement System of Keonjhar District, Orissa.* Unpublished Ph.D. Thesis submitted to the University of Poona, Pune.

Mohanty, P. 1991 The Mesolithic Culture of Keonjhar District. *Orissa Review*, September Issue, pp.4-7.

Mohanty, P. 1992 Stone Age Research in Orissa: An Overview. *Man in India*, 72(2): 207-232.

Mohanty, P. 1993 Mesolithic hunter gatherers of Keonjhar, Orissa, India. *Asian Perspective*, 32 (1):87-104.

Mohanty, P. 1998 The Mesolithic Culture of Keonjhar District, Orissa: A New Perspective. In Dutta, A. (edited) *New Perspective in History and Archaeology of Eastern India*. New Delhi: Books and Books.

Mohanty, P. 2000 Mesolithic Culture and Ethnography of Keonjhar District, Orissa. In (pp. 114-52) K. K. Basa and P. Mohanty (edited) *Archaeology of Orissa*.

Mohanty, P. and B. Tripathi. 1997-98 The Prehistoric, Proto historic and the Early Historic Cultures of Orissa. *Pragdhara* 8:69-98.

Mohanty, P. and Baba Mishra. 1998 Recent Archaeological Researches in Orissa with special reference to the Early Historic Phase, *Man in India* 78 (3 & 4), pp.205 – 221.

Mohanty, P. and B. Mishra 2001 Early Historic Kalahandi, in Orissa Revisited. *Marg* (Special Monograph Issue- Mumbai,) PP. 17-26.

Mohanty, R.K. and M.L. Smith 2006 Excavation at Sisupalgarh 2005. *Man and Environment* XXXI(1):27-32.

Mohanty, D 1999 *Archaeological Exploration around Sankerjang District; Angul, Orissa.* Unpublished M. A. Dissertation, Department of Anthropology, Utkal University, Bhubaneswar, Orissa.

Mohapatra, G.C. 1957-58 Exploration in District Dhenkanal, Mayurbhanj, *Indian Antiquary*, p.4l.

Mohapatra, G.C. 1976 Geo-tectonic developments, sub-Himalayan lithic complex, and posty-Siwalik sediments, *Union International des Sciences Prehistoriques et Protohistoriques, Colloque VII,* Nice.

Mohapatra, G.C. 1981 Acheulian discoveries in the Siwalik Frontal range, *Current Anthropology* 22 (4).

Mohapatra G.C. 1985 The lower Palaeolithic in India. In (pp. 1-8) K.N Dikshit (edited) *Archaeological perspective of India since independence*, New Delhi: Books & Books.

Mohapatra, G.C. 1958-59 Exploration in Districts Keonjhar and Mayurbhanj. *Indian Antiquiry*, pp. 36-38.

Mohapatra, R.P. 1986a *Archaeology in Orissa* (Sites and monuments) 2 Vols. Delhi: B.R. Publishing Corporation.

Murty, M.L.K. 1966 *Stone Age cultures of Chittoor District Andhra Pradesh.* Unpublished Ph.D Thesis, Poona.

Murty, M.L.K.1985 Upper Palaeolithic Culture in India. In (pp. 15-25) K.N. Dikshit edited *Archaeological Perspective of India Since Independence.* New Delhi: Books and Books.

Nayak, S 1999 *Excavation at Sankerjang, District-Angul, Orissa.* Unpublished M. A. Dissertation, Department of Anthropology, Utkal University, Bhubaneswar, Orissa.

Niyogi, D. 1981 Geomorphology and Morphotectonics of the Neogene-Quarternary sediments in India. *Field conference on Neogene Quaternary boundary, India, 1979, Proceeding.* M.V.A Sastry, et. al.(eds.).

Ota S.B. 1982-83 New research design in the prehistoric research in Orissa with special reference to pebble industry of north Boudh-Kandhamal district. *Manav* 1 (I): 160-180.

Ota S.B. 1986 Mesolithic culture of the Phulbani District, Orissa with special reference to the heavy duty tool component. *Bulletin of the Deccan college post graduate and Research Institute* 45:47-56.

Paddayya, K. 1968 *Pre and Protohistoric Investigations in Shorapur Doab*. Unpublished Ph.D. Thesis, Poona University.

Paddayya, K 1970 The Blade Tool industry of Shorapur Doab. *Indian Antiquary*, 4. pp.1-4, 165-190.

Paddayya, K. 1973 *Investigations into the Neolithic Culture of the Shorapur Doab, South India*. Leiden; E.I. Brill.

Panigrahi, K.C. 1981 *History of Orissa* (Hindu Period). Cuttack: Kitab Mahal.

Pattnaik, J. 2000 Ceramics of Lalitgiri ; A Buddhist site in Orissa. In (pp. 456-72) K. K. Basa and P. Mohanty (edited) *Archaeology of Orissa*.

Piggott, S 1950 *Prehistoric India*. Harmondsworth: Penguin.

Pradhan, D., P. Mohanty and Jitu Mishra 1996 Manikapatna: An Excavation Report. *Puratattva* 26;120-123.

Pradhan, D., P. Mohanty and Jitu Mishra 2000 Manikpatna: An Ancient and Medieval Port on the Coast of Orissa. In (pp.473-94) Basa, K.K. and P. Mohanty (edited) *Archaeology of Orissa*.

Pradhan, S. 1987-88. Megalithic remains in the upper Mahanadi Valley of the Orissa. *Journal of Ancient Indian History* 17:1-2, 16-22.

Prusty, H. and P. Mohanty 1995 Langudi; A Unique Rock-cut Buddhist site in Orissa. *Bulletin of the Deccan College Research Institute*. Poona 53:325-327.

Prusty. H., P. Mohanty and J. Mishra. 1997 Langudi: An Early Historic Buddhist site in Coastal Orissa. *Puratattava* 27:100-104.

Ramachandran, T.N. 1951 Find of Tempora Painting in Sitabinjhi, District Keonjhar, Orissa. *Artibus Asiae,* Institute of fine arts, New York University XIV (1-2):5-25.

Ray, P.K. 1977 Recent Archaeological Excavations in Orissa. In (pp. 539-40) M. N Das (edited) *Sidelights on History and Culture in Orissa*, Cuttack.

Renfrew, C. and P. Bahn. 1991 *Archaeology : Theories, Methods and Practice*. Thames and Hudson.

Sahi, M.D.N. 1979 Iron at Ahar. In (pp. 365-66 D.P. Agrawal and D.K. Chakrabarti (edited). *Essays in Indian Protohistory,* New Delhi: B.R. Publishing Corporation.

Sahoo, D. 2013 Archaeology before history a Kardi, District-Boudh. *SEARCH, A Journal of Arts, Humanities and managements* 1:86-103.

Sankalia, H.D 1956 The microlithic Industry of Langhanaj, Gujrat. *Journal of Gujarat Research Society*, No.13.

Sankalia, H. D. 1960 Houses and Habitations through the ages. *Bulletin of Deccan College Research Institute*, XX.

Sankalia, H.D 1973 *Ramayan Myth and Reality*, Delhi.

Senapati, N.1986 *Orissa District Gazetteers: Keonjhar*. Cuttack: Orissa Government Press,

Senapati, N. and P. Tripathy. 1972 *Orissa District Gazetteers: Dhenkanal*. Cuttack: Orissa Government Press.

Seshadri, M. 1962 Stone Age Tools from Salvadgi, Bijapur District Mysore State. *Journal of the University of Mysore*, 25:1-5.

Sharma, G.R. 1960 *Excavation at Kaushambi* 1957-58. Allahabad, Department of Ancient Indian History, Culture and Archaeology.

Sharma, G.R. 1965 In *Indian prehistory*: 1964, (ed.)V.N Mishra and M.S Mate, Pune,

Sharma, G.R. 1969 *Excavation at Kausambi*, Delhi.

Sharma, G.R. 1980 *Beginning of Agriculture*, Allahabad.

Shaffer, J.G. 1978, Bronze Age Iron from Afghanistan: its implications for South Asian Protohistory, Mimeographed paper.

Singh, P.K. 1985 *Palaeoanthropology of Central Orissa*. Unpublished Ph.D. Thesis, Utkal University, Bhubaneswar.

Singh, P.K. 1988 Cultural Succession of Prehistoric culture in central Orissa. In (pp.87-99) K.L. Bhowmik (edited) *Cultura of the Past.* New Delhi: Inter India Publication.

Singh, P.K. 1988-89 Neolithic Culture of Central Orissa. *Manav* 3:275-281.

Singh, P.K. 2000 Stone Age Cultures of Central Orissa. In (pp. 102-13) K. K. Basa and P.K Mohanty (edited) *Archaeology of Orissa.*

Sinha, B.K. 1990-91 Excavations at Golabai Sasan, District: Puri, Orissa. *Puratattva* 21:21-23.

Sinha, B.K. 1992-93 Excavations of Golabai Sasan, District Puri, Orissa. *Puratattva* 23:48-50.

Sinha, B.K. with an appendix by S.K. Ghosh Maulik and P.K. Das. 2000 Golabai: A Proto historic site on the Coast of Orissa. In (pp.322-55) K. K. Basa and P. Mohanty (edited) *Archaeology of Orissa.*

Soundarajan, K.V. 1958 Studies in the Stone Age of Nagarjunakonda and its neighbourhood. *Ancient India* 14:49-113.

Soundarajan, K.V. 1985 Middle Paleolithic in India. In (pp. 9-14) K.N. Dikshit (edited) *Archaeological Perspective of India Since Independence.* New Delhi: Books & Books publisher and distributor.

Spencer, H. 1867 *Principle of Biology.* New York : D. Appleton & Company.

Spencer, H. 1870 *Principle of Psychology*, Two Volume, New York: D. Appleton & Company.

Stirling, A. 1825 An account, geographical, statistical and historical of Orissa proper of Cuttack. *Asiatic Researches* 15:163-338.

Subbharao, B. and R.N.Mehta 1955 Excavation of Vadnagara, *Journal of the M.S. University of Baroda.*, IV, I.

Sukla, D.N. 1958 *Hindu Cannons of Iconography and painting*, Vastu Sastra Vol-II, Lucknow: Vastu-Vanmaya Prakasana Sala, Shukla-Kuti faizabad Road. pp. 239-248, 325-334.

Thapar, B.K. 1976 Prehistoric and Protohistoric Remains (From food gathering to food Producing) In (ed.). *Orissa Review: Monumental Special*, Cuttack: Government of Orissa Press, pp. 1-14.

Thapar, B.K. 1985a Fresh Light of the Neolithic Cultures of India. In (pp. 37-43) K.N Dikshit (edited) *Archaeological Perspective of India Since Independence.*

Thapar, B.K. 1985b *Recent Archaeological Discoveries in India.* Paris: UNESCO.

Tripathy, Balaram 1996-97 Archaeological Exploration in Boudh District, Orissa; A Preliminary Report. *Bulletin of the Deccan College post graduate and research Institute*, pp.47-57.

Tripathy, Balaram 2000 Archaeology of Boudh; Central Orissa. In (pp.392-417) K. K. Basa and P. Mohanty (edited) *Archaeology of Orissa.*

Tripathy, Balaram 2001 *Archaeology of Boudh district, Orissa: with special reference to the Early Historic Settlement Pattern.* Unpublished Ph.D. Thesis, Deccan College Post Graduate and Research Institute (Deemed University), Pune.

Tripathy, K.C. 1973 South Orissa Prehistory- the first record of stone age tools. *Asian Perspective* 4: 47-59.

Tripathy, K.C. 1980 *Lithic Industries in India: A Study of South Western Orissa.* Delhi: Leeladevi Publications.

Tylor, E.B. 1871 *Primitive Culture.* New York: J.P Putnam's Son.

Varma, R.K. 1964 *Stone Age Cultures of Mirzapur District.* Unpublished Ph.D. Thesis, University of Allahabad.

Varma, R.K. 1970 *Bharatiya Pragitihas*, Pt. I. Allahabad.

Varma, R.K. 1985 The Mesolithic cultures of India. In (pp. 27-36) K.N. Dikshit (edited) *Archaeological perspective of India since Independence*, New Delhi: Books & Books.

Worman, Jr. Eugene C. 1949 The Neolithic Problem in the Prehistory of India. *Journal of the Washington academy of Science* 39 (6): 181-201.

Yule, P, B.K. Rath and K. Hojgarred. 1989 Sankerjang in metalizeithicher Bestattengs platzin Dhenkanal Vorgebirge Ostindiens. *Anthropos* 84:107-32.

Yule, Paul and B.K. Rath with an appendix by Karen Hojgaard. 2000 Sankerjang - A Metal Period Burial site in the Dhenkanal Uplands of Orissa. In (pp. 285-321) K. K. Basa and P. Mohanty edited *Archaeology of Orissa.*

Yule, P.2006 *Early Historic Sites in Orissa.* New Delhi: Pragun Publication.

Index

C

J

K

L

M

N

PLATES

Pl.1: River section at Ban[illegible]adar

Pl.2: General view of the river section at Baisnavadar site.

Pl.3: Palaeolithic artefacts from Barikaguda (Soida Hudi) site.

Pl.4: Microliths from Dalo Puruna Diha site.

Pl.5: Microliths and Neolithic artefacts from Kadamdar site.

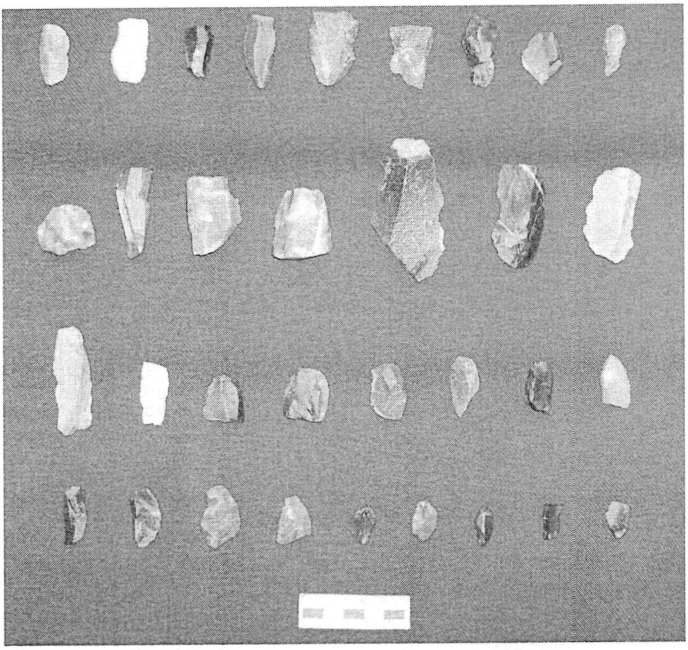

Pl.6: Microliths from Rajamunda site.

Pl.7: Microliths from Atanaka Reserve Forest site.

Pl.8: Microliths and Neolithic ring stone from Karadapal-I site.

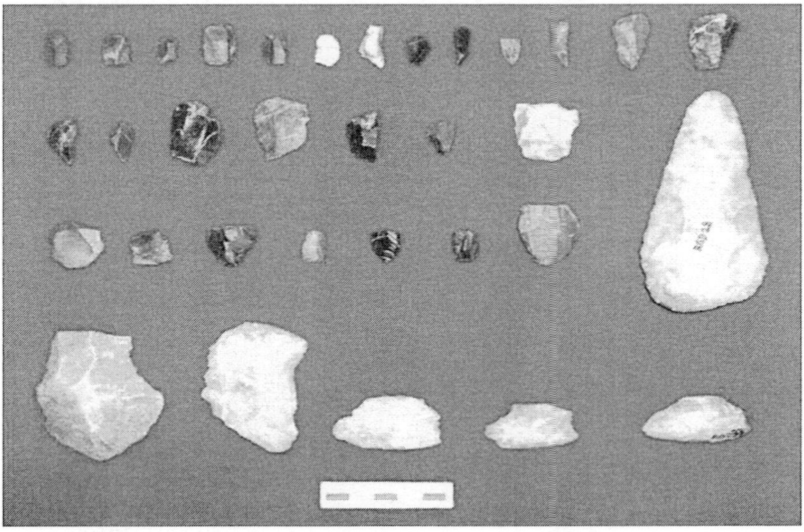

Pl.9: Microliths and Neolithic artefacts from Rugudidiha site.

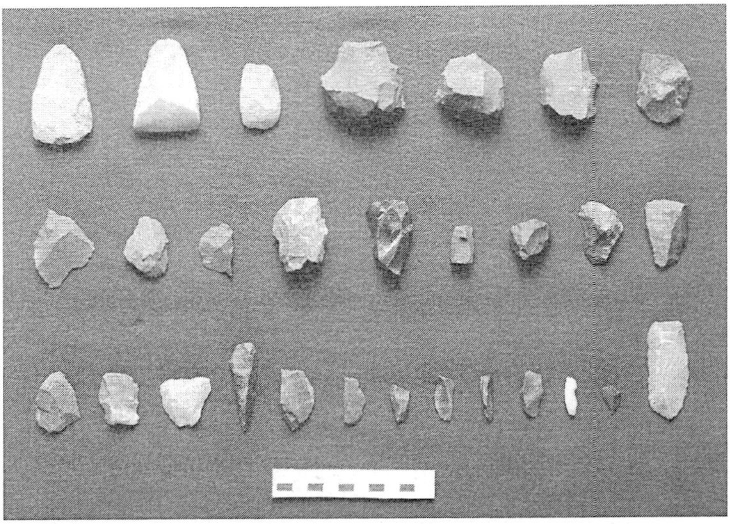

Pl.10: Neolithics and Microliths from Sorbeda Dautasala site.

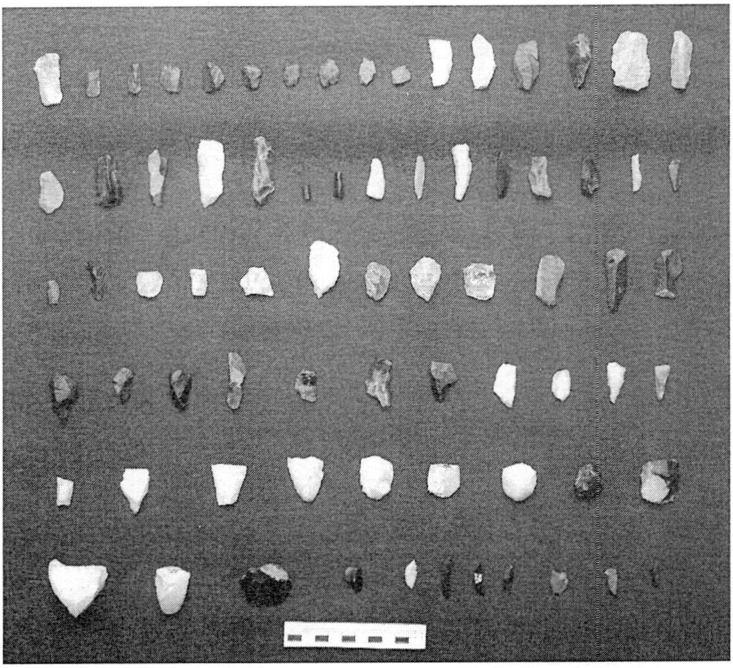

Pl.11: Microliths from Kadamdiha site.

Pl.12: Microliths from Karadapal-II site.

Pl.13: Microliths from Mohanpur Shiva Mandir site

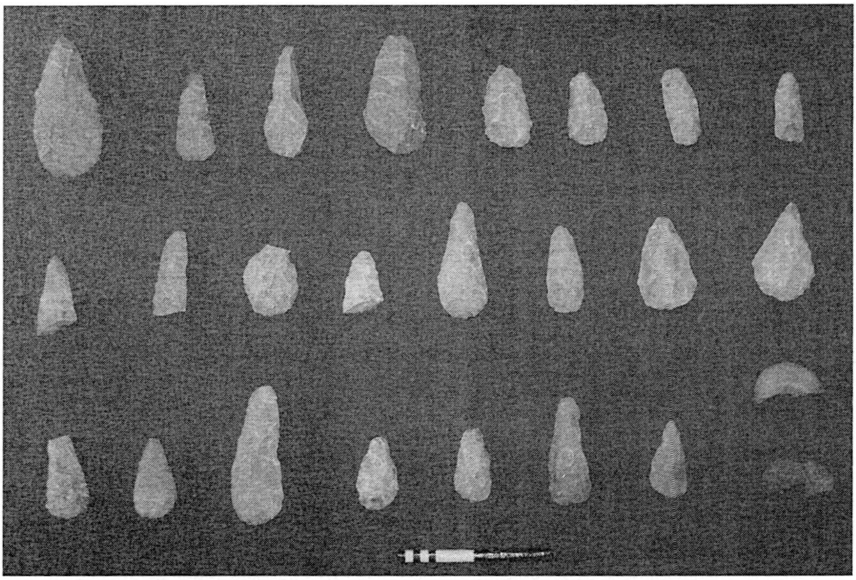

Pl.14: Neolithic artefacts from Baisnavadar site.

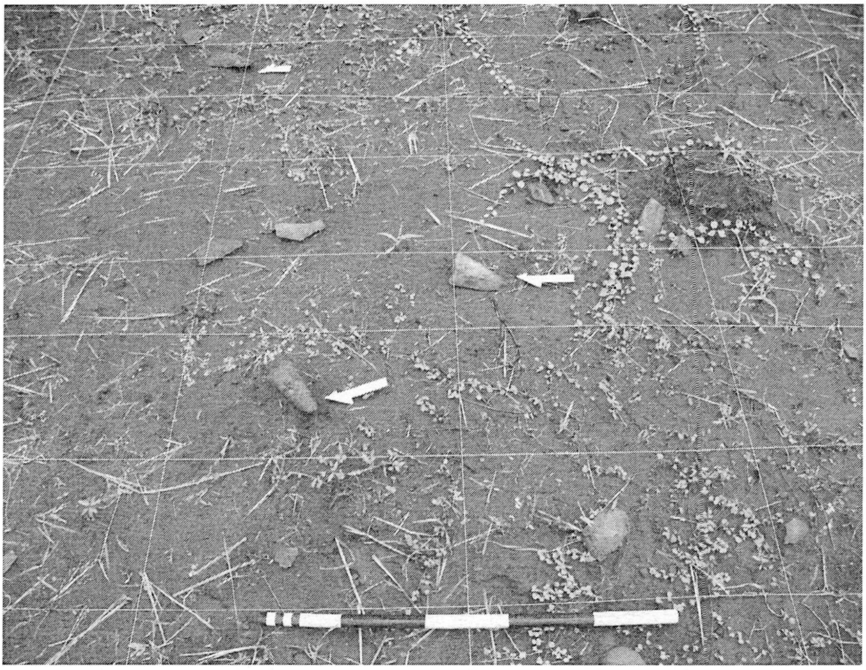

Pl.15: Close-up view of grid showing Neolithic artefacts from Baisnavadar site.

Pl.16: Close-up view of water channel showing Neolithic flakes at Bisriguda Site.

Pl.17: Close-up view showing adze and broken axe at Bisriguda site.

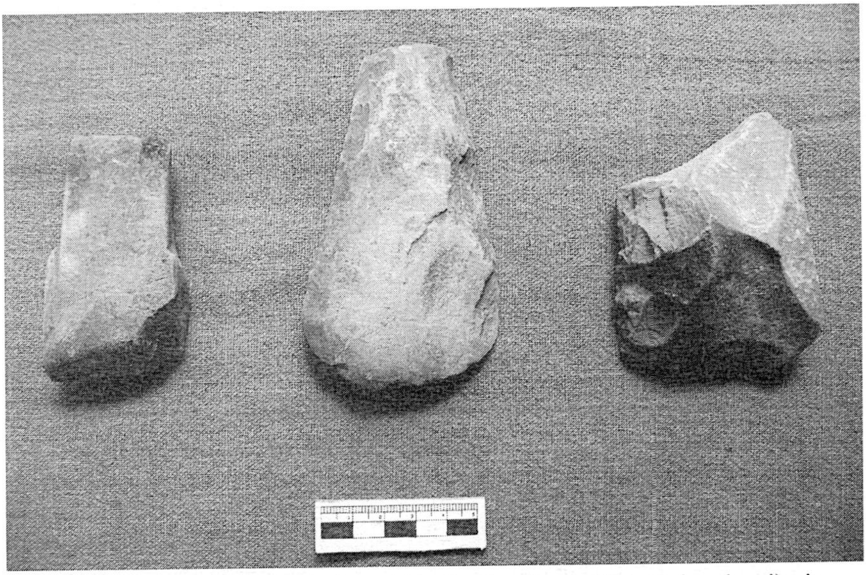

Pl.18: Neolithic artefacts from Khalinala (Jamudiha Gaiguthani) site.

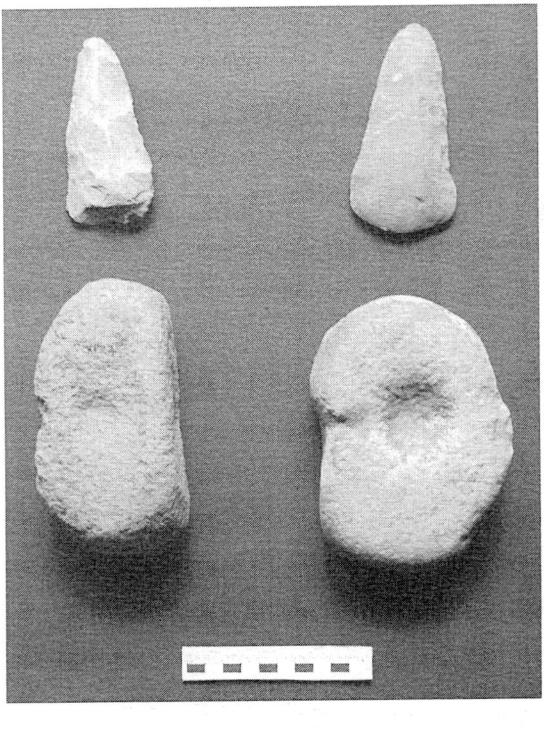

Pl.19: Neolithic artefacts from Kamparkala site.

Pl.20: Neolithic artefacts from Rajamunda site.

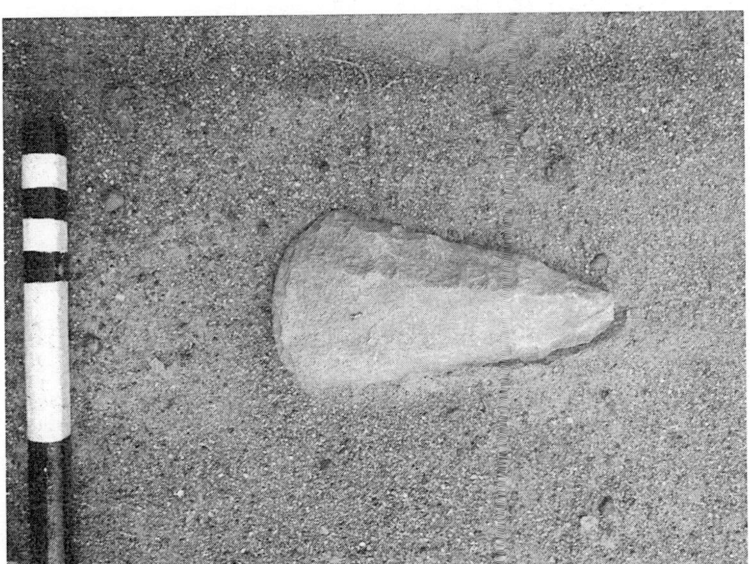

Pl.21: Close-up view of Neolithic axe at Tentulimula Gaiguthani site.

Pl.22: Neolithic artefacts from Tentulimula Gaiguthani site.

Pl.23: Neolithic artefacts from Jalanda Hatapada site.

Pl.24: Neolithic artefacts from Jalanda Munda sahi site.

Pl.25: Neolithic blank and flakes on ground at Kakharua Protection Forest site.

Pl.26: Close up view of used Dolerite block at Kakharua Protection Forest site.

Pl.27: Neolithic artefacts from Kakharua Protection Forest site.

Pl.28: Close up view of exposed Neolithic axe at Radodiha site.

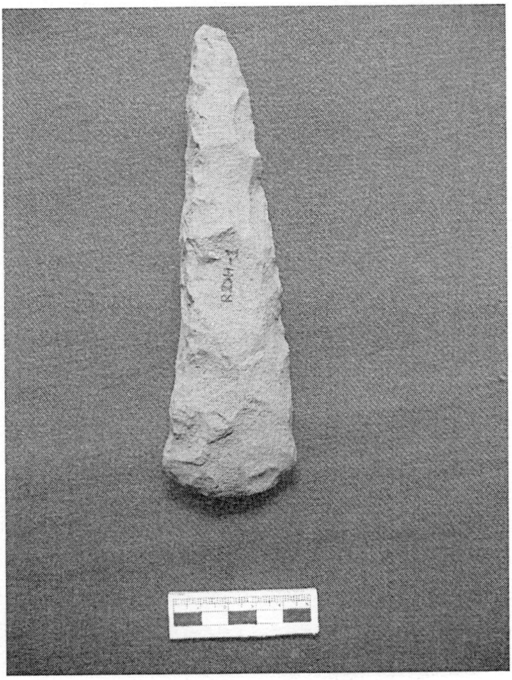

Pl.29: Neolithic axe from Radodiha site.

Pl.30: Close up view of Bar-celt at Sorbeda Kudur site.

Pl.31: Bar Celt from Sorbeda Kudur Neolithic site.

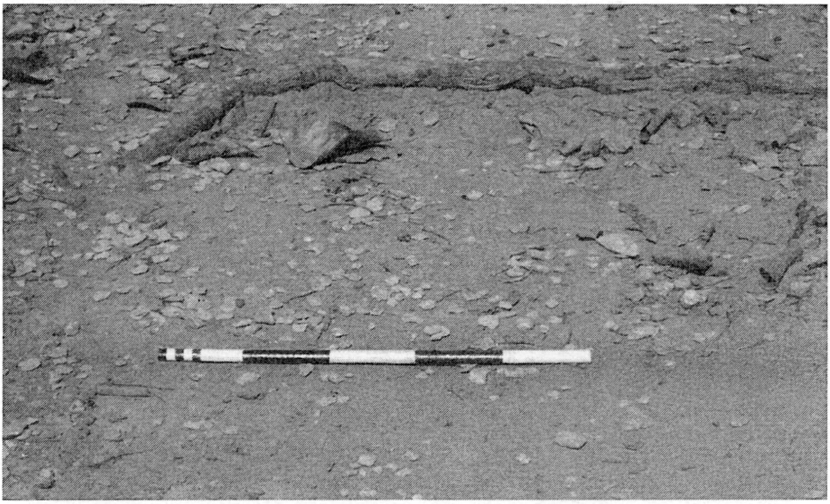

Pl.32: Largely exposed Neolithic flakes at Bijagota Hatapada site.

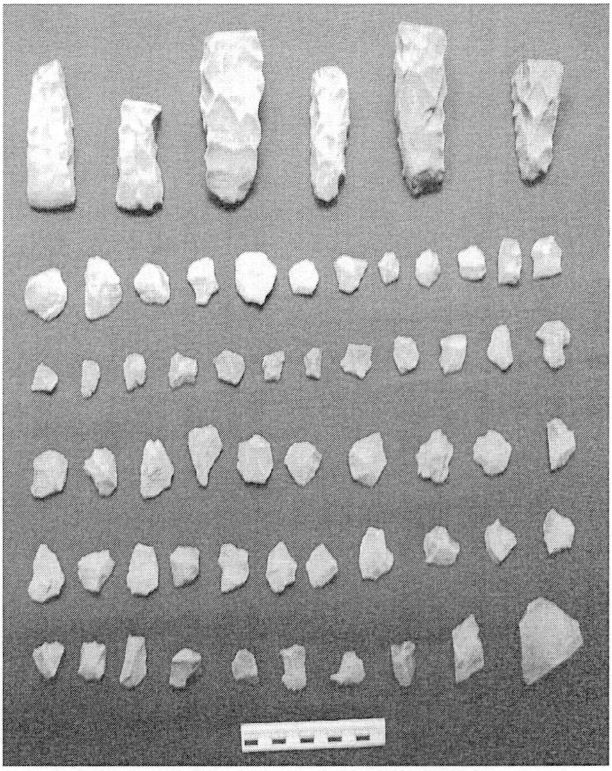

Pl.33: Neolithic artefacts from Bijagotha Hatapada site.

Pl.34: Exposed section at Katiragarh site.

Pl.35: Close up view of sculptures at Katiragarh site.

Pl.36: Two partly exposed miniature temples and Amlaka at Katiragarh site.

Pl.37: Fragment part of laterite pillar block at Katiragarh site.

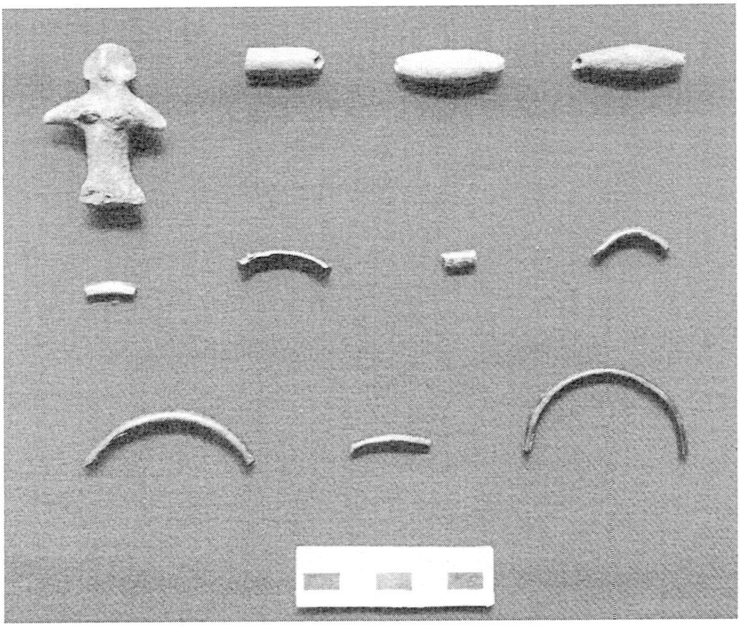

Pl.38: Terracotta figurine, terracotta beads, glass bangles from Katiragarh site and Rado MIP.

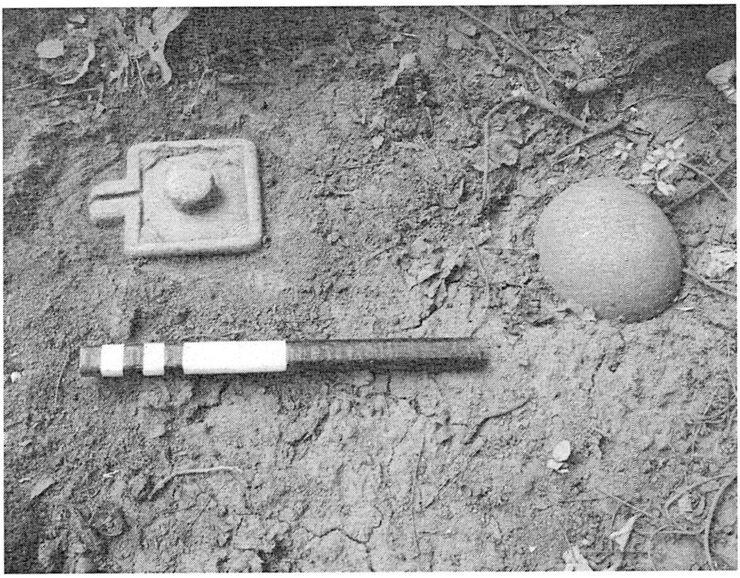

Pl.39: Close up view showing Shiva linga at Katiragarh site.

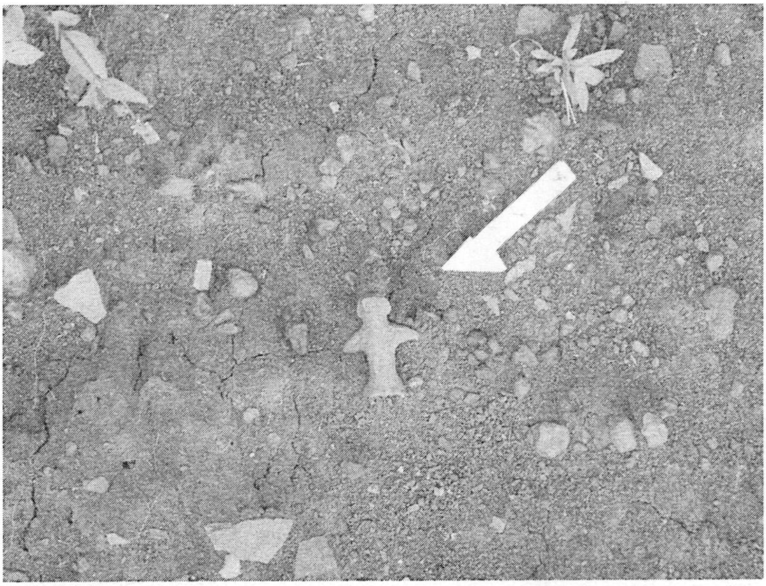

Pl.40: Close up view of terracotta figurine at Katiragarh site.

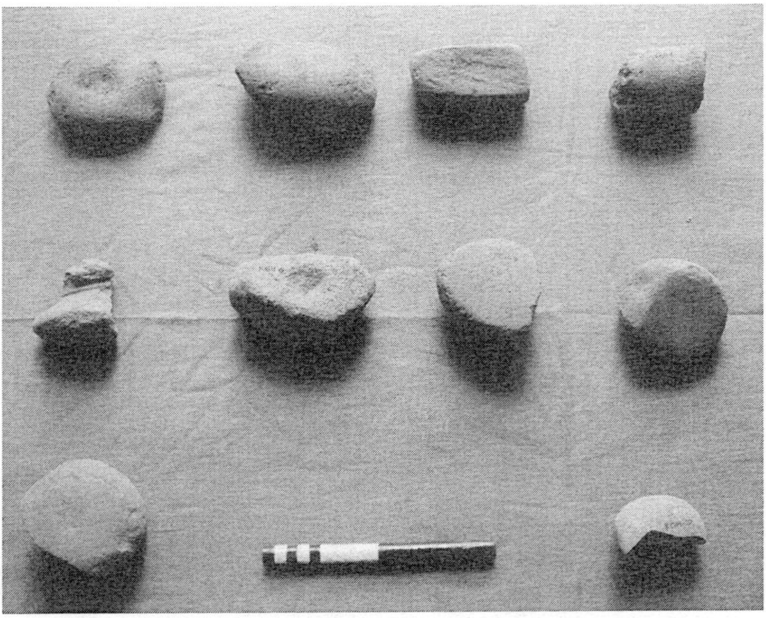

Pl.41: Pestle, dabber and dimple scar rubber
stone fragments from Katiragarh site.

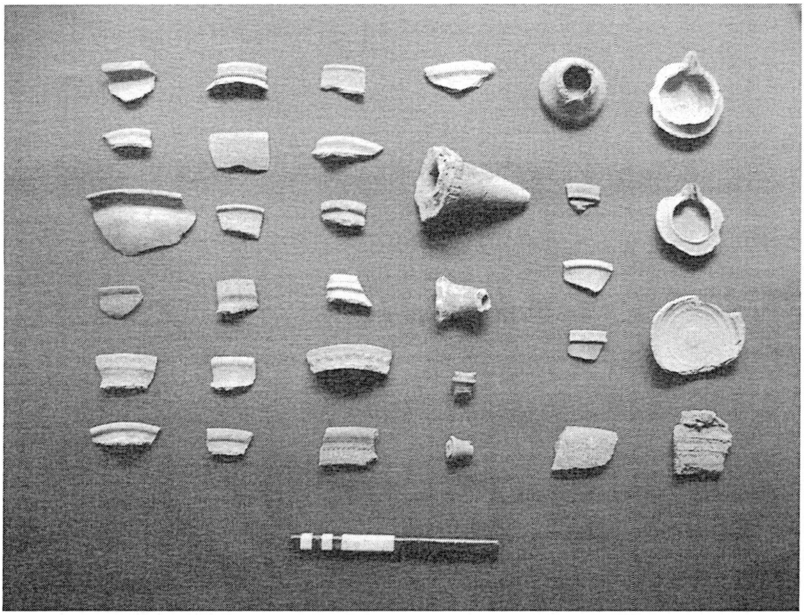

Pl.42: Potsherds, lamps and spout fragments from Katiragarh site.

Pl.43: Close up view showing Shiva linga at Nemliloti site.

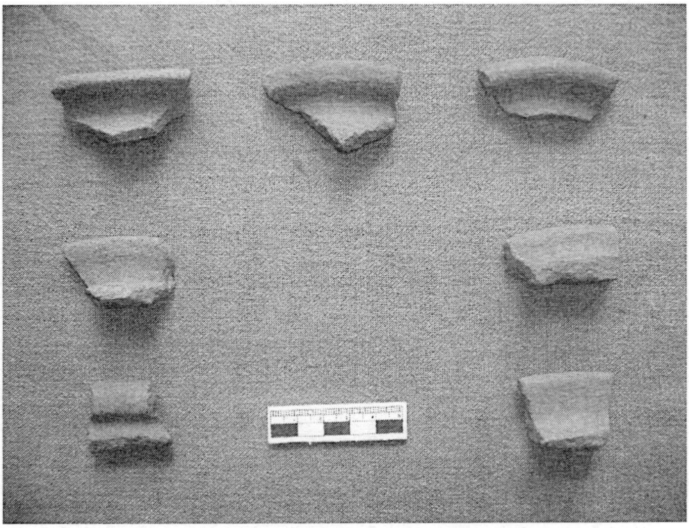

Pl.44: Potsherds of Rado MIP site.

Pl.45: Quern and muller fragments from Dalo Puruna Diha site.

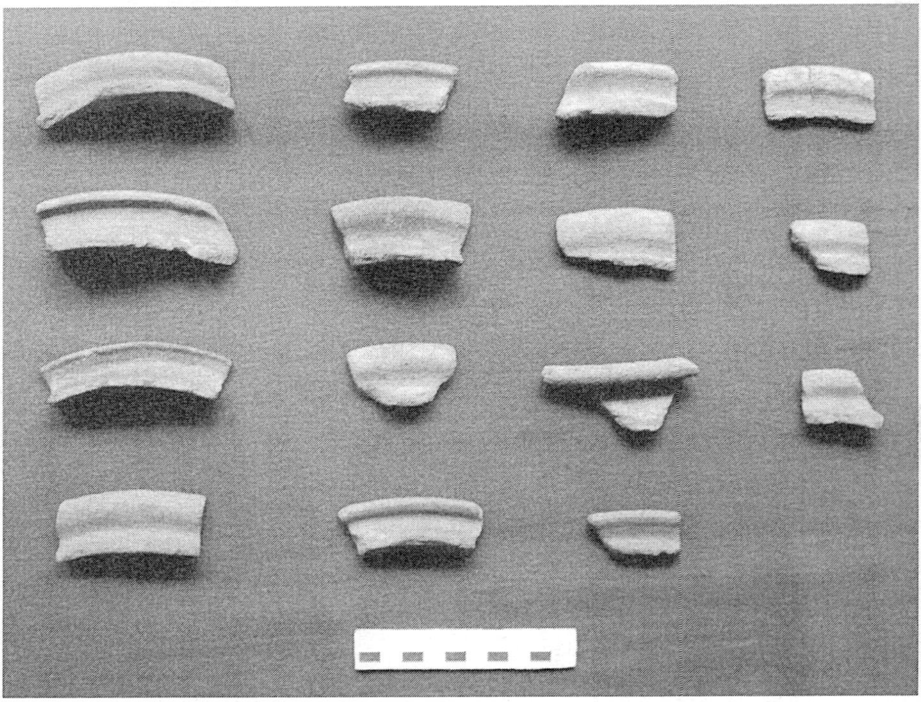

Pl.46: Potsherds from Dalo Puruna Diha site (Jamar diha).